PAT SUMMERALL'S
SPORTS IN AMERICA

PAT SUMMERALL'S
SPORTS IN AMERICA

**32 CELEBRATED SPORTS
PERSONALITIES TALK
ABOUT THEIR MOST
MEMORABLE MOMENTS
IN AND OUT OF THE
SPORTS ARENA**

PAT SUMMERALL
AND JIM MOSKOVITZ
WITH CRAIG KUBEY

HarperCollins*Publishers*

HarperCollins books may be purchased for educational, business, or sales promotional use. For information, please write to: Special Markets Department, HarperCollins Publishers, Inc., 10 East 53rd Street, New York, New York 10022.

FIRST EDITION

Designed by Joseph Rutt

Library of Congress Cataloging-in-Publication Data
Summerall, Pat.
    [Sports in America]
    Pat Summerall's sports in America : 32 celebrated sports personalities talk about their most memorable moments in and out of the sports arena / Pat Summerall and Jim Moskovitz with Craig Kubey.—1st ed.
        p.   cm.
    ISBN 0-06-270186-X
    1. Athletes—United States—Biography.   2. Sports—United States—History.   I. Moskovitz, Jim.   II. Kubey, Craig.   III.   Title.
GV697.A1S825   1996
796'.092—dc20
    [B]   96-26873

---

96 97 98 99 00 ❖/RRD 10 9 8 7 6 5 4 3 2 1

Contents

ACKNOWLEDGMENTS

The authors thank the wonderful people of Continental Airlines and their representatives at Courtlemagne Communications, without whose help and support this book would never have been possible. Continental and Courtlemagne made certain that we had the finest air transportation to myriad destinations across the United States as well as to Europe and Latin America. Specifically, we want to thank Courtlemagne's president, Chuck Lisberger, as well as Melissa McSorley, Heidi Shimoda, Joy Osaka, Caroline Rostad, and Maria Tsilimidos, all of whose professionalism, good humor, and fine work ensured this book's timely completion and the radio show's day-to-day success. At Continental, we'd like to acknowledge its dynamic leadership duo of Gordon Bethune (CEO) and Greg Brennerman (COO), as well as marketing pros Bonnie Reitz, Richard Metzner, Rosalind Calvin, Eric Kleiman, and Elizabeth Diamond.

We are also grateful for the support and hard work of Joyce Moskovitz, whose abundant creative talents were essential to the completion of this book. Kudos have also been earned, many times over, by those who have vitally assisted the radio series throughout the past seven years, most notably Robert, Faye, Andrew, Stephen, and Paula Forbis and Ken and Edna Adelberg.

The authors thank RLR Associates, Ltd., and especially Robert L. Rosen, Christine K. Tomasino, and Jonathan Diamond for the countless tasks they undertook to put together the complicated project that resulted in this book; in particular we thank Chris for her incisive editorial guidance and Jonathan for literally and figuratively "being there." We also gratefully acknowledge Robert Wilson and others at HarperCollins for their support, understanding, and enthusiasm during this project.

Craig Kubey thanks Laura Goodman and the Secretariat, her Davis, California, secretarial firm that professionally transcribed the interviews that form the basis for many of the chapters in this book; in particular he notes the efforts of transcriptionists Doris Miner, Mary McGlone, Jeanette Buck, Susan Shah, and Lori Hendrix. In addition, he expresses his gratitude to Stan Morrison, Joe Carlson, John Sproul, Ray Minella, Ken Kubey, and Bob Thau for their advice and other assistance during this project. Finally, he thanks his family—Maki, Karen, Alan, and Elizabeth—for their patience during his work that contributed to this book.

Jim Moskovitz dedicates this book to Mayer and Charlotte Moskovitz.

Craig Kubey dedicates this book to promising athlete Elizabeth Kubey, age two.

ON BEING INTERVIEWED

BY ROGER KAHN

You enter the examining room slowly because you are bare-foot. In fact, you are not only barefoot, but nude. The surgeon's assistant has confiscated your clothing.

You are also uncomfortable. You are also broke. The surgeon's receptionist has seized your wallet, which contained your new Master/Visa Card, with no credit limit, issued by the Irresponsible Banking Company of America.

But wait. Just half a moment. What really is going down here? Are you actually facing surgery and chaos?

Easy, podner. None of the above. Your anxious fantasies have run amok.

You are about to submit to an interview, one that will air from coast to coast. Just the prospect of all those people listening crams your brain with wild anxieties.

Courage, friend. Try not to be embarrassed. Use no expletives. And don't worry about panicking.

Everybody does.

The work of Pat Summerall and his associate, Jim Moskovitz, command such thoughts to mind. I knew of Pat first as a place-kicker, a bigfoot attached to the New York Giants football team. Later he emerged as a triple-threat sportscaster. He came to that assignment armed with a subdued but assured style, a splendid voice, and keen intelligence. His employers called him "Super-Summerall" in advertising copy. Pat is a big, square-jawed fellow and it is rumored that with the right pair of spectacles he is a dead ringer for Clark Kent. Jim Moskovitz is a polymath, a word you may have to look up. (Hint: Jim got a lot of A's when he was at

Stanford.) Being interviewed by this pair is challenging, stimulating, and sometimes even fun.

Let me pause here for a little background. My next book, *The Press Box: When Baseball Was a Game and Writing It an Art,* is my nineteenth. For almost every one the publisher has sent me on the road for a so-called book promotion tour. Authors like to complain about these tours. The flights are bumpy. The hotel lost their laundry. They miss their mommy. I never complain. If someone wants to send me around the country first-class to talk about my work, I'll make the time. Put differently, isn't it better to be desired than ignored?

In making all these trips, one notes that the quality of interviewing varies. One pleasant, vague lady, hosting *Good Morning, America,* opened up: "I haven't read your book. What's it about?" This plea of ignorance may have suggested to two million Americans: "If she hasn't read the book and she's getting *paid* to read it and interview this bloke, why on earth should I read it?" I wanted to snap, "My book is about 400 pages, ma'am. Bye, bye." I didn't, but the interview was awful.

I remember an ebb in Philadelphia. *The Boys of Summer* was published in March 1972. Three weeks later, Gil Hodges, one of the principals in the book and a personal friend, died of a heart attack. Interviewing me for a five o'clock news show, hard by the Schuylkill, a journalist began: "Do you think Gil Hodges' death is helping sales of your book?" Answer? I had none.

At the high end, Johnny Carson was funny and informed. (His staff prepared most of the questions, but Carson was wonderful at adapting to unexpected turns.) Dick Cavett's intelligence keeps you alert and makes you nervous. When David Hartman presided at *Good Morning, America,* he seemed really to care about your answers. Maureen Reagan, the President's daughter, interviewed me for a morning show in Los Angeles. She'd filled a legal pad with notes, spoke fluently and intelligently and, like her Dad, was the epitome of charm.

This Summerall-Moskovitz duo is first of all informed. Their subjects know that and come to respect them. That's a starter. If the interviewer really knows a subject's life and career, that sets a climate. These fellows know their athletes and they speak the lingo of wide-outs, circle change-ups, and topspin lobs.

The interviews in this book make for an invigorating read. Do I agree with everything? Hardly. Is it true that "everybody" believes that Pete Rose bet on baseball? Bill James, the baseball historian, does not. Neither does Marvin Miller.

Baseball Inc.'s case against the flawed Mr. Rose was a murky proceeding in which the defendant wasn't allowed to confront his accusers. His lawyers were not given a chance to cross-examine them. And Rose's accusers were convicted felons.

Of course, Rose can make a case for himself. He does just that from his niche inside this book, where you'll find him chattering away, between Cal Ripken, Jr. and Monica Seles.

Enjoy.

Introduction

have had the good fortune to have known and observed many of the greatest legends in the history of sports. I played with some and against others, and I have broadcast the exploits of many more. Then, beginning in 1990, I began hosting a radio show that brought me close to dozens of sport's most fabled names.

The show was called *Instant Replay*. It is now known as *Pat Summerall's Sports in America*. The show airs for two hours on weekends in most major markets in the United States, and it has become better and better over the years. In its current format, I interview two or more sports figures "live on tape."

Over the years, countless people have complimented the show on the extraordinarily colorful and entertaining interviews we have broadcast. These interviews have been so attractive because of the superstars we have featured and because of what they have said.

Our interviews are not like most—those quick, machine-gun, five-minute segments in which short questions alternate with short answers. Instead, we have often gone a full two hours with a single athlete or coach. Many of the interview responses extend for more than a minute. As a result, sports figures reveal their lives and personalities in depth and detail. Sometimes what they reveal is inspiring, sometimes it's distressing, but it's never boring. And on our show, sports personalities often say things they don't say anywhere else.

In this book, we present the best of the best: the highlights of our most memorable interviews. Over the years, we have conducted hundreds of interviews. Here we publish parts of just thirty-two, all conducted in 1990–96, and even then we have room for only the most fascinating portions.

We present these legends: From football, Jim Brown, Joe Montana, Joe Namath, O. J. Simpson, Jerry Rice, Frank Gifford, Terry Bradshaw, and John Madden. From baseball, Mickey Mantle, Pete Rose, Ted Williams, Hank Aaron, Cal Ripken, Roy Campanella, and Jim Bouton.

From basketball, we present Kareem Abdul-Jabbar, Larry Bird, Bill Bradley, and John Wooden. From other sports, Wayne Gretzky, Arnold Palmer, Greg Norman, Monica Seles, Arthur Ashe, Jimmy Connors, George Foreman, Sugar Ray Leonard, Don King, Mario Andretti, Scott Hamilton, Frank Shorter, and Michael Johnson.

In these interviews, you'll find out how young children turned themselves into amazing athletes. You'll see that even some of the most imposing sports figures faced moments of failure, self-doubt, and crisis: crossroads that nearly took them not to Yankee Stadium or the Super Bowl but to oblivion. You'll learn the techniques that make for a league-leading hitter or an Olympic champion sprinter. And you'll hear hilarious tales usually told only in the pro sports lockerroom.

Some people still hold the image of the "dumb jock," but in this book many of the most prominent sports figures of the century reveal impressive intellects and descriptive vocabularies. They have captivating stories to tell and they tell them well.

Some people think that in today's world of multi-million-dollar contracts, all the noble traditions of sport have been swept aside. Yet many athletes, like Kareem Abdul-Jabbar and Joe Namath, show a reverence for their coaches. Others, like Sugar Ray

Leonard and Michael Johnson, tell how they overcame adversity to excel at the highest level. Many honor the players who suffered under unfair contracts and paved the way for free agency. Players from baseball, basketball, football, and tennis acknowledge their debt to Jackie Robinson.

No sports figure in this book seems obsessed with money. Almost all seem passionately dedicated to learning and training and executing in order to do one's best, whether it is to hit a baseball or a puck, to throw a football or a jab, to sink a shot or a putt, to run down a lob or to run through a finish line. Many, like Larry Bird and Wayne Gretzky, also show that they get as much gratification from an assist as from a score.

This, then, is a book for the sports aficionado and for the casual fan; a book for those who saw Ted Williams play and for those who've barely heard of him; a book for those seeking entertainment and for those searching for inspiration. It's been exciting and uplifting to get to know the athletes and coaches presented here, and I'm more than pleased to present these legends to you. Happy reading!

Pat Summerall

PAT SUMMERALL'S
SPORTS IN AMERICA

HANK AARON

Henry (Hank) Aaron stands alone. Of all the men who have ever played major league baseball, Hank Aaron has hit the most home runs: 755.

That much is well known. After all, Aaron broke the record of the most storied player in the history of the sport, Babe Ruth, who had hit 714, a number most fans assumed would never be equalled.

To get there was hard. It was more than just hitting 755 home runs against major league pitching—it was facing racism, which caused Aaron's professional career to begin not in the major leagues but in the Negro leagues, and which dogged him as he pursued the most famous record in baseball, a record held by a legendary player who happened to be white. Often Aaron had to come to the plate facing not only a ninety-five-mile-an-hour fastball, but also a death threat received at his hotel before the game.

Less well known than the home run record are Aaron's other accomplishments in his twenty-three years with the Milwaukee Braves, the Atlanta Braves, and, finally, the Milwaukee Brewers. Aaron is the all-time major league leader in runs batted in, with 2,297, and he is in good company: next on the list come Ruth, Lou Gehrig, and Ty Cobb. Aaron is the all-time leader in extra-base hits, *with 1,477; next come Stan Musial, Ruth, and Willie Mays. He is first all-time in total bases, with 6,856; he is followed by Musial, Mays, and Cobb. In other all-time categories, Aaron is tied with Ruth for second in runs (2,174); he is second in at-bats (12,364); he is third in games played (3,298); he is third in hits (3,771); and he is twelfth in slugging percentage (.555).*

Hank Aaron led the National League in batting average in 1956, when he hit .328, and in 1959, when his average was .355, the highest in the majors that year. Aaron led the NL in home runs four times: in 1957, with 44; in 1963, with 44 again (tying with Willie McCovey); in 1966, with 44 one more time; and, finally, the next year, with 39. He was the National League RBI leader in 1957 (132), 1960 (126), 1963 (130), and 1966 (127); no player has won the NL RBI title more often. In 1957, Aaron was voted the league's Most Valuable Player.

Aaron also led his Milwaukee Braves to the National League pennant in 1957 and 1958; each time the team faced the New York Yankees in the World Series, winning in 1957 and losing in 1958.

I saw Aaron play when he was a second baseman in Class A in Jacksonville. This was before anyone realized how good he would be. He was a very good second baseman. He didn't have power yet. But he had speed and he had an arm. He got that power as he developed physically.

Mickey Mantle was my friend, but Aaron was a better hitter. I think the figures reflect that. Maybe Aaron didn't have more power than Mantle, and he wasn't a switch-hitter, as Mickey was.

I spent some time with Aaron in April 1996. We were at the same table for about two hours. I was amazed at his knowledge of sports other than baseball. We talked about football, and he was asking me about the coming NFL draft—who was going to go first, whether there were any good quarterbacks, where the sport was going. Some say he's kind of short with people, but when I was with him, he couldn't have been more courteous to the people who lined up for autographs. He seemed very comfortable with them.

These days, when so many children must have the best available equipment at the earliest age—regulation balls, expensive leather mitts, bats of perfect size, hitting gloves—it's startling to learn about the beginnings of the all-time home run king:

We didn't have a baseball team in Mobile, Alabama. I had to start playing with soda tops and rag dolls and things like this. I heard of baseball, of course, when I was seven or eight, but I never owned one until I was about thirteen or fourteen.

I don't think I really ever had a professional teacher to teach me anything about baseball. My father did the best he could with me as a baseball player. But I think I learned myself by going out in the backyard, throwing the old broken tin caps up in the air, swinging at them.

I'll tell you a story. I know this is going to be hard to believe. I lived in the South, when they built the houses in a V shape, with the tin top. I used to take rags from my mother's and sister's old dresses. They were old dresses, of course, but I used to steal them out of the house. And I used to ball up the old rags and pretend they were a baseball. It got so I could just barely throw it to the top of that roof, and it would just barely go over, and I could run around there and catch it before it got down the other side.

There weren't that many kids around thinking about baseball at the time, and I just did things I imagined. Like I would draw three or four lines and throw a top up in the air and pretend to hit it, and if I hit it over the first line it would be a single, the second line a double, the third line a triple, and the last line would be a home run. That's how I learned to play.

If I found somebody to play with me, then we would pitch to each other, and if the ball was not hitting a certain area, we would be out. All of these things I created myself, as a kid growing up in Mobile. I enjoyed!

And then comes the name that arises in the stories of so many legendary black athletes in and out of baseball. The name is Jackie Robinson:

I never thought about playing baseball as a living until Jackie Robinson broke into baseball and gave all black kids in the South and across this country a hope that if they were good enough, they could play professional baseball.

I never thought about it. My mother, in fact, discouraged me from playing baseball. She wanted me to go to college, get an education, and come back home and be either a schoolteacher or whatever else was available for blacks at that time.

As a child, Aaron had the good fortune to see Robinson play when the Dodgers were barnstorming through the country:

The Dodgers had a farm club there, the Mobile Black Bears. The Dodgers used to come through the South all the time and play them, or the Braves used to come through. Jackie used to come through two or three days earlier and always used to come to the school, either the school or right there at the drugstore, and used to talk to kids about baseball and what to expect in life.

I would be right there with my mouth wide open, listening to every word he would say. When I got to professional baseball, I did have a chance to talk to Jackie many, many times before he passed away. In fact, he and Campanella and Don Newcombe and all of the great Brooklyn Dodger players used to travel with the Milwaukee Braves heading south, so quite naturally I had a chance to talk to Jackie quite a bit.

Jackie Robinson was my hero. He was the man who inspired me to be where I am today. Not only as a baseball player, but as a human being. As good a player as Jackie

Robinson was, he felt like he needed to do more in order to make people understand that no matter what kind of obstacles are in your way, you can go around them, jump over them, but somehow you always kept things in perspective and you could go out and get the job done.

The way I'm trying to think about Jackie Robinson is the same way we all in this country are trying to keep Dr. Martin Luther King's dream alive by keeping the Jackie Robinson dream alive, by trying to keep focusing on the fact that although I was a baseball player, as good as I was, there's still some discrimination in this country toward blacks. I think that's the dream, and that's the thing that Jackie Robinson wants me and every black ballplayer in this country to focus on and let people know we're not satisfied with what's happening.

When Jackie Robinson first broke into baseball, Branch Rickey told him that no matter what happened, he couldn't strike back. Of course, when Jackie had been in the big leagues for a long time, he felt like it was time for him to be vocal and let people understand that he was a human being, too, and that he didn't need to continue to take the abuse.

Baseball became the ticket out of poverty for Hank Aaron and his family:

The thing I liked about baseball was that it gave me an opportunity to be one-on-one with the competition. Nobody stood there but me, the pitcher, and the catcher, and it made me feel good to try to stand there and outguess the pitcher. Also, I felt like I had enough talent to play professional baseball, and I'm not talking about minor-league ball; I'm talking about major-league ball.

Also, it gave me the opportunity—coming from a large family—to make a decent enough living to help my brothers and sisters to get out of some of the poverty they were in. And that's what I needed to do.

I was not pushed into baseball by my mother and father. I played baseball because I loved it. I played baseball because financially it was going to be very rewarding for me, and I played it because it was a lot of fun.

Hank Aaron came to baseball late enough to have a long career in the major leagues, but early enough to get a taste of the Negro leagues:

Most players who came out of Mobile—McCovey and Billy Williams and some of the other great players—only played recreation baseball. That was the only type of baseball that we had to play. We played a lot of softball, but actually no baseball.

And from that point, I went into the Negro American League, and I guess I developed my skills there that showed the scouts in the National and American League that I could play professional baseball.

For Aaron, life in the Negro leagues was easy. And it was hard:

It was easy for me in a way, and yet it was hard for me in a way. It was easy because, being nineteen years old, everything was easy. And yet it was hard because although my habits as far as eating and things like that weren't different than they were in Mobile, I wasn't eating as often as I was in Mobile. We were only getting two dollars a day meal money. And when you play in Washington, D.C., and have to drive to Chicago without eating, it makes things tough.

I had a friend who was my roommate. He lives in Charlotte, North Carolina, now, and I speak with him quite often. He used to call me "Little Bro," because at the time I was the smallest and youngest person on the ball club.

We used to take our two dollars and put them together. We would buy a loaf of bread and some peanut butter, and I

would insist upon having some jelly. I said there's absolutely
no way I'm going to eat peanut butter, because I did that
when I was in Mobile, and it choked me to death on this bus.

I think the Negro leagues taught me some valuable,
valuable lessons about what life is all about. Yet I saw some
older players—I was eighteen and these players were thirty-
some years old—and they were still hoping one day that they
could get to the big leagues. And I saw these players, and I
said there's absolutely no way, even I know these guys are
much too old to get to the big leagues, and even I know their
talent must be a little bit better to get to the major leagues.

It taught me some valuable lessons. Hey, you're young,
you got to make it now, you got to get to the big leagues as
quick as possible, and when the time comes you got to take
advantage of it. I was playing with the Indianapolis Clowns,
and my paycheck was a hundred fifty dollars a month. It
certainly wasn't that much money, but the money absolutely
didn't matter. I was getting some time to play against people
that had a little bit more experience than I had. I had an
opportunity to play against pitchers that I had not seen
before, and also to be away from home. And that's the most
important—being away from home, because being a black
player, away from home for the first time, I didn't know what
to expect, because we were living in segregated hotels, we
were going to segregated cities. It was a learning experience
for me.

For Hank Aaron, baseball was a job, but it was also an escape:

I've always loved playing baseball. Baseball to me was a
way of getting away from some of the outside pressure. It was
a way of doing something that I knew absolutely well that I
was good at. I knew that I was a good ballplayer. I knew when
I got between the white lines to play baseball, I had the
supreme confidence in what I was doing.

The public may forever remember Hank Aaron as the all-time major league home run leader. That's not how he thinks of himself:

Believe it or not, I never thought of myself as a home run hitter. I always thought of myself as a complete player. I'm not taking away the fact that I hit more home runs than anybody else, but I always felt I could do other things. I know no matter what happens to Henry Aaron, I'm going to always be labeled as the man that broke Babe Ruth's record and hit more home runs than anybody else in baseball. But I always want people to remember me as a complete player.

In the Negro leagues and as a rookie with the Milwaukee Braves, Aaron certainly didn't look like the future home run king:

I was skinny and scrawny. I wasn't strong enough to hit a home run. I was too poor, really. And as I grew a little bit and got a little stronger, I started eating the right foods. I started to generate a little bit of power. But when I first started playing baseball, nine, ten, thirteen home runs were as many as I could hit.

I think power came with the confidence. So it all worked together. I think it was about seven or eight years into my career that I gradually started feeling a lot of confidence. I started feeling like nobody, no matter who was out there on the mound, could get me out. Maybe one time, maybe twice, but not the third time. I felt like I had the upper hand—I knew what he was going to throw to me, and I had a chance to hit the ball out of the park.

Aaron's approach at the plate was a mix of intuition and discipline:

Believe it or not, I guessed about ninety-five percent of the time. I not only guessed, but I also looked for the pitches in certain areas. Just because I looked for a curveball didn't necessarily mean that they'd throw me a curveball. I look for a pitch inside, outside, up, down. If I don't get my pitch, I was disciplined enough to wait the second time to get my pitch in order to hit it.

I could see the pitch before it left the pitcher's hand. I could tell when he was in his motion whether it was a fastball, curveball, change-up, or slider. I wish I could transplant it and tell somebody else what it's all about. If I could, I'd've bottled it and given it to my sons!

Ted Williams talks about the same thing. Stan Musial talks about it. When you're really hitting the ball well, no matter who you're facing—the pitcher out there can be Bob Feller or Sandy Koufax—and you see that ball, you can tell exactly whether it's a fastball or a curveball. Because I think that when you're up to the plate, you've got these blinders on; you see nothing, you hear nothing.

You can have forty-five thousand people in the stands. They can be just screaming and hollering and doing whatever they want to do, and you're just looking directly at that pitcher. I look at tennis, and they've got to have absolute quiet before they make a shot. Yet when you come up with the bases loaded and forty thousand people screaming, it calls for nothing but concentration.

Some players shrink from pressure. Aaron thrived on it, especially when it came from an opportunity to help his team:

Just give me an opportunity to get myself in that situation of playing when the pressure's on. I love playing under pressure. I loved trying to perform under pressure. I'm not saying I'm going to come out best all the time. But I love to be up there with the bases loaded and the pitcher's pitching to me. I feel like I've got a much better chance of hitting than he has of getting me out.

I love to be in the field when the bases are loaded and the ball's going to be hit to someone. I want the ball to be hit to me, because I want to catch it. I want to make the last out.

Put them all together—all of the home runs, the slugging percentages, the batting average—I think the run batted in is very, very, important. I've known some ballplayers, without calling any one particular name, who just couldn't deliver with runners in scoring position. They would get out.

Now you take that same hitter with no runners on base, and he was a different type of hitter. The guy we call the "meat and potatoes guy" is the guy who drives in that all-important run, scores that all-important run; he's the guy who's going to win championships. It's not the guy who's going to hit .350. It's not the guy who's going to hit forty-five home runs, because that same guy may hit forty-five home runs and drive in seventy-eight runs. But a guy may hit .280 and drive in a hundred and thirty runs for you. So who is important to your ball club? It's that guy that drives in the runs.

I think I did a little more concentrating when hitters were on base. I think I put a lot of pressure on myself to make sure that I was the one to drive in that runner from first base, second, or third. And especially when the bases got loaded, I told myself hey, I've got to get me a good pitch to hit out of the ballpark.

As Aaron approached that magical 715th home run, the one that would place him one past Babe Ruth, he contemplated the moment:

People said, "Oh, Hank, when you hit the home run, are you going to run backward?" I couldn't do that. I had to be myself. I did the same thing when I hit seven-fifteen as I did when I hit number one. I made sure I touched every base, and then when I got to home plate, I made sure I put my foot on home plate, because the umpires were watching me. And if I had missed that—can you imagine hitting seven-fifteen and they say, "You got to do it again"?

And I'd say, "Boy—." No way I could have done it again. I had to be the same person that I had been throughout my baseball career. I drive up to the curb sometimes in my daughter's car, an old, ragged car, and I hear people, especially young kids, and they say, "That's Hank Aaron? Why, he should be driving a Mercedes" or whatever you call it.

I say, "For what? I do what I think is best, and I'm treating myself that way—as long as I'm comfortable, I'm satisfied."

KAREEM
ABDUL-JABBAR

Bill Walton calls Kareem Abdul-Jabbar the best player he ever
played against. Among the players Bill played against were
Larry Bird, Magic Johnson, and Michael Jordan. When you think of a
man who's over seven feet tall—Kareem is seven-feet-two—you envision a guy who's kind of gangly, who's not well coordinated, who grew
so fast that his coordination didn't develop along with his physique.
You think of a guy who stumbles all over himself. Even a phenomenal
player like Chamberlain you didn't consider by any means graceful.

But when I first saw Kareem play at Power Memorial High
School in New York, he was always very graceful. He had a great
shooting touch. During his pro years, his famous "Sky Hook" was
almost unstoppable.

Also unlike some big men, Kareem was a great player at both
ends of the court. Obviously, he could score. On defense, in addition
to grabbing a lot of rebounds, he was an intimidating force in the
middle. When Kareem was with the Lakers, people wouldn't take it to
the hole, because he was a very good shot blocker.

Before he changed his name, Kareem was Lew Alcindor. He was

a three-time high school All-American at Power Memorial, and the school had the number-one Catholic team in the country. Lew went west to play under John Wooden at UCLA. It was culture shock: the eastern ethnic world of Manhattan meets the blond surfer world of Southern California. Even so, Lew led the Bruins to the national basketball championship all three years he played on the varsity: 1967, 1968, and 1969.

In all three years, he was also the NCAA tournament Most Outstanding Player. In both 1967 and 1969 he was the national college Player of the Year.

Alcindor went on to star in the NBA with the Milwaukee Bucks and, more memorably, with the Los Angeles Lakers. He was the number one choice in the 1969 draft and broke in as Rookie of the Year for the 1969–70 season. In Milwaukee, he led his team to one NBA championship, over Baltimore in 1971. The same year, he changed his named to Kareem Abdul-Jabbar.

Back in L.A., beginning in 1975, he led the Lakers to five championships. These were over Philadelphia in 1980, Philadelphia again in 1982, Boston in 1985, Boston again in 1987, and Detroit in 1988. The mid-to-late-eighties Lakers teams, featuring players such as Magic Johnson, James Worthy, Byron Scott, Michael Cooper, and Kurt Rambis, were among the greatest teams of all time.

Kareem was MVP of the NBA six times: in 1971, 1972, 1974, 1976, 1977, and 1980. He was MVP of the NBA playoffs in both 1971, at age twenty-four, and 1985, at age thirty-eight.

When he retired in 1989, he had played twenty seasons in the NBA and was the all-time leader in more than twenty statistical categories. Among the categories in which he remains at or near the top:

Career playoff records:
Years played, eighteen.
Points, 5,762 (average, 24.3).
Field goals, 2,356 (of 4,422 attempts, for a .533 average).
Second in free throws, 1,050 (average, .740).
Third in rebounds, 2,481 (average, 10.5 per game).

Career regular season records:
Years played, twenty.
Games played, 1,560.
Points, 38,387 (average, 24.6).
Field goals, 15,387 (of 28,207, for a .559 average).
Third in rebounds, 17,440 (average, 11.2 per game).
Personal fouls, 4,657 (but with only 48 disqualifications).

Annual leadership:
Scoring average, 1971, 31.7.
Scoring average, 1972, 34.8 (tenth highest in NBA history).
Rebounding average, 1976, 16.9.
Field goal percentage, 1977, .579.
Blocked shots, 1975, 4.85 per game.
Blocked shots, 1976, 4.12.
Blocked shots, 1979, 3.95.
Blocked shots, 1980, 3.41.

Kareem's introduction to basketball was not auspicious:

I first picked up a basketball in the public grade school in my neighborhood. I was about six or seven years old. I remember spending one recess just trying to fling the ball through the hoop underhanded. I couldn't even get the ball up over my head. That's how strong I was.

Baseball was really what I had my heart in. It's just something we played almost year round in my neighborhood. We'd take a little bit of time off for football and basketball, but as soon as it got warm, we got to stickball and baseball, and we stuck with that until it was too cold to play and we were chased indoors.

Interspersed in there I tried a little basketball, but as I went through Little League, I got taller and taller. It seemed to me that I would be an ideal pitcher, but I didn't have the control at that point.

HANK AARON

KAREEM ABDUL-JABBAR

ARTHUR ASHE

LARRY BIRD

BILL BRADLEY

TERRY BRADSHAW

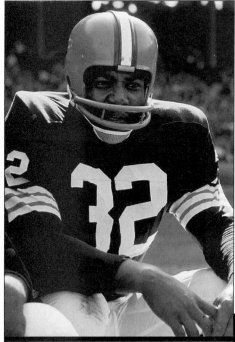

JIM BROWN

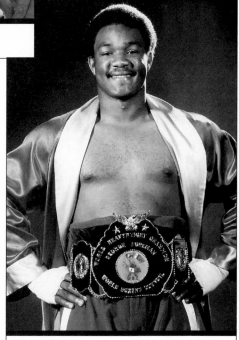

GEORGE FOREMAN

FRANK GIFFORD

WAYNE GRETZKY

KAREEM ABDUL-JABBAR • 15

Also, as I was getting taller, I was going from being a preadolescent into my teenage years, started getting up over six feet tall, and I just seemed to have the right body for basketball, and everything seemed to just fall in place.

All the other things I had done as a kid, baseball, football, swimming, running, really helped me in basketball. I just seemed to be prepared for it, and I started learning the fine points of the game.

Basketball was a different thing to me at different times of my life. When I was in high school, it was really fun, and it was a challenge just to master the game, to learn the game and to master my own body, my coordination, and all the skills I needed for the game. And then from that point on, it became more of a profession. It was the way I earned my way through college. Then it became a full-time profession for me, and it was always fun, but it was in a different context at each stage.

Most players are recruited as juniors and seniors in high school. Kareem heard from colleges a little earlier:

I started getting college offers in the ninth grade. It was a very strange thing, because I was still basically just entering adolescence, but in another way I was also entering the adult world, and I was kind of viewed more in that vein than anything else, and it was like part of my youth was taken away from me. I was kind of thrust on the national stage. I know people my age who tell me they remember reading about me in *Scholastic* magazine when I was in the eighth and ninth grade. That type of thing affected my life.

Kareem's coach at Power Memorial, Jack Donohue, prohibited him from speaking with the press:

For awhile, I think Coach Donohue's policy of not letting me talk to the press did me a lot of good, because it helped me focus on what I needed to be paying attention to, which was doing well in school and playing what I wanted to play in, in growing up rather than providing good copy.

But things went on that way after I got into college, and then it started to be a problem. I think my freshman year in college, it also was a good policy, but as I started playing varsity college ball, the demands got to be so great that some accommodation had to be made.

Kareem was interested early in his life in civil rights:

I think it all started for me when my body consciousness really stirred. It was something that I really couldn't avoid, because we watched the civil rights movement unfold on television, and it was really something to see, the type of thing that really you couldn't be neutral about.

It really affected me deeply and made me want to be something to be proud of and get the respect that I desired as a human being, just from seeing what was happening in the South and also in New York City.

A number of my friends went down to Chase Manhattan Plaza to protest Chase Manhattan Bank's involvement in investments in South Africa. I think it was like '61 or '62, and I just saw the polarization and hostility that that whole consciousness was provoking, and it was really something to observe.

Power's Coach Donohue introduced his players to pro basketball:

Our gym was located only eleven blocks from the old Madison Square Garden, which was on Forty-ninth Street. The teams would come up to our gym and practice, and Coach Donohue would get free passes to the Garden.

So we would go down and see the professional teams play, and he always made it a point to tell us to go and watch the Celtics. The Knicks would play the second game, but the first game would be the Celtics. I would watch Bill Russell and watch how he helped his teammates, how he made everybody a great defensive player by finishing off the defensive plays and starting their fast break and giving them the defensive pressure that made them impossible to beat.

The next day, Coach Donohue would ask us, "All right, look in the box score. How many guys got more than twenty points?"

We'd all look and scratch our heads and say, "Listen, nobody got twenty points."

He says, "Right, you see that, but how many guys scored in double figures?"

And the Celtics always had six or seven guys in double figures. He says that's how you win basketball games. You spread the ball around, you play tough defense, you take the best, easiest shots that you can, and you always try to make each other better. He showed us how to do it on the court. And everything after that was just application of those principles.

When Kareem was sorting through recruiting offers, he chose UCLA:

The main reason I went to UCLA was I liked the idea of playing ball at a school that had been doing so well. They had won the NCAA two years in a row, and they had good guys going to school there. I'd be playing with good athletes, it was an excellent academic school, and it gave me a chance to escape home. It had everything; it didn't have any downside to it.

One of the things it had was John Wooden:

I think the best way to describe Coach Wooden is somebody who really had dissected and really understood the composition of the dynamics of the game. He knew how A led to B if certain things were happening or led to something else if other things were happening, and he taught us how to adjust to each situation and still execute our game plan no matter what was happening.

He just constantly drilled it down, just tore all the situations apart and had us work on it, on the fundamentals of it, offensively and defensively. And we just applied ourselves, without really having to think about it; someone has to be at a certain point. We could just look at the court and know what was needed from us.

Coach Wooden kind of kept a distance in one way. He was not intrusive. He wanted everybody to know that they were expected to do well at their studies and everything, but he did not try to intrude in your life. But he was there for you if you wanted to go talk to him.

UCLA could never have been as successful as it had been without the leadership of Coach Wooden and his understanding of the game. His ability to train and motivate young men was exceptional, and he knew how to pick people who could play for him. He didn't want certain types of athletes. No matter how much physical talent, they had to be able to understand certain concepts. They described him as the Wizard, and you could call him that, because he understood it all inside out and from front to back.

In some sports settings, intimidation can be a big factor. Kareem says that's not the case in the NBA:

Intimidation really doesn't work. It might work against a rookie or someone who hasn't really competed at a high level very much. But for people who've really been out there in the fires of competition, the intimidation factor does not become a big issue.

You know what you can do, you know that you can do A, B,

and C and you can't do one, two, and three, and the successful players are not intimidated. They go out and compete.

As the top college player in America at a time when pros did not compete on the U.S. Olympic basketball team, Kareem would have been the most prominent player on the U.S. basketball team at the 1968 Olympics in Mexico City. He chose not to go:

A lot was being said as to whether or not the Olympics were a political event. If they were, I, along with a lot of other black athletes, felt that we should make a certain statement because the Civil Rights Act had not yet been passed and it was very important to all black people that this legislation be passed and that our needs and our rights be protected if we were going to go represent the United States. I was very much on the side of those who wanted to make sure that we did not get taken for granted.

Some people thought Kareem was hostile to the press. That was a misinterpretation:

There are always certain people who don't like you, but the overwhelming majority of reporters I dealt with were at least trying to be objective, and that's really all I wanted. I had a few people that were on my case just because it was me, and there's nothing you can do about that.

Although over ninety-seven percent of journalists try to conduct their job with some ethical standards, the one or two times it happens to you personally makes you hate all of them and makes you suspicious of all of them. Unfortunately, I was very suspicious in those days, and my suspicion was a lot of times interpreted as hostility.

Kareem is a basketball player who found special inspiration from a man who played a different sport:

With hindsight, it's easy for me to see how much of the example of Jackie Robinson that I absorbed. He was a very competitive person, but with a lot of quiet, intense pride. He wasn't demonstrative, he didn't yell and howl a lot, but when he went on the field of competition, he was this serious warrior, 100 percent, and he played for the jugular and played to win and showed a lot of skill and cunning. I really admired him; he was my first hero and I kind of absorbed his style.

Another idol was Wilt Chamberlain:

I met Wilt either before or after my freshman year of high school, and he had already heard about me and heard that I might be a good player, and I was like totally blown away that he would even know my name. I would see him at the Rucker tournament in Harlem. He had given me his phone number, because even though he was playing for Philadelphia, he lived in New York, and he'd commute to Philadelphia for the games.

So every so often I'd call him, and he'd let me use some of his jazz albums and stuff like that. It was a very interesting time to be around a superstar like that and see how his life could be, all the things he had, all the comforts, beautiful women, going to the Riviera, this place, that place. And he talked about it like it was nothing, and it was like blowing my mind. I remember he had this one beautiful girlfriend from Denmark that I fell in love with. Much to my dismay, it had certainly not even the faintest possibility of happening, but, boy, there were a few days I sat drooling on his couch.

I never really saw myself as being able to live like Wilt. I had to try and live like me and had to develop my own identity. I kind of evolved into it my own way—fortunately, because it would have been a tragedy if I had become a carbon of Wilt. I would rather be who I am, and I think it's worked out for the best.

The highlights of Kareem's pro career were the three NBA final series against the Boston Celtics. In 1984, Boston prevailed. In 1985 and 1987, it was Los Angeles:

The eighties saw the Celtics and Lakers go at it a number of times, and I think that was probably the most enjoyable and the most challenging, and it lasted a while. It was theater for several years, and it didn't just pop out of nowhere and disappear quickly. It had a great prelude with Magic's competition against Larry Bird in college. People transferred it from the college game to the pro game, and I think that's when the pro game started to gain huge amounts of fans.

What's the secret of Kareem's success? His answer shows his modesty and his power of analysis:

I think I was just fortunate enough to play in a position that does not get renewed with great talent very often. The shorter you are, the more people there are competing for the space, but when you can play the pivot well, there aren't a whole lot of very good pivotmen who come along. And my commitment off the court to conditioning and the fact that I didn't mind training twelve months a year really helped me physically to be able to keep the pace and not get worn out mentally.

MARIO ANDRETTI

Born in Montona, Italy, Mario Andretti moved to the United States in 1955 at the age of fifteen, settling with his family in Nazareth, Pennsylvania. He has become one of the most daring—and successful—drivers in the history of auto racing. He is second to A. J. Foyt among all-time leaders in IndyCar victories, with 52. Like Foyt, Andretti (though retired from the IndyCar circuit) remains an active driver. Andretti is the all-time leader in pole positions, with 67. He was the IndyCar annual champion four times. Andretti has earned more than $11 million on the track.

He also is the senior member of the most impressive father-son duo ever seen in auto racing: 27 IndyCar victories make Mario's son Michael sixth on the all-time winner list. Perhaps most impressive, Mario Andretti is the IndyCar driver who has crossed over most successfully to the Formula One circuit, where he was World Champion in 1978 and where he is fourteenth on the all-time victories list, having won 12 races.

With all his success, you might think he would be overconfident, even arrogant. Not at all. When I've seen him, he's never been anything but courteous. But on the track he's as aggressive as any driver.

Andretti knows that pressure is highest when a driver has to pass:

Those are the excited moments. You make that chancy move that could mean the position. Sometimes the position means coming in second or first, and usually a lot depends on the competitor—as to how you go about it. There are times when you can really trust the men you're working with, and you can really have a good time doing it. There are other times when you can't trust them, and it's miserable because you don't know what's going to happen.

Yet sooner or later, you've got to take that chance. And if you get away with it, fine, but many times it's a really close one. Other times, you're both on the wall.

There are no two moves alike. Each one is a brand new experience. After you've had some negative experiences, it really works on you, when you're trying to decide. Yet you know you don't have all the time in the world to ponder a situation either. You know you've gotta go for it. That's what keeps it fascinating.

Observers who don't closely follow auto racing may think racing is simply a matter of steering an awesomely fast car in the right direction. But, as Andretti explains, the driver must be equal to a very physical task:

The importance of the physical aspect in auto racing is probably the most misunderstood aspect from a fan's standpoint, mainly because it's a nonparticipant sport. You could watch a tennis match and pick up your racket, and you go out there and bat away with your buddy, and you know you get tired. Even though you can go to a driving school, it's some sort of facsimile car—nothing like a true blue.

So when I'm away from a race car, say three weeks—which is probably as long as I'm away any time during a year—when I get back in, I can only endure three, four, five laps and that's it, and I gotta come in and sort of get myself back. And I'm somewhat dizzy because of the g force.

You almost have to get reacquainted and tuned in: your wrist aches and you're out of breath because you are not in sync with your breathing control and you ache all over. So the physical aspect is important—even more today because of the additional g forces that you're experiencing out there.

The age factor is something I'm very interested in because I'm undergoing my own experiment here. I'm at a stage when I should be retired from all racing. I should be on the sidelines, cheering on my kid. But I've chosen to test myself. I want to see if the desire can supersede the deterioration of the physical side.

Experience and desire will probably keep me in it because I keep my adrenaline flowing. And I feel that my reflexes are still O.K. I know that I'm coming close to a lot of limits, but I'm just trying to see if I can defy the norm.

ARTHUR ASHE

Arthur Ashe played a unique role in the history of tennis. He had a combination of eloquence, modesty, and grace rarely found in athletics or any other field. He maintained dignity throughout the many harsh challenges he faced, from racism to a heart attack at thirty-six to AIDS (contracted during a heart bypass operation), which took his life.

With a 115-mile-per-hour serve, a backhand of almost infinite variation, and an amazing cool on the court, Arthur Ashe was the first black male player to win a Grand Slam tennis championship. He won the U.S. Open in 1968, the Australian Open in 1970, and Wimbledon in 1975. As a child, he confronted racism in his native Richmond, Virginia; now the citizens of that city, capital of the Confederacy, have erected a statue of Ashe on Monument Avenue, a five-mile boulevard previously reserved for Confederate heroes of the Civil War.

I first knew Arthur only from watching him play. I covered the U.S. Open when he won it in 1968. Later he worked in the CBS booth with Tony Trabert and me. He was very well-spoken, very low-key but dedicated to whatever he did on the court or in the broadcast booth. When he was about to do a broadcast, he prepared thoroughly, unlike *so many former pro players who just sit down with no prior prepara-tion.*

As a breakthrough black player, Arthur Ashe followed in the foot-steps of Jackie Robinson:

> I grew up as most black kids in the South, in a city like Richmond, dreaming of being Jackie Robinson. He was the first black player to play major league baseball this century, he wore number 42, and he played second base, so when the baseball tryouts at the public park where I lived began every summer, every kid wanted to play second base and wear number 42. And I did play baseball, and I was always a pretty good athlete, but I wasn't very large, so I eventually wound up concentrating on tennis and got to be pretty good at it.

But Ashe did not concentrate so hard as to ignore the world around him:

> I was very aware of what was going on. The sit-ins started in '59, and the other black students at UCLA and I were very aware of what was going on back East and in the South, with black college students, many of them athletes, involved in sit-ins.
>
> In fact, the first sit-in at the Woolworth's lunch counter in Greensboro, North Carolina, eventually involved athletes from the school. So we were very aware of that, even though most of the black student athletes at UCLA were born in California and raised in California and therefore did not suffer the same sort of racism one would find legally sanctioned in the South. But we certainly followed it.
>
> And you had the Olympics in '60 and '64, where South Africa was an issue. And there was one other trend that started in the early sixties, which we couldn't help but notice: the granting of independence to most of the former anglophone and francophone colonies in Africa. Harold

Macmillan and Charles de Gaulle spearheaded that effort at
least from Europe, and so you had countries like Nigeria;
Ghana; Guinea; Ivory Coast; Kenya; Tanganyika, now
Tanzania; Uganda all gaining independence in the same time
frame. So you have this African independence movement
paralleling the U.S. black social revolution and the sit-ins. It
made for a very heady period.

*Ashe helped integrate tennis not only in the United States but also
worldwide, starting with the Davis Cup:*

We were slated to meet South Africa in '68. South Africa
was a very contentious issue as far back as 1960, the last year
they were in the Olympics. Fortunately, they lost to West
Germany in a match played in France, under armed guard
with no spectators. In 1974 South Africa won the Davis Cup
by default because they were supposed to play India in the
final, and India refused to play them.

I got very involved in 1968, when, at a players' meeting,
Cliff Drysdale, a South African, told me that I wouldn't be
able to play in the South African Open in Johannesburg that
November. And I remembered that the same thing had
happened to me when I was twelve years old.

My coach, Ron Charity, took me over to the white park in
Richmond, Virginia, when I was twelve, just to try to see if I
could enter the official USTA tournament, and I was turned
down. And so here's the second time this had happened to
me, strictly because of race, and, of course, there's a
difference between twelve and twenty-five, so I just decided
that, well, if I cannot play in South Africa, then the
tournament should not count for world rankings. And so I
began to get very involved in that issue.

LARRY BIRD

Larry Bird was one of the greatest long-range shooters in the history of the National Basketball Association. He was also one of the greatest passers. His stunning combination of skills made him the dominant NBA star of the mid–1980s. In 1981, he led the Boston Celtics to the NBA championship over Houston. But Larry Bird is best known for taking the Celts to the finals in four straight years, from 1984 through 1987.

Each time the team faced the superbly talented Los Angeles Lakers, a team that featured Kareem Abdul-Jabbar, Magic Johnson, and James Worthy. In 1984 and 1986, Boston won the finals; in 1985 and 1987, L.A. was the champion. The series of four Boston–Los Angeles finals presented a rivalry unseen before or after in the NBA.

Bird also has his share of statistics. In the history of the NBA play-offs, he ranks fourth in points, with 3,897, for an average of 23.8 per game; he trails only Abdul-Jabbar, Jerry West, and Michael Jordan. He is second in assists, with 1,062, and is behind only Magic.

He led the NBA in free-throw percentage in 1984 (88.8 percent), 1986 (89.6), 1987 (91.0), and 1990 (93.0).

On the list of all-time leaders for regular season points, Bird is fourteenth with 21,791 points, an average of 24.3 points a game. He *accomplished these figures over thirteen years, while every player above him on the list except Michael Jordan accumulated his total over a career of fourteen to twenty seasons.*

Bird was the NBA Rookie of the Year in 1980. He was Most Valuable Player of the finals in 1984 and 1986. He was MVP of the All-Star Game in 1982. He was MVP of the NBA in three straight years, 1984 through 1986; no one has ever won it four times in a row, and the only players to match Bird were Bill Russell and Wilt Chamberlain.

Bird was more than a shooter and passer. He could also get the key rebound. But I think his greatest quality was that he was a leader. He and Magic Johnson have been the ultimate team players, excellent passers who got everybody involved on both ends of the court.

As a basketball fan, I probably enjoyed watching Larry more than any other player I've ever seen. That's because he did so many subtle things. In fact, he was so subtle that a lot of people didn't realize what he was doing. For instance, he was supposed to be one of the great trash-talkers of all time, but fans never thought he was saying anything to anybody. He also was wonderfully effective in the way he would block out under the boards, but you were never conscious that he was doing that. I think he lulled even his opponents to sleep, and then all of a sudden they lost.

Larry Bird grew up poor in the basketball-crazed heartland of Indiana. His family moved sixteen times in seventeen years because it often couldn't pay the rent. Larry enjoyed many sports, but basketball was number one:

When I was growing up, I was into just about every sport. I played a lot of baseball and football, a little bit of basketball. I don't think I really caught onto basketball until probably my sophomore year in high school. That's when I really got involved and started playing a lot and getting interested in what the coach had to say and what he was trying to teach you. From that point on it has just been part of my life.

I really enjoyed walking into our gym every night. On the

wall there was a sign that said "Seating Capacity, 2,800." Being from French Lick and knowing that we had just twenty-two hundred in our town and we were going to fill it every night probably gave us a little more inspiration to play hard.

As a six-foot-six senior, Larry Bird led the Spring Valley High Blackhawks to their best season ever. Bird finished second in the state in scoring, with a 30.6 point average, and was third in rebounding, averaging 20.6 boards a game. This impressed Bobby Knight enough to give Larry a full scholarship to Indiana, but Bird spent only twenty-four days with the Hoosiers. He attended a junior college and then enrolled at Indiana State:

At Indiana State the fans started coming a little bit at a time. It wasn't a mad rush at the gate to get in. We started off our first game, and I think it was like three or four thousand people, then it got up to six thousand and then eight thousand. The next thing you know, they had "Sold Out" signs on the marquee outside, and then you noticed people in town would recognize you a little more.

I think the big turnaround was the time in my sophomore or junior year when I was on the cover of *Sports Illustrated*. Then you got recognition from around the country and around the world. Every time you'd go out, people would recognize you, not only in Terre Haute [where Indiana State is located], but in Indianapolis or Chicago.

That was pretty difficult on me because I never did like to be around a large group of people in a room, and I didn't like to go out in public where everybody noticed you. I liked to live my life quiet and in the background. Then all of a sudden you're thrown in front of everybody. It was a tough adjustment, and it's still tough at times.

One of Red Auerbach's shrewder moves in a career of shrewd moves with the Boston Celtics was to draft Larry Bird as the sixth choice in the 1978 college draft even though Larry was a junior and intended to play his senior year. Auerbach intended to sign Bird at the end of the 1979 college season, just weeks before he would lose rights to him:

I was drafted by the Celtics in my junior year, and there was a lot of speculation that I was going to come out, but there was only one reason I went to college, and that was to get a degree. And I was going to stay there until I achieved it, and I didn't care if it took me eight years.

I think it's too easy in life to get something started and quit. Basketball has been great to me and it's going to set me for the rest of my life, but it's not the only thing in life. I think you have to have an education, and you have to strive to keep doing things that you want to achieve.

That senior year gave the Indiana State Sycamores their best season ever: the team was 33–0 and number one in the country when it met Magic Johnson and Michigan State in the 1979 NCAA final in Salt Lake City. The battle was so intensely anticipated that it drew the biggest TV audience in the history of college basketball:

You get in the NCAA tournament, you play a game, and you don't worry about getting to the Final Four or winning the whole thing. You just worry about your next opponent. The next thing you know, you're in the final game against probably the greatest team in college basketball that year. I'd seen Michigan State play. They not only had Magic Johnson, they had three or four guys that could just flat play.

We were very fortunate. We lucked out along the way. We had some good games and some bad games. We felt our free throw shooting was going to get us sooner or later, but it never did. We made it to the final game and played against a team that had a lot of tools that we didn't have.

We were just very fortunate to get where we got, because

we didn't have four or five guys that could run and jump and shoot night in and night out like they did. They had the better team, and they won [75–64]. I was disappointed that we lost, but I think I was sad knowing that it was the last game I was going to play for Indiana State University.

Even though the players lost, the university treated the team as though they'd won the championship. The Sycamores' plane from Salt Lake was escorted by four Indiana Air National Guard F–100s, and the team was greeted at Terre Haute's small airport by five thousand cheering fans:

That's something that will be with you the rest of your life, because in a city like Terre Haute, it might never happen again. The one thing about the people of Terre Haute is that they sensed early on in my senior year, when we started off winning ten or fifteen games in a row, that this might be a once-in-a-lifetime thing. Not only did the older people or the middle-age citizens get involved; young kids, everybody got involved. That's what made it so special. So we were their team, and we put them on the map, and they were proud of us as much as we were proud of them, and it all just worked out.

In the NBA Bird had less speed and jumping ability than most players. He compensated with hand-eye coordination, quickness, and a burning desire to compete:

I had to practice a lot to get my skills down, but once I mastered them, everything else was pretty easy. I think this league is overrated at times, because you look at guys who can jump high and dunk and have a forty-seven-inch vertical jump. Then they go out there and get three or four rebounds a game. To me, that's just a waste of talent.

A coach in high school said that if you boxed out and did

the fundamentals and learned the game the way it's supposed to be played, which I tried to do, you'll be able to outsmart and master these guys that have so much physical ability. You'll be able to go out and take their game away from them.

During his NBA career Bird was famous for showing up for practice before anyone else and for staying after all the other players had left. But even that didn't paint the whole picture. Those who knew him well knew he sometimes would sleep on the court after practice, getting up just in time to practice for the next day's game:

In high school we used to do that, to sleep on the mats if we had a Sunday or a Saturday night practice, two practices a day. You know, get something to eat and come back and lay around and sleep in the gym and wait for practice to start.

I probably don't work as hard as I used to because of the injuries. I've had a lot of injuries the past couple of years, and it's sort of held me back. I haven't been able to do the things that I like to do, but I'd say the first eight to ten years in the league, and the four years in college, I worked pretty hard to establish a reputation and to get my game as good as I could possibly get it.

Bird enjoyed the NBA but found that the tough schedule of the pro league required certain compromises:

The NBA lacked some of the magic, because in college you might just play two times a week. Here you play four days a week most of the time. You're not able to play at your best every time, because fatigue sets in. But both college and pro basketball are very valuable, and both of them are very special. The college league is one thing, the pro league is another. I enjoyed playing both of them. Every night we step on the court, I enjoy the game.

One aspect of the NBA game Bird didn't like was the banging:

I don't know how a boxer feels when he steps in the ring, but when you step on the basketball court, you know you're going to get bumped and pushed and banged around. I think a lot of altercations start when the officials are very lax in their job. If a guy comes down and fouls a guy and holds a guy three times in a row and they don't pick that up, something's going to happen. I don't blame them totally, but I think a lot of things happen because they miss a lot of what's going on out there.

When I first came into the league, they said it was a real rough, tough league. But now it's getting to where you hold and push, and I think it takes a lot away from the game when a guy goes up for a shot and somebody grabs his arm or hits him on the arm, and everybody's got their own little style where they knee a guy in the hip or push him underneath the basket. To me, that's not basketball, but I get paid to do it, and most of the nights it's a pretty nice game.

Bird had special respect for his 1986 Celtics, which won the NBA championship, four games to two, over the Los Angeles Lakers. An important part of their success was their sixth man, Bill Walton:

Bill's a great talent. It was unfortunate that he had a lot of injuries before he got there, but if he didn't, he probably wouldn't have gotten here. I think Bill could have been one of the greatest centers of all times if he stayed healthy. It's a time in my life I'll never forget, because I feel that the '86 team that the Celtics had was the best team that I've ever seen in the professional league since I've been here.

In the NBA, friendships meant so much to Larry Bird that it hurt:

In this league they come and go so fast. You have a lot of guys that are here for maybe a year, year and a half, and they're gone. There's no telling how many guys have come and gone since I've been here, and a lot of my good friends have come and gone. It seems like every year I've had a good friend who's left. So it's been tough, and now I sort of just go my own way because it's just been too hard on me to get to know somebody and then they get traded a couple weeks later.

Famed as an unselfish player, Bird often derived as much gratification from passing as from scoring:

It's according to how the flow of the game is going. If you're into the game, and you're scoring and it seems like you can't miss, sometimes that's the best. But if everybody's involved, and you're cutting and you're moving and you've got the ball in your hands, and you thread the needle two or three times in a row, taking a chance of getting it deflected or stolen, sometimes that's the enjoyment I get out of the game. I like to make a long pass. I like to play quarterback a lot, where I throw the long pass and hit the guy right on the money. That's always been a big jolt for me.

JIM BOUTON

Jim Bouton was either the greatest pitcher ever to be a star writer or the greatest writer ever to be a star pitcher. That is, he wrote Ball Four, *the best known insider's book in the history of sports, and part of the book was about his years as a star pitcher with the New York Yankees. Known as the "Bulldog" for his tenacity in tough games, Jim Bouton rarely missed a start. In a career that took him from the Yankees to Seattle to Houston to Atlanta, he had good years and bad, but at his best he was about as good as they come. After going 7–7 as a rookie with New York in 1962, he had a record of 21–7 in 1963. In the American League that year, only his teammate Whitey Ford won more games, 24. Bouton's winning percentage, .750, was also second in the league, exceeded only by Ford's .774. Bouton's ERA was just 2.53, fourth in the league. He allowed just 6.89 hits per nine innings, third best in the AL. His six shutouts were second in the league. In the World Series, he lost the only game he pitched, but his ERA was a mere 1.29.*

The next year Bouton went 18–13 with a 3.02 ERA. His 271 innings placed him third in the AL. In the World Series, he was 2–0 and had an ERA of 1.56, giving him a lifetime Series ERA of 1.48. Bouton had twelve complete games in 1963 and eleven in 1964. He

*started thirty-seven games in 1964, making him the American
League leader.*

*He was thrilled when, at age twenty-three, he was called up by the
Yankees:*

Playing for the Yankees in 1962 was like a dream. I was
walking around in a fog. It was like I couldn't believe it. I had
a silly grin on my face a lot. I remember coming home from
my first week with the Yankees and having dinner with my
family and saying, "Well, today Mickey said this and Ellie said
that." I was on a first-name basis with Mickey Mantle and
Roger Maris and Elston Howard and Whitey Ford. I said,
"The other day, Whitey said to me . . . "

It was funny to me, to be talking about these guys. They
were teammates of mine. What was I doing here? I really had
no business being on the New York Yankees even though I
knew I had ability and I believed in myself. It seemed like
making the big leagues and being on the Yankees was too
much of a dream come true.

I felt the Yankee mystique. I felt during ballgames that we
would win a game. The other team knew they were playing
the Yankees, and that would cause them to make a mistake,
and we'd go ahead and take advantage of it and win. So there
was a tremendous feeling of confidence that you had walking
out to the mound as a Yankee pitcher. On the other hand, you
had to have good stuff because the batters didn't roll over
and play dead. The Yankees couldn't throw their scrapbooks
out on the mound and win, but there was an element of
waiting for something to happen.

It was great fun to be in the big leagues and to be a
Yankee. The most fun for me was having fans come up and
ask me for my autograph. If they didn't come up and ask me
for my autograph, I'd sort of hang out so they would. I
enjoyed it. A lot of the Yankees didn't like giving autographs,
because they'd been in the big leagues for ten years. They

were hounded by the news media and by fans always wanting a piece of them and so, to them, it was a real nuisance. But to me, it was fun. It was a novelty, it was exciting.

Sportswriters wanted to talk to me, they wanted to do an article, put my picture in a newspaper. Hey, that would be great! It would be great to see my picture in the paper! It would be great to have them write an article about me! Hey, somebody wants my autograph! So I really enjoyed that part of being in the big leagues.

I remember before a World Series game in 1964, we were in St. Louis staying at the Chase Park Plaza Hotel, and I was hanging around the lobby waiting for people to come up and talk to me about the game tomorrow.

"Hey, what are you going to pitch to these Cardinals here? Can I have your autograph? Who are you?" So I got a big kick out of it. Even kids who didn't know me because, being with the Yankees, at least as a rookie, nobody knew who I was, really, compared to Roger Maris and Mickey Mantle.

I had some very funny incidents. I remember a father and son coming across the lobby to get my autograph, and the son was running ahead, and his father hollered out to him, "Who is that, Son? Who is he?"

The son said, "It's only Jim Bouton, Dad."

His father said, "Well, get his autograph anyway."

Kids would come up to me and say, "Are you anybody good?"

I'd say, "Well, not yet, but get my autograph now, and maybe it'll be worth something in a few years."

Yankee veterans were very friendly to the rookies and, I think, made it possible for them to adjust. They included us in their pranks and their horseplay and stories. Every once in awhile they'd invite us out to dinner, which was a big thrill.

I remember my first game at Yankee Stadium, I pitched a shutout against the Washington Senators. It was the worst shutout in the history of baseball. I walked seven guys, and I gave up seven hits. So I pitched the entire game from the stretch position, stranding fourteen runners. It was the longest game. Hector Lopez made three leaping catches in left field. After the ballgame was over, I came walking into the clubhouse, and Mickey Mantle, of all people, had laid out a path of white towels from the door over to my locker so I could walk on white towels to my locker. That was probably one of the biggest thrills of my career.

In Bouton's rookie season, 1962, the Yankees were on their way to their twelfth pennant in fourteen years, and Mantle was on course for his third season as American League MVP:

He was the most exciting ballplayer to watch, because he had this tremendous power from both sides of the plate. Left- or right-handed. Left-handed, he would sweep the ball. He was a low-ball hitter left-handed, so he'd sweep a low pitch and golf it into the upper deck in right field. I remember he won the third game of the '64 World Series, the game I was pitching. It was a 1–1 tie going into the ninth inning, and he said in the dugout, "I'm going to hit one out of here off of Barney Schultz."

Sure enough, Barney Schultz threw a knuckleball that broke down about ankle high, and Mickey just golfed it right into the stands for a home run. We won that game two to one. It was my first World Series win. But then, right-handed, Mickey would tomahawk the ball. Like chopping a tree with an ax. He would hit these tremendous line drives into the seats right-handed.

So there's two different swings and two different kinds of home runs. Of course, he had this tremendous speed. It was really exciting to watch him. Particularly in Boston, to be sitting in the dugout along the third base line and watch Mickey steal third base from second. To watch him come

charging right at you, because your dugout was so close to
the field it looked like he was going to run right into the
dugout. It was a tremendously exciting experience to play
ball with Mickey Mantle.

He was also great fun in the clubhouse. He was a real
practical joker. I remember one time he got up a raffle.
Everybody put in five dollars. He was raffling off a ham and
then he drew a number out and it was my number. I had the
winning number. So I went over to his locker and I said,
"Here's the winning number, Mick, where's my ham?"

He said, "Well, there is no ham."

I said, "What are you talking about?"

He said, "Well, that's one of the hazards of entering a
game of chance."

Then, of course, there was always the Mickey Mantle
fishing tournament in Florida. The whole team would drive
down to the Loxahatchee canals and fish in the Everglades.
You'd go down with your roommate, or you'd pair off with
somebody. Two guys to a boat. Everybody would take off
from the dock about eight o'clock in the morning, and you'd
come back at noon, and whatever boat had the most fish
would split the prize with whoever had the biggest fish.

I think everybody would kick in fifty bucks or a hundred
bucks or something like that. So there was a lot of money in
the pot, but Mickey and Whitey would always win. Most fish
or biggest fish, because they were very good fishermen. I
was a terrible fisherman, and so was my partner and
roommate, Phil Linz.

One spring, we were driving down there, and on the way
we passed this fish store. This is like seven o'clock in the
morning. We backed up real quick and pulled into the store;
they were just opening up. We said, "We'd like to buy a large
fish."

He said, "Well, we don't have anything, but look in the
freezer back there." So we went to the freezer out back and

here was this huge sea bass, about thirty pounds. Enormous fish. We said, "What do you want for this?"

He said, "Oh, that's no good, it's been there for about three years. You can have it." We took this huge sea bass, which barely fit into the bottom of this big cooler we'd bought for our lunch and beer and everything, and we snuck this fish out there.

Fished all morning, didn't catch a damn thing, came back to the dock and, of course, knew we had the winner in our boat there. The only question in our minds was would we be able to thaw this baby out in time for the twelve o'clock weigh-in?

So we get back there, and we're the last ones in, because we want to make a dramatic entrance with the winning fish, with this trophy thing that we've got, and sure enough, they're all lined up on the dock and Mickey's got about twenty-five bass, and Whitey's got about six, and everybody's caught some fish, and they say, "What did you guys get?"

We said, "We only caught one, but it could eat all of those fish for breakfast and still have room for more."

They said, "Get outta here!" So we hauled this thing out of the water. We had it on a stringer, and it kept coming out of the water and coming out of the water, and we flopped this thing down next to the other fish. It looked like a whale next to minnows. So we won the largest fish category. But there were questions over the years. Mickey would come to me every spring and say, "You know, the more I'm thinking about it, you'd better explain to me—how come our fish were all green and flopping around and yours was gray and just laid there?"

Bouton found similarities between Yankee stars Mickey Mantle and Roger Maris:

Roger Maris and Mickey Mantle were very similar in the kind of personalities they had. They were both very popular in the clubhouse. They got along well with the other guys. Fun to have around. Good teammates. Everybody liked them. They played when they were injured. And they were just good competitors, good all-around ballplayers.

Roger Maris was a good defensive outfielder in addition to his hitting ability. But, also like Mickey, Roger had difficulty, I think, coping with the big city. They were both from small towns—Roger from Fargo, North Dakota, Mickey from Commerce, Oklahoma.

I don't think they ever really adjusted to the fame they had. I think they felt that if they could just play baseball by themselves, if they could do it without the nuisance of fans always hollering and wanting their autographs and reporters asking dozens of questions, everything would be all right. They never really learned to cope with that part of it. They never felt comfortable about it.

I don't think the Yankees prepared ballplayers very much for what it would be like to be a major star or have the demands placed on you that a major athlete has. I think the players didn't have as much fun playing baseball as they could have had, had they been able to handle the press and fans better, if they had had some instruction on how to do that.

I found it easy, I think probably because I grew up in the New York metropolitan area [Rochelle Park, New Jersey] and also on the South Side of Chicago. I had had experience with dealing with lots of people, and also I never expected to be a big star. So when I became a star—I was never a big star, but when I became a twenty-game winner and a pitcher in the World Series—I thought it was great fun. I thought it was like a special bonus in my life. I enjoyed all the benefits around that, autographs and fan mail and that kind of stuff. I think Roger and Mickey expected that they would be real good, and so it wasn't so much of a thrill or a surprise to them, and then all the extra stuff was sort of a nuisance, a necessary evil that went along with the good stuff.

When Jim Bouton pitched in the Series, he pitched against the best:

The first World Series I pitched in was against the
Dodgers in 1963. I drew Don Drysdale as my pitching
opponent, and unfortunately Drysdale pitched the best game
of the World Series. Remember, the Dodgers swept us in four
straight that year with Koufax and Drysdale. Koufax won two
games. Drysdale beat me one to nothing. I gave up a run in
the first inning. I had always wished that I had pitched
against Koufax, because I would have beaten him. I gave up
one run and Koufax gave up two runs in each of his games,
even though he struck out fifteen guys. It would have been
fun seeing "Koufax Strikes Out 15 and Loses, 2–1."

*Jim never regained his form of 1963–64. He went 4–15 in 1965,
3–8 in 1966, 1–0 in 1967, and 1–1 in 1968. After the 1968 season, the
Yankees traded Bouton to the Seattle Pilots. At about the same time, he
began writing* Ball Four. *Published in 1970, it did well, very well:*

I didn't expect that *Ball Four* would sell as many copies as
it did. The publisher had only printed five thousand copies,
on the grounds that nobody would want to read a book by a
marginal pitcher on the Seattle Pilots.

But when baseball commissioner Bowie "The Ayatollah"
Kuhn called me into his office and tried to get me to sign a
statement saying the book wasn't true, *now* people wanted to
read the book the baseball commissioner didn't want them to
read.

So the publisher had to print another five thousand a week
after that, then fifty thousand, one hundred fifty thousand, and
I'm happy to say that *Ball Four* has sold about five hundred
thousand in hardcover and about four and a half million in
paperback. It's been translated into Japanese. I feel I owe a lot
of that to Bowie Kuhn, which is why I dedicated my second
book to him. I figured it was the least I owed the man!

The reason the commissioner was angry with *Ball Four* was not locker-room scenes. It had to do with the fact that *Ball Four* told people how tough it was to make a living at baseball. And they were afraid that a congressman, a judge, a jury, maybe an arbitrator, would read that and decide to take away baseball's antitrust exemption.

They were abusing the contractual advantage they had over the players. Ironically, this is exactly what happened in 1975 at an arbitration hearing in New York, the famous Andy Messersmith case where ballplayers became free agents. I was the only former player called to testify at that hearing, and Marvin Miller, the executive director of the players' association, told me just to read passages from *Ball Four*, which I did. *Ball Four* was accepted as legal evidence against the owners, because it was based on contemporaneous notes, and so whatever part *Ball Four* played in helping players become free agents, I'm very proud of that.

Eventually, Ball Four *made the* New York Times *best-seller list for seventeen weeks, breaking the record for sports books. What people thought about* Ball Four *had a lot to do with whose ox was gored. Many baseball players thought Bouton had invaded the privacy of the players he covered. Many outside of baseball praised Bouton for raising the consciousness of the media and the fans, especially about the inadequate conditions and pay that prevailed before free agency:*

I thought it would be controversial, but I didn't think it would create the firestorm that it did. I didn't think sportswriters would be writing three and four columns about it and that there would be such outrage over the book. And I didn't think players would be that upset by it.

I thought most ballplayers would see that it was a funny book, lots of funny stories, and that basically it told a ballplayer's point of view. *Ball Four* was the first book to tell people how difficult it was to make a living in baseball. I thought a ballplayer would read that book and say, "Hey, yea! This is our story. This is how owners mistreat us and take advantage of us. I'm glad somebody wrote this down. This is good."

That's how I felt. But the players focused on the few negative things I had to say: Mickey Mantle hits a home run with a hangover, the ballplayers run around the roof of the Shoreham Hotel, and that sort of thing. I certainly didn't name any names when it came to sexy stories, and in terms of not meeting curfew, keeping late hours, and drinking too much, that was not a big surprise to most people who have been around a ball club. It's just that they never read it before.

Different players reacted differently:

It depended on the player, really. My roommate on the Houston Astros [Seattle traded Bouton in August of the 1969 season], Norm Miller, thought it was great fun and exciting when *Ball Four* came out. Reporters were calling my room all the time. He became my personal secretary, screening calls for me.

He thought it was funny, as did a number of other players on the Astros. Then there were some, like Joe Morgan, who didn't like the book. So it really depended on their point of view, I guess, or how they came across in the book.

Most of the Seattle Pilots guys didn't like the book, but Tommy Davis did, Gary Bell did, Steve Hovley did. I think some of the guys are still angry about it, and I guess there's nothing I can do about that.

Foreshadowing the book he would write, Jim Bouton fought with the Yankees' management in the days before free agency:

The minimum salary was seven thousand dollars. And they would fight you tooth and nail for five hundred. And you

had no bargaining ability at all. They would tell you to sign
this contract, and if you didn't want to sign this contract, you
would quit baseball and become a plumber or a doctor or
something, go park cars.

You had no choice. The only leverage you had was to
hold out. And I held out every spring. I held out my first
spring training. The first contract I ever signed with the
Yankees I signed two minutes before the national anthem on
opening day.

I was seven and seven that year and won my last three
games when I was a pretty important pitcher for us down the
stretch, and the following year they offered me a two
thousand dollar raise. Seven to nine thousand dollars, if I
made the club. If I didn't, I'd go back down to seven
thousand. I said, "Why are you planting that doubt in my
mind? Don't you want to encourage me?"

Dan Topping, Jr. was in charge of the lower echelon
players. I told him, "I'm not going to sign this contract."

He said, "Well, then, you'll just have to go home."

I said, "O.K., I'm going home."

So the morning I was ready to leave for the airport, he
called up the hotel and said, "All right, get over here, we'll
sign you. We'll give you your $10,000."

I said, "Forget it. I was asking for ten thousand five
hundred or eleven thousand."

He said, "All right. I'll split it in half. I'll give you ten
thousand five hundred."

So that was my salary the year I won twenty-one games. I
was twenty-one and seven. Well, I figured now was my time to
get what I was worth, so I asked for a raise to twenty
thousand. They wouldn't give it to me. They offered me a five
thousand dollar raise. I had to hold out for two weeks in
spring training to get an eight thousand dollar raise.

I mean, they took advantage of you. They had us over a
barrel. They literally stole our money. All the players before

free agency never got paid our fair share of the money that was made in baseball.

I think today major league baseball should make it up to those guys. I think they owe it to the older players to repay them retroactively for the money they could've earned had there been a fair system of paying, just like the National Football League did. They took players from the past and simply gave them a bonus for a certain sum, a certain amount of dollars for every year they played.

They could go back and say, "For every player who played before free agency, we're going to give a two thousand dollar bonus for every year in the major leagues." So if you spent ten years in the major leagues, you'd get twenty thousand. They could certainly afford this.

Except the old players don't want to go to the owners for the money. They want to go to the modern players and say that modern players should give them some of the money that they're making. But it's against labor laws for modern employees to bargain in behalf of former employees. So even if the modern players wanted to do that, they wouldn't be allowed to. No. It's up to the owners to take care of the older players, and they can do it by the very simple system I've suggested.

BILL BRADLEY

Bill Bradley has a pretty good resume. He graduated from Princeton with honors in American history. He received a Rhodes scholarship for study at Oxford, where he did graduate work in politics, philosophy, and economics. In 1978 he was elected to the United States Senate from New Jersey. Now the senior senator from that state, Bradley will retire from the Senate in 1997 after three terms. A run for the presidency may lie in his future.

Incidentally, Bill Bradley played a little basketball. He was a three-time All-American at Princeton. In 1964 he was the captain of the U.S. Olympic basketball team, which won the gold medal in Tokyo, beating the Soviet Union in the final game. In both 1964 and 1965 Bradley was named The Sporting News College Player of the Year. In 1965, the same year he won his Rhodes Scholarship, Bradley also won the James E. Sullivan Memorial Trophy, awarded annually to the athlete who "by his or her performance, example and influence as an amateur, has done the most during the year to advance the cause of sportsmanship"; he was the first basketball player ever to win it.

Bradley went on to a storied ten-year career with the New York Knicks. Bradley's team, coached by Red Holzman, won the NBA

*championship in 1970 and 1973. In 1982 Bill Bradley was elected to
the Basketball Hall of Fame.*

*Bill was a very good shooter from the sides and from the corners,
but not from out in front. He was not a player who could take the ball
in the backcourt and manufacture his own shot; he was not a guy to
take it to the hole or a guy who could pull up and shoot a jumper.
Rather he was a player who needed a set play to get him an open shot;
once he got the open shot, he could hit it.*

*His career at Princeton was nothing short of remarkable, espe-
cially when you consider the style of ball the team played. When
Bradley played there, the style was very much the same as that of the
Princeton team that upset UCLA in the first round of the NCAAs in
1996: a ball-control, set-play basketball team. Yet Bradley was such
an outstanding college player that he still holds the NCAA Final Four
record for most points in a single game, with 58 in the consolation
round of 1965. For him to score that many points on a ball-control
team is just astonishing.*

Bill Bradley's entry into basketball was dictated by his height:

I grew up in a small town in Missouri called Crystal City,
3,492 people, on the banks of the Mississippi River. There
were ninety-six in my high school graduating class, and the
town had one stoplight. If you were six-foot-one in the eighth
grade, six-foot-three in the ninth grade, and six-foot-five in the
tenth grade, there was only one thing that you were going to
do, and that was play basketball.

At age fourteen I went to a basketball camp run by "Easy"
Ed Macauley, the great Celtic and Hawk basketball player. He
said, "Look, if you're not practicing, remember, somebody,
somewhere, is practicing, and if you two meet, given roughly
equal ability, he's going to win."

I never wanted to lose for lack of effort, so from that
moment on I worked awfully hard at the game. Always, in
that small town, the objective was to win the state
championship, and every year we got close. My last year, we

lost the final to one of the largest, most prestigious high schools in St. Louis, but we lost by only one point.

Bradley nearly went to school in Durham, North Carolina:

I'd actually signed an athletic scholarship to go to Duke. Then the night before the freshman class at Princeton was to convene and three days before the freshman class at Duke was to convene, I changed my mind and switched to Princeton. I arrived there at 9 P.M., the night before the freshman class had their first meeting.

Why Princeton? I thought ultimately that was the best place I could get an education. I had broken my foot playing baseball in August of that year. I contemplated the world without basketball, then decided I'd rather go to Princeton than to Duke.

I had no scholarship. My father, who was a small-town banker and therefore didn't qualify on the basis of need, had to pay my way each of the four years I was there.

At Princeton, Bill Bradley became an almost instant superstar. He gained fame as a shooter and passer. As a freshman he averaged 30.6 points and hit 57 straight free throws; as a senior he averaged 30.5 points on 53.3 percent shooting and made 89 percent of his foul shots, highest in the country. He was also known for his almost palpable intellect on the court, shown by how he would break free for a shot, how he would give up a good shot if he could pass to a teammate who had an even better one. When Bill Bradley left the Princeton basketball floor for the final time, 3,500 people gave him a standing ovation that lasted for five minutes. Bradley's team made it farther into the NCAA tournament than any other team in Ivy League history, qualifying for the Final Four in 1965:

The high point athletically was the Eastern Regional in my senior year, when we played Providence. We were supposed to lose. This was the great Providence team—I think they were number three or four in the country at the time—and instead, we beat them 109 to 69. (Bradley scored 41 on 70 percent shooting.)

It was the best game we ever played. In the second half we hit something like twenty-two out of twenty-six shots. We went on to the Final Four and played Michigan, whom we had lost to in the Holiday Festival Tournament, narrowly, a couple of months earlier. We lost to Michigan in the semifinal.

Unlike many athletes, Bradley didn't see the classroom as merely a route to the basketball court:

I've always thought that sports supplemented your education. For me, going to Princeton from the small town in Missouri really changed my life. It opened up new social horizons, challenged me intellectually on levels that I never thought existed, and it brought me to New Jersey, which I've had the honor of representing for the last eighteen years.

So it did change my life. If I look at those years, the excitement of the education was the important thing. Writing a senior's thesis about Harry Truman, working with some of the best minds in America as advisers for papers, being captured by the library in a very fundamental sense. To a large degree, my life at Princeton was a triangle: my dorm room, the library, and the gym. In some senses, I thrived in that atmosphere.

The other aspect of Princeton was that it was a worldwide university, meaning there were people there from all over the world, and simply by going there, you got to know people from all over the country, all over the world, and form friendships that really have lasted a lifetime.

One might think that when Bill Bradley was at Princeton or at Oxford or in New York, he would sometimes have longed for the small town from which he came. He didn't:

I never did get homesick. I live things through and then when they end, I move on. I don't ever want to go back. I always think of that town. When I used to train in high school, I'd run through the fields down to the banks of the Mississippi River. I used to stop and watch the river flow, and I'd watch the things that were in the river that were scoured from half a continent, as they flowed all the way down to New Orleans. Then I'd look at the limestone bluffs behind me, listen to the wind blowing through the cottonwood trees, and I'd think, "You know, I'm always going to be as much from this small town tucked between two limestone bluffs on the banks of the Mississippi River as I am from anywhere," and that is true.

But when I left, I left. When I finished basketball, I finished basketball. I never really looked back, partly because I feel I've always been very lucky to have had a quality experience in each of the places I've been and to have had tremendous friends and people who taught me an awful lot, and I express this sense of gratitude. But there are new horizons, there are new places to go and new things to do, and the exhilaration of attempting those things has always outweighed any kind of wistfulness I might have had about the past or those other places.

One of the places was the Olympics:

The best basketball in the world is not played in the Olympics; it's played in the NBA. So it's not the greatest basketball, but it is the Olympics. The opening ceremony, winning the gold medal and standing on the platform with the medal around your neck, watching the flag going up the pole with the national anthem being played and chills going up and down your spine—that's a tremendous moment, and I certainly will never forget it. And then the closing ceremony, where you walk in as individuals, not representing your country, and the friends that you've met in the Olympic Village, the power of the Olympic ideal that is so real to anybody who participates, that was a tremendous experience in my life, and I feel very grateful.

The other day I was on a program with Al Oerter, who won the gold medal in the discus in '56, '60, '64, and '68. In one of these Olympics, he wasn't doing well, and Rink Babka, who was his teammate, was in first place, and Babka said to him, "You know, if you simply made this change in your technique, you'll probably be able to do a little bit better." So Oerter made the change, and he ended up winning the gold medal. That's the epitome of the Olympic experience: it's that you want to strive to be your best, and you help other people to be their best, too.

Though Bradley's Olympic basketball team was all amateurs, he accepts the invasion of the pros:

I think it's probably fine to allow the pros to play. It does reduce the experience for college kids, but every other team in the world has had its pros. In 1964, we played the Russians in the finals, and two years later I was playing for the Simmenthal Meat Packing Factory [of the professional Italian Basketball League] in Milano, Italy. For the European Cup championship, in the semifinal, we played the Russian team. I went out to warm up and saw the exact same team that represented the Soviet Union in the Olympics, except now they were called the Soviet Army Club Team. They were basically pros.

It is not only Olympic basketball that has changed since Bradley's days. It's also college basketball:

I think there's no question that college sports have become big business, and the NCAA Final Four is only one example of that. The only bill I've ever passed in the Congress that's affected sports was the NCAA "Right to Know" bill, where anybody who gets a college scholarship has a right to know how many kids in that school actually graduated in five years. So you can get some idea of whether your child is going to be exploited or whether he or she is going to get an education. But as long as the emphasis can remain on education, as long as there's some standard for athletes, and it doesn't take away from their education, it doesn't bother me.

Bradley's detour to Oxford delayed his career in the pros. He finally signed with the Knicks two and a half years after he was drafted. During Bradley's years with the team, it was full of legends: Willis Reed, Walt Frazier, Cazzie Russell, Dave DeBusschere, Dick Barnett, Earl Monroe, Jerry Lucas. With the Knicks, Bradley was a strong outside scorer and deadly free throw shooter. His Knicks teams made the playoffs for eight consecutive years, from 1967–68 through 1974–75, winning the NBA championship twice, both times over the Lakers. There was a special aura that surrounded the Knicks of Bradley's time:

I think it was an extraordinary group of human beings and a kind of perfect blend of talents on the court. Everybody knew what he had to do in order to have the team win, and each of us realized that no one of us could be as good as all of us could be if we played together. I think that it captured the imagination of the whole metropolitan area, as well as a big chunk of the country. That was just when pro basketball was taking on prime-time TV.

We won in 1970 and again in 1973. Traveling around America with this group of human beings, playing a game I loved, allowed me to see the country whole for the first time, really, as well as to live in a predominantly African-American world. I think that gave me some unique perspectives on the issues of race that have been valuable to me as I've served as senator from New Jersey.

I doubt that many players could have made it in the NBA after a two-and-a-half-year hiatus. But Bill's remarkable transition was not enough for the demanding fans of New York. The fans seemed to expect him to be just as successful as he had been at Princeton, where he dominated almost every game he ever played. So they were disappointed:

Being away from the game was like taking someone away from something he depends on for life. I hadn't had my fill of the game, clearly. It was kind of an artificial break, so when I was shooting around at the gym at Oxford I realized, "Look, it's time to go back and time to test yourself against the best." When I did come back, my first year in the NBA was not exactly a heroic return. I was "the Great White Hope," the person who was going to set the town abuzz and bring the team the championship. Instead, I was a slow-footed white guard, unable to get over the picks in tough situations.

Somehow or other, I was a giant disappointment to the New York fans. So I would come out of games to boos regularly. People would throw coins at me, spit on me as I'd go to the locker room. People would stop me in the street and tell me what they thought of my abilities. Cab drivers wouldn't pick me up; if they did, they'd give me an earful.

In all my years in politics, I've never encountered constituents that duplicate the experience of that searing first year in the NBA. So what I did was basically hunker down and say, "Look—remember Ed Macauley—if you're not practicing, somebody somewhere else is." So I just kept working. Then, in my second year, the break came, which means the person who was playing forward, Cazzie Russell, broke his ankle. I was moved from guard to forward and found my natural position, then remained on that team, in that position, for the rest of my career.

Bradley believes the NBA helped him make it in politics:

I think the NBA experiences helped me get elected, first of all because people in New Jersey knew me. There used to be three hundred people in a hall, as opposed to one hundred, when I first started running, which always meant I could fail before three hundred, as opposed to one hundred, if I didn't have anything to say. But if I had something to say, it was a real advantage. So it was an advantage in my first election. And I think that the experience of living in a world that was more or less African-American had a very formative effect on me. It gave me a chance to see the world through the eyes of my teammates, it gave me a chance to see how they saw things and how the world reacted to them.

I never will forget, for example, one morning I went down to the coffee shop in L.A., and Earl Monroe was there. His left eye was swollen, so I said, "What happened?" The night before, we had played a game in New York and then we flew to the Coast. He had dazzled 19,500 people in Madison Square Garden. A couple of hours later, a thousand feet from center court, he was hailing a cab outside the Garden to send a friend of his back to her apartment, and some guys on the street corner started calling him "boy."

One thing led to another, and they came to blows. A guy came to his rescue from the post office across the street and put him in a cab to the airport, but there he was, the morning after, with a swollen face and a deep, bitter anger. If I hadn't been there at that point, I wouldn't have seen that. The irony of having this occur, this act of denigration only a thousand feet from where he was the hero, was kind of an irony that I've never forgotten.

The NBA also gave me a chance to get to know my teammates as individuals, as people, their rich family backgrounds, the kinds of things they strived for. It re-emphasized something I'd known since childhood, which is that seeing somebody as an individual is what you have to do. You've got to look beyond the skin color or the eye shape.

What now, after the Senate?

I'm leaving the Senate, but I'm not leaving public life. I think the Senate is the best elective job in the world, but I don't think it's the only place that you can serve. It is also a very time-consuming job, in terms of committees, sub-committees, caucuses, back-and-forth to your state, mastering the complexity of legislation. It means if you're doing that, you don't have time to do other things that are in the public interest, such as trying to energize movements for fundamental campaign reform in states across the country or trying to think through the next chapter of this American story: the economic transformation that is making us wealthier and more competitive but is also shrinking the outlook for middle-class Americans, who are working longer for less and are only one or two paychecks away from falling out of the middle class.

Also, the story that I think is going on in the country in more and more places: people searching for some meaning in their lives that is deeper than the material. So I'm going to stay very much involved in those two areas and in the issue of racial healing.

We now get to my wife's question: "O.K., what's the job?" Which, at the moment, there's no answer to. The commitment and the direction is clearly set; the real issue is how it will evolve professionally.

I have a plan, in the sense of knowing that that is what I'm going to do. What I'll have to do is create the structure to make that happen.

People ask, "You going to run for president some day?" My response is "Look: in 1992, I went through a number of personal traumas. My wife developed breast cancer, mastectomy, and chemotherapy; I had two friends who died in airplane crashes, my parents were in the latter stages of their lives, with advancing emphysema, one went blind, had heart and cancer problems, and a friend committed suicide. After living through that year, I realized that catastrophe can overtake the best-laid plans. So you simply have to lead life every year, figure that you've given a hundred percent of your service, and work on things that you believe are critical to our becoming a better country. And then the future evolves. Ultimately the old proverb is right: you've got to plow the field before you reap the harvest. Maybe someday I'll take a crack at the presidency, but there's no way you can really plan that. You have to just work every year and see how it evolves.

TERRY BRADSHAW

Terry Bradshaw had as much raw physical talent as any quarterback ever to throw a pass. I remember when Terry came out of Louisiana Tech, one of the scouts said, "If somebody doesn't take him as a quarterback, we're going to draft him as a tight end." He could throw the ball from one end of the field to the other. Of course, somebody did take him as a quarterback: the Pittsburgh Steelers made him the number-one draft pick of 1970. Terry played with the Steelers until his retirement following the 1983 season.

Terry Bradshaw may also be the most underrated quarterback of all time. He was underrated regarding both his intellect and his ability on the field.

Early in his career, Terry was falsely saddled with the image of a "dummy." Maybe it was because of the bias some northerners have against anybody with a southern accent; maybe it was because, as all young quarterbacks do, Terry made some judgment errors in his first years in the NFL. Regardless of the reason, the label hurt him deeply.

It's almost incredible that he could be underrated as a quarterback, because his credentials are stunning. In the entire history of the Super Bowl, only two men have quarterbacked four winning teams. One is Joe Montana, and the other is Terry Bradshaw, who did it in

1975, 1976, 1979, and 1980 (he was 4–0 in the Super Bowl). Only three teams have won four or more times: the 49ers have done so five times, but once with Steve Young; the Steelers have done it four times, each time with Terry; and Dallas has done it four times, but twice with Roger Staubach and twice with Troy Aikman.

In 1978, Terry was voted Most Valuable Player in the NFL by the Associated Press and by Philadelphia's Maxwell Club, which presents the Bert Bell Trophy. Terry is in the Pro Football Hall of Fame.

As time passed, Terry built on his tremendous natural ability, acquiring the touch necessary to become one of the great quarterbacks. Still, he remains underrated.

Part of the reason is Joe Montana, whose career partly overlapped Bradshaw's. If you look at the statistics, year by year, game by game, Bradshaw is not as impressive as Montana. But if you saw both of them play, as I have, Terry certainly was every bit as good a quarterback. A different type of quarterback, but just as effective.

Bradshaw had such a strong arm that a receiver could be covered almost as well as you can cover a receiver, and Terry still had the arm strength to get the ball in there, with speed and precision. Montana's style was different: he had such great anticipation that he'd throw the ball before a receiver ever broke, knowing where he was going to be. So one was a touch quarterback, and the other was almost a brute strength quarterback.

Of course, Terry's statistics were not exactly weak. Here are some from the Super Bowl list:

He ranks seventh in career passing efficiency, with a rating of 112.6. He is number two in career passing yardage, with 932.

He shows up twice on the list for yards per game: at number five with 318 yards against Dallas in 1979 and at number seven with 309 against Los Angeles in 1980.

On the list for touchdown passes in one game, he's tied for third, with four TDs in 1979.

Still, Bradshaw was always more of a winning quarterback than a statistics quarterback. He—along with players like Mean Joe Greene, Jack Lambert, Rocky Bleier, Franco Harris, Mel Blount,

John Stallworth, and Lynn Swann—took the Pittsburgh Steelers to eight consecutive appearances in the playoffs, and he never shined brighter than when it was most important: in the Super Bowl.

In 1975, his Steelers beat Minnesota, 16–6. In 1976, they won against Dallas, 21–17. In 1979, the Steelers beat Dallas again, this time 35–31; Bradshaw completed seventeen of thirty passes for 318 yards and four touchdowns and was voted MVP of the game. A year later, Pittsburgh beat Los Angeles, 31–19. In that game, Bradshaw, who had completed fourteen of twenty-one passes for 309 yards and two touchdowns, was again voted MVP.

Terry Bradshaw retired from the NFL after the 1983 season. He is now a successful football analyst with a network called Fox.

Before Super Bowl XIII in 1979, Hollywood Henderson of the Dallas Cowboys said, "Terry Bradshaw couldn't spell cat if you spotted him the C and the T." I have two answers to that: One, Terry and Pittsburgh beat Dallas, as they had in Super Bowl X. Two, I figure Hollywood didn't know Terry as well as I do. I've worked with Terry for years, and I've never found him lacking in intelligence. At CBS and Fox he has presented incisive analysis and has done so articulately. Terry was smart on the football field, too: he could recognize defensive coverages and get the job done. And unlike many quarterbacks, Terry called all his own plays. He did so for all of his fourteen years in the NFL:

Look, I got a southern accent. I flunked the ACT test [but later took the SAT and got a 1,046]; it took me five years, according to the so-called geniuses, before I could ever become a quarterback. They're saying they won in spite of me and I say, "Hey, fine. Look, I'm not going to win the world over here, I'm not looking to be the greatest quarterback. I don't even care if my name is never mentioned as one of the greatest. It doesn't bother me. It doesn't faze me."

That's a lie. It does bother me. Yeah, it does. It does bother me, but I can't control it, so why fight it? You know, you can only upset me if I choose to let you. I can become very egocentric here and very defensive and start naming off all the things I do better than Montana and some of these other guys, but what good does it serve me? It sounds like sour grapes and does no good.

Hey, look, we won four Super Bowls, I got four Super Bowl rings; thank you very much, I'll see you later.

Montana couldn't run my offense, it was too deep. He runs a systemic offense, one-two-three, one-two-three. I ran a read offense where it's very deep, and you read coverages, and it's different. His scheme is designed for him. I admire him. I love his talent, but I won't let people shoot me down.

Terry Bradshaw has countless colorful stories to tell, and he tells them well. I'll concentrate on tales from his early days, from junior high through his first years with the Steelers.

Terry's ability as an athlete first showed itself during his days as a Little League pitcher. As just a nine-year-old, he stunned his fellow players with a perfect game, two no-hitters, and six shutouts. Still, his love was football. But at first his love for the game was unrequited: he couldn't make the team at Oak Terrace Junior High School in Shreveport:

I think probably the first thing you become very familiar with in any sport is failing, losing, not starting, not being that good when you're playing. It's very hard to accept when your dream is to be a quarterback in the National Football League.

My earliest association with football was failing, not making the team. I mean you can't get into pro ball if you can't make the team, see?

We were at Oak Terrace Junior High School, and we'd been to the coach's meeting in the gymnasium, where he gave a talk and then he hand-picked the team. You didn't practice and try out, you were hand-picked. I saw him in P.E., and I was switching schools, and so this guy hadn't seen me in P.E., and therefore he didn't know who I was or anything, didn't know I could throw the football. And I didn't get a uniform. I didn't get picked.

So I went out and I was watching them practice. Do you know how devastating that is to go out and see these guys practicing, knowing they don't love it as much as you and you know their dreams aren't to go in the National Football League? At least that was the way I looked at it.

So I'm sitting over there just eaten up inside with jealousy and envy and hurt, and the ball rolled over by me, right in front of me, actually. They were warming up, and I just stood in front of it to hide it from everybody, and a little bitty ball boy came running over, and I wouldn't let him have the ball.

So he went back, I suppose now to complain to the coach. And there were a few kids standing over there that had also been rejected, and I grabbed one of them and said, "Come on, let's go over here and throw." So we got off the football field, went on down on the P.E. field, which was about a hundred yards away, and I started throwing the football.

I'm sending him out and man, in eighth grade I could throw it sixty yards. I mean, I cranked that sucker up. And I'm cranking it. I'm showing off is what I'm doing. I'm auditioning, because I want me one of them dang uniforms, man. I got business to do.

Here I'm just running him long and long and throwing it, and jump passes, and then the coach saw me and he came after me. He started walking. And I saw him, then I thought, "Hey, I got this football. This sucker, he's coming, he wants his football back."

So I started walking, kind of getting away from him because I was scared. Then he kind of jogs, and I started jogging. Then I took off running. I hit the cyclone fence, screaming and hollering for my mama. This guy's grabbing me by my ankles and pulling me down. Finally he gets me down, tears are flying, and he says, "Boy, I never seen anybody throw a football like that. What grade are you in?"

I told him I'm in the eighth grade. And he says, "God, come on in, we're going to get you a uniform." Well, he had told us they didn't have enough uniforms, but now all of a sudden they got a uniform. So he takes me in and I got my uniform.

But then, surprise, the coach had the strong-armed quarterback play middle linebacker, too:

That was very disappointing, because I didn't want to tackle anybody. Girl cheerleaders like them when they throw touchdown passes, man. I mean, there was this girl, Dorinda Shaw, and I had my eye on her and I figured if I got that uniform and threw a few touchdown passes I'd win her heart. But you don't get anywhere tackling.

Not only didn't I like to tackle; it hurt. The first game I got to play, I went out and had like fifteen tackles and maybe six or eight sacks all by myself from the linebacker's spot. I could jump and beat the guard-center gap before they could block me, and it was fun.

I sprung my knuckle on my hand and had a huge knuckle, and the cheerleaders liked that, so I said, "Well, this might be all right." But when we got in passing situations, the coach would take me from linebacker and put me in to throw the football, so it wasn't all that bad.

At Woodlawn High School, Bradshaw again struggled before he made it:

The first two years I went to Woodlawn High School, which at the time was one of the top five in the state consistently—great coach, Lee Hedges, Hall of Fame coach now, winningest coach ever in high school football in Louisiana.

I went over there and sat on the bench and played junior

B-ball. They had a quarter by the name of Trey Prather, who was a great All-American, and he signed with LSU and eventually quit school and went to Vietnam and got killed.

But I played behind him for two years and then finally started my senior year. And we had one returning letterman who was a nose, Donnie Beauman, and we were picked last in the district, first time ever the school had been picked last other than when it first came into the league. And we won the district.

At Lafayette High School there was a kid by the name of Ross Brubaker, who was a *Parade* All-American fullback/linebacker drafted later by the Bears in the second round. Lafayette High School was one of the top ten high schools in the country, and we went down there in Lafayette and beat those suckers. That was the best game I ever played in high school.

We didn't throw the football in high school. I averaged nine, ten passes a game, but I threw for a lot of touchdowns. Nine, ten passes, I could throw three touchdowns, fifty-to-sixty yarders, stuff like that. Be three-for-ten and ten touchdowns. It was kind of fun, really.

Even today when I talk about football, I will go back to high school, because that's when it was fun, with the crowds, and we had these great rivalries. And that's where there's the first excitement of football, where you went out and you were introduced to the crowd. We had big crowds, in Shreveport, thirteen to fifteen thousand at all of our games.

As a pro, Terry Bradshaw kept looking for that fun he had found at Woodlawn High:

Why would anyone in their rightful mind want to do something that's not fun? Well, you've heard people say, "Well, I can make a lot of money."

"But are you happy?"

"No, but I'm making a lot of money."

How sad that is to me, to do something just for the love of money, when you don't enjoy it, when it's not fun, when you don't love it. So I was lucky. I never could get the kid out of me in football.

It was a joy to go out and cut up in practice, and I never took things too serious. I knew what was going on, but my attitude was, "O.K., I'm well prepared, now I can have some fun, I can giggle and cut up and pull pranks and get in those big games and have fun." It should be fun; it's just a game; come on, folks. And that's how I approached it, and that's why I had so much fun with reporters and people, pulling jokes on them, lying to them, creating all these stories, just because it was fun.

I was serious about playing, very focused on what I was doing, very much aware of how important the games were and especially big games and that sort of thing. So aside from my love and having fun with the game, I took it very serious. You wouldn't want to misunderstand and think that I was some idiot out there jumping around and screaming, hollering, laughing, and cutting up; that wasn't the case at all.

I took it very serious, but even that was fun. It was just a neat feeling. It never got the best of me; I never got too carried away with the big game coming up. And I think that's one of the reasons I was able to play well in big games, because I didn't let them affect me.

I just kept them in their proper perspective, and it was easy for me to do it, because I had always done that my entire career in football, from junior high to high school and on up. It wasn't "Well, this is the Super Bowl, now it's time for me to panic." Of course not. Now is the time for me to really have some fun. Now is the time, this is what you live for.

One index of just how strong Bradshaw's arm was came from another sport. In high school he set the national record in the javelin:

You don't make any money throwing the javelin. You don't make a dime. And throwing that javelin was just something that this coach said: "Boy oh boy, if you'll throw this javelin, you'll develop arm strength." Well, you don't run back in the pocket with a football stretched out back over your shoulder. But he just felt that since I could throw the football, I could throw the javelin.

Bradshaw turned down two hundred scholarship offers from college track teams and went to play football at Louisiana Tech:

My junior year, I split time with Phil Robertson, and he's now a millionaire making duck callers. He used to come to work with fish scales and squirrel tails hanging out his back pocket, and duck feathers, barefooted and talking about ducks and squirrels and deer. That's all he cared about. And I'm trying to get into the NFL, and this guy's starting ahead of me, and all he wants to do is shoot stuff. He'd show up late for practice.

"Say, where you been, Phil?"

"Uh, uh, tell you, them ducks is flying high today. Flying high today. Been down there, I got twenty-six."

Well, the limit's three, and he got twenty-six. They used to just slaughter those things.

Anyway, he got knocked out. Best thing that ever happened to Phil, he got knocked out cold in this one game against a tough Delta State team. I got a chance to start and played real well and started the rest of the year off and on. And then the following year, Phil got into his life's chosen work, he got into making duck callers, and that sucker is rich, man."

College football was the ultimate. It wasn't Notre Dame, and it wasn't the University of Miami, but to me it was. McNeese State and Nicholls State and Delta State, that's the big time for me, boy. I enjoyed it. At least I was playing.

Bradshaw was one of the all-time greats in the NFL, but he claims he threw the ball better at Louisiana Tech than at Pittsburgh:

I never threw the football like I threw in college ever again. After my rookie year, I lost all my confidence. I couldn't ever snap it off again. Back when we were doing a deal at Woodlawn High School this year, I was throwing in the backyard, and I was snapping it off like I threw then. Just whistling it. But I lost it. I lost my passing touch, my motion, totally lost it. I lost every ounce of confidence I had. I could no more make a pass spiral or do anything. People find this hard to believe, but for five or six or seven weeks I might be throwing it one way real good and then, hell, it'd go bad in a game, and I worked on so many ways of throwing the football, I'd just go to something else.

Hold it low, hold it high, try to throw like Namath, throw it like this, push it with my shoulder. I went into Super Bowl XIII, best game I ever played for a half, that was a whole new way of throwing a football: I set the ball on my shoulder and pushed it. But it had to sit there; I couldn't snap it off. My mind would freeze up if I had to snap a ball off. And all because of my rookie year.

I never had a standard way of throwing a football after my rookie year. It hurt me in productivity because I would've been a lot more accurate my way of throwing, I would've been a lot more aggressive, I'd've had better games.

At the beginning of his pro career, Terry floundered under the hostility he felt from Steelers head coach Chuck Noll. But then Babe Parilli became quarterback coach in Terry's second year in Pittsburgh:

Babe Parilli came in, patted me on the back, took me aside, stroked me, encouraged me, built up my confidence, 'cause I was at an all-time low. And when things would go bad, Chuck would stay out of it and Babe would come in.

Babe was the one who led me to Lou Rickey, who used to hypnotize me to help me get my confidence back. I still use the words today: "Relax, confidence, concentrate." Right in the middle of the game, crucial play, I'd call out one word, "Relax." Call out, "Confidence, confidence, confidence." It was just amazing. Damnedest thing. I used it my entire career. I could just pull those words out and just, boom. Babe brought that to me. I love Babe Parilli; he saved my career.

JIM BROWN

As far as I'm concerned, Jim Brown was the greatest football player of all time. From playing against him, I know what an awesome, awesome weapon he was. You couldn't stop him.

I've been asked, "How varied were Jim Brown's talents?" My answer: "As varied as they needed to be." I've been asked, "How fast was Jim Brown?" My answer: "As fast as he needed to be."

I remember trying to tackle him. It wasn't a question of could you knock him down—as it was when you took on most backs, even most good backs—because you couldn't knock him down. The question was, could you hold on and how long could you hold on?

I was in the Pro Bowl with Jim several times. The other players always wanted to race him. He would say, "Okay, we'll race; I'll stay after practice." And lots of very fast players raced him—world class sprinters, guys who said they had run 9.4 in the 100-yard dash—but nobody ever beat him.

He was an incredible all-around athlete. I went on a barnstorming basketball tour with him for Sports Illustrated in the off-season one year, and I learned that he was a very good basketball player. He'd get under the boards and all of a sudden people would come flying out and he'd have the rebound. A man whose judgment I respect saw Brown play lacrosse at Syracuse, and this man says that Brown was not only the greatest football player of all time, he was also the greatest lacrosse player.

Jim Brown led the NFL in rushing yardage in eight of his nine seasons. (In the only other season, 1962, he had a broken wrist but still led the team in receiving.) One of those seasons, 1957, was his first, when he was named NFL Rookie of the Year. In 1963, Brown ran for 1,863 yards (an average of 6.4 per carry) in a fourteen-game season; before Brown, Steve Van Buren of Philadelphia held the season record at 1,146. Though he retired after only nine seasons, Brown ranks fourth on the all-time NFL rushing list with 12,312 yards on 2,359 carries, behind only Walter Payton (thirteen seasons, 16,726), Eric Dickerson (eleven seasons, 13,259), and Tony Dorsett (twelve seasons, 12,739).

Of the twenty-five top rushers of all time, Brown has the highest average per carry, 5.2 yards (next is Barry Sanders at 4.9). He has the second highest number of rushing touchdowns, 106, behind only Payton, who had 110 in thirteen years. On the all-purpose running list, he is in third place (behind Payton and Dorsett but ahead of Dickerson), with a total of 15,459 yards: 12,312 rushing, 2,499 receiving, and 648 on returns.

In total touchdowns, Brown is behind only Jerry Rice (139); he had 126, 106 rushing and 20 on receptions. He was named NFL MVP by the Associated Press or United Press International or both in 1957, 1958, 1963, and 1965. He is the only player to win the award more than three times (and only Johnny Unitas and Y. A. Tittle won it more than twice).

Jim Brown went on to a successful career in motion pictures. Soon he was admitted to the Pro Football Hall of Fame in Canton, Ohio. Later he founded the Black Economic Union, which promoted minority success in business.

Like many legendary athletes, Jim Brown's athletic dream was not exactly Jim Brown's athletic reality:

My dream was to be in athletics and just be a student. I played a lot of different sports: the decathlon, baseball, track and field, lacrosse, and football. It just happened that football panned out best, and after college I realized I should be a professional football player.

I enjoyed all sports then and now. I didn't compare them; it wasn't necessary because they all had their own season. I played both track and lacrosse at Syracuse University.

Since Brown enjoyed many sports, it's not surprising that his role models did not come from football:

I think the term "role model" is a very overused term. I don't think it's very complimentary, because it depends on your upbringing, your church, how you turn out as an individual. Joe DiMaggio was the guy; I really liked the way he played. I liked his style, his demeanor, his performance. And then, of course, Jackie Robinson, who broke the color line, was a tremendous asset to my life because he had to perform under such adverse conditions and he did it so well. He was a very outspoken individual.

Like Arthur Ashe, Jim Brown was active in the civil rights movement:

I was in the movement since I was a little boy, fighting for my equality, my respect in this country. I never thought that I was a part of the civil rights movement when it just became popular. As a black kid, I was dealing with the inequalities that were put upon me. I had an attitude where people said I was some kind of malcontent, some kind of incorrigible.

I didn't understand why they would say that, because I wanted to be free like everybody else. I've always been what you might call a revolutionary—although I don't call myself that—because you want to be treated equally, fairly within society.

When the so-called movement came along, my position was to form an organization called the Black Economic Union, which dealt with economic development of minorities within the framework of the American economy. We had eight offices across the country, and we started many black businesses. We got a grant from the Ford Foundation back in 1967 for over a million dollars.

I always felt that this was my country, that I had to fight to enjoy it fully. And the way I thought best to fight was through economic development.

Eventually, every fan knew Jim Brown could star on any professional football team. Earlier, though, he had to prove he could play in college. And there was racism:

Kim Malloy, who was a graduate of Syracuse and a great lacrosse player, helped a lot of kids go to school. He wanted me to go to Syracuse, more than Syracuse wanted me. Without my knowledge, he had the community finance my first year, to show Syracuse I was good enough to win a scholarship. It was very difficult for me, not being wanted in the beginning.

Syracuse was a reflection of society at large. There was a certain amount of racism there. You had only a few black students, about twenty, and very few black girls to date. If you dated a white girl, it was like committing a crime. I was used to racism anyway, because the total society at that particular time was full of racism and discrimination.

I had good times because I socialized with blacks. There were some good people up there. I found that Syracuse represented America; there were some good white people, and there's always a form of discrimination or racism.

I played basketball. The football team didn't want me; they wanted me to play line or become a punter. They had a black quarterback, Avatus Stone, who had disappointed them and gone to Canada and dated many, many white girls.

It was a miserable time, the first two years at Syracuse. On the other hand, it had been a great time for me: a progressive school with great teachers and great coaches and a great attitude, even though it was a very affluent school.

In my last year at Syracuse, it became much better; they accepted me, and I was able to help them recruit Ernie Davis [who won the Heisman Trophy in 1961], who was the type of black individual they wanted. But those were very trying days for me overall. My memories were not the same as memories of high school.

How did Jim Brown deal with the racism he found at Syracuse?

You deal with racism, as we had to deal with slavery. There were times when slaves, under all kinds of duress, had fun, but that's not the kind of fun I'd like to have. You can't isolate football if you're a person like myself. There are some black superstars today that do that. They think they're European or Anglo-Saxon because they achieve a certain amount of superficial fun.

We always found ways to overcome certain kinds of thinking and have what you might call fun. We laughed at ourselves a lot, we joked about our conditions. We made fun of racism, and we had a chance to go out and dance and do those kinds of things.

Whenever you're an oppressed people, you are very conscious, as I was at Syracuse, that the fun is always secondary, because you will always be reminded that you aren't quite equal, that you always had to be better than anyone else and prove yourself and be approved of.

It was only gradually that Jim Brown recognized he would have a career in pro football:

Nothing is clear, because nothing in sports happens automatically. You have the ability to compare yourself to people around you: how fast they are, how fast you are, strength, quickness, the kind of hands you have.

I knew I was an outstanding athlete, but you don't know what's ahead of you. There's always a caution that you must have when you approach a different level: from college to pro is quite different, as is high school to college.

I expected to do well, but I would have to look at the situation, size it up, and be honest with myself. A lot of times your abilities do not dictate what's going to happen within your career, because if you go into a bad situation you can usurp all your abilities.

Some players look back at their greatest thrills. Jim Brown sees his career differently:

I didn't deal in thrills. As a sportsman, as a professional, I looked at things as any army general might look at going to war. I wasn't looking for thrills; I was looking for results and the ways to get those results, and I dealt with my own mind as much as I've ever dealt with any coach's mind.

I was always hoping a coach would put in the kind of plays that would allow me the best chance of getting results. On many occasions that did happen, and on a lot of those occasions I had my own chance to put my input into that, because in order to be consistent in the NFL you're going to have to be able to be flexible.

That's because the defense is always studying you. They're plotting ways to stop you, they're overloading a particular play that they know you like. They look at your feet, they look at your hands, they look at the weight that you put on your hands to see where you're going. So the main thing is always thinking ahead, always studying ways to do something differently to get successful results.

*Jim Brown gives credit to his coaches but also sees coaches as a
potential hindrance:*

My development came with my high school coach, Ed
Walsh. Ed was a very brilliant man who conceived many high
school innovations. I took his coaching very seriously
because at the time I needed the things he taught. I would
always refer back to his coaching over everybody else's
because I think he taught me more about technique than
anyone else. But even with him, I thought on my own at night
and even at practice on things I could do to get better results.

It's very difficult to coach a running back about running
style because you're usually born with your style. You can try
to perfect a player by improvement in certain areas, but
everybody has a different body, and since running is made
up of many, many things—speed, balance, acceleration,
quickness, strength, and brains —you have to use those
things like an artist, because you can't just use one, two,
three, four; you have to mix them up, reverse them, and do
many, many things with them.

I've always respected coaches, but I've also felt that a
coach can hurt you more than he can help you. I was always
glad I didn't have a coach that would hurt me by limiting my
abilities. [Cleveland Coach] Paul Brown started to do that, a
couple of years before he let me deal with all my abilities,
which became more enjoyable for me because I had free
expression to throw passes, catch passes, run inside, run
outside, do anything you can do out of the backfield.

*Jim Brown matured as a running back, but he didn't get old as a
running back:*

I had no age involvement in my career, any losing of
steps. I left at twenty-nine as MVP of the league. I also don't
think about and refer to what other people do. I've got great

admiration for the things people do, but I know a lot of things they do I can't do, and I know they aren't me. I think experience helps you because as a six-year veteran, you're more familiar with the system and yourself.

Brown came from New York, but liked playing in Cleveland:

Cleveland was a great setting for me. They had border lines as far as communities. They had Little Italy, which you couldn't go up in. The east and west side, which was basically based on color. And I enjoyed being with my black brothers and sisters and going to the black clubs. I was living basically a black life except playing football and being in the stadium. One thing about Cleveland: the fans were terrific. We got eighty thousand people in that stadium; it was fantastic. Blue-collar guys, knowledgeable football fans, and they always treated me very well. My memories of Cleveland are pretty good, especially from the standpoint of the fans.

Most players have to wait years before their team has great success. Not Jim Brown: in his first year, 1957, the Cleveland Browns made it to the NFL championship game (they lost to Detroit, 59–14). The Browns had qualified for the championship game every year from 1950 to 1955, winning the NFL championship three times in six years. Jim Brown gives much of the credit to Coach Paul Brown:

When I play I'm looking to win, and when you win you're looking to get into the championship game. I've always felt that way. I've never been with losing teams. I wasn't like a kid just happy to be there; I wanted to be there and win.

Paul Brown was a genius from the standpoint of his innovation in professional football. He had many championship teams under Graham and Motley. He was innovative from the standpoint of the face mask and messenger guards and playbooks and the way he'd run his camps. His success is almost unparalleled.

In Paul's later years, football changed somewhat. A lot of new coaches came in with different ideas, and Paul was a little too conservative for us. We never bristled at the messenger guards or anything like that, but his conservatism, we felt, was holding us back.

And at the time a young owner out of New York bought the team and sort of used us. He said the players are disgruntled, so we're going to get rid of Paul, but in reality Art Modell wanted to get rid of Paul anyway. It wasn't really because of us, because we called a meeting to sit down with Paul to talk about being less conservative, but that meeting never came about because of Art Modell. My idea of Paul is that he was a tremendous coach and innovator in football for most of his years and got too conservative near the end of his career.

Jim Brown set many records and his teams won many games, yet he measured himself by a different standard:

Winning could never be the only thing, because you have so many guys on the team; everybody's not equal, everybody's not playing, everybody's not getting what he wants. So my attitude was to excel, to play the best I could play. I wanted to dominate.

If I gained 95 yards instead of 100 and I played a good game and we won the game, then I knew I did a good job. I didn't care about the 100 yards; that gets ridiculous.

What we have in our system are true players and then the people who make money off those players. As a gladiator, as a warrior, I was on the field dealing with a totally different concept than those observing me, and those observing me set all the rules on records. And those rules and records are not correct as far as performance is concerned. So usually when people talk to you about records, they're talking to you about what they have set up. Every time I touched the ball, I wanted to do well, and that doesn't mean a touchdown either, because that's stupid.

There are players not designed for a touchdown. Sometimes he's designed for a first down or one yard, and sometimes you want to break it, because you know it's a play that you can break, so if I maximized myself in every situation, then I was satisfied.

I never did that, so I was never satisfied, and that's the thing nobody ever understands. I was not satisfied because I made errors I should not have made. My standards were that high. I think about those errors more than the things I did successfully because I expected success and I wanted to strive for it, but I didn't expect to make an error that I should not have made or to get tackled when I should not have gotten tackled—that was the way I thought about it.

Other people would look at statistics and say, "Oh, he got 120 yards," and I'm thinking of the two plays that I made the error on, so I lived in a different world from the standpoint of the general public or even the coaches or the broadcasting people. And that's not to say that I'm any better, it's just that I took my performance very seriously, I had a level of intensity and a level of dedication that I don't think very many people relate to.

To some people, football is a game. To Jim Brown, it was a war:

Football players are trying to hurt each other. You're trying to hit a guy so hard that he might not want to run the ball anymore or might not want to block anymore. Players can say what they want to say. They're not trying to maim anyone, or paralyze anyone, but if they can hit you hard enough to hurt you, knock you out, hey, that's a feather in their cap. So you've got to do some damage, and you've got to protect yourself, and the greatest way to protect yourself is to perform well. If you're performing well, they're not going to have a chance to hurt you.

It is a war when you play from a sincere level because you've got to put your head in places that you normally wouldn't, you've got to do things to endanger yourself that you wouldn't normally do. And people are trying to knock your head off all the time, so if you're a fighter, you would like to knock the guy out. You don't want him to die, but for thirty seconds you don't mind if they're down for the count and then get up and are all right.

Football is like that. Other sports are not necessarily like that. I don't think basketball is that way; it shouldn't be that way. In basketball the object is not to hit someone; the object of baseball is not really to hit someone.

So yes, it was like a war. I took it that way. I know they were after me. They were plotting. They were finding ways to discourage me, even to hurt me. That was a tremendous challenge. I knew if I performed well and made a few of them miss, run over a couple of guys, that I would've won, especially if my team won the game.

In a game that is a war, intimidation plays a leading role:

People are afraid of being made to look foolish. So if you are a particular kind of character and you don't say too much and you perform at a high level and you're tough and you don't complain and they can't see weakness within you when they hit you, that's got to be somewhat intimidating.

If you warm up in a strange way, if you have strange personality traits, that can be intimidating also, especially when you get certain kinds of results. So I calculated things on the one hand, but it was almost my own personality on the other hand. You can't fake being tough. Either you're tough or you're not. You can't fake being fast or quick or having great maneuverability. You take those things and you maximize them and get every edge you can get, whether it's psychological or physical, there's no doubt about that. I was a thinking player. I thought almost 24 hours a day when I was awake, about ways to improve my performance.

Jim Brown retired at or near his peak, after winning the 1965 NFL rushing title with 1,544 yards, a 5.3 yard average, and 17 touchdowns:

Football is a very short-lived profession. The key to life is to leave before you're invited out. If you have an understanding of the business you're in, then you know there's a time to leave where you maximize your position. So I maximized my position by leaving at the right time. I had a three-picture deal with Paramount. I had just done *The Dirty Dozen*. I also made a western called *Rio Conchos*. I had a consulting contract for five years, and I had deferred payments, so I was pretty well set to move, and only foolish people try physical things the same way all their lives.

I'm always amazed when people ask me why I left at the peak of my career. When you look at your overall quality of life, versus being a football player, football is very minor in the scheme of world politics and the scheme of what's going on in our society.

I enjoyed it, I got paid for it, I left on my own terms. I think that bothers a lot of people right now because people like you to hang around so they can get rid of you on their own terms and then bring you back and approve of you. No one's been able to do that with me, and that won't ever happen in my life.

ROY CAMPANELLA

Roy Campanella began his professional baseball career at the amazing age of fifteen with the all-black Baltimore Elite Giants of the Negro National League. He went on to star with the team in 1937–42 and 1944–45, playing in the Mexican League in the intervening season. He signed with the Brooklyn Dodgers in 1946, the year after the team signed a man named Jackie Robinson. Robinson moved up from the minors in 1947, Campanella in 1948. Campanella thus became one of the first black players to play in the majors.

As a catcher with the Dodgers, Campanella became the National League Most Valuable Player in 1951, 1953, and 1955. In 1953, he batted .312, hit 41 home runs, and drove in 142 runs. The RBI figure not only led the NL that year; it was also the highest in the league since Joe Medwick's 154 in 1937.

Campanella's career earned him a place in the National Baseball Hall of Fame. Tragically, however, his baseball days were cut short in a January 1958 automobile accident that left Campanella paralyzed from the waist down.

I was enormously impressed with how Campanella adjusted to his new life. Despite all the adversity he went through, despite the fact *that he was confined to a wheelchair, he still conducted his business in Harlem, and until the end he remained a celebrity in New York. He showed no bitterness, no "Why me?" attitude. He was a gentle man and a gentleman. His remarkable character in the wake of tragedy turned him from star to legend.*

Some players may take the "Big Show" for granted. Not Roy Campanella:

It meant so much to me just putting on a Dodger uniform for the first time. And it was right here in Dodgertown [the Dodgers' spring training facility in Florida]. The spring of '48. They purchased my contract from the St. Paul Saints, a Triple-A farm club of the Dodgers.

I joined the Dodgers in the farm club system in 1946, and I went to Nashua, New Hampshire, in the New England League. Jackie was with Montreal, and Don Newcombe was with Nashua.

It was all new now. Nobody had ever had any black players. It was different to all of your teammates and around the league. Now I played in the New England League with Nashua, and that area wasn't too bad, but there was a difference. Once we got to the big leagues it was a little worse 'cause you couldn't stay in some of the hotels with your team; all you could do was play ball and then go back to a black hotel and live there until the next day you had a game to play. We got some catcalls from the stands, but, thank God, it all worked out.

[Future Dodger manager] Walter Alston was my manager at Nashua. The first meeting we had in the clubhouse, he said, "If I ever get put out of the game, Campanella, you are to manage the team."

I pretty near fainted. And that was the first time he had met me. But he did get put out of a game. One night in Lawrence, Massachusetts, we were losing in the ninth inning by one run. I put Don Newcombe up to pinch-hit with a man on base, and he hit a home run, and we won the game. Alston said, "You're my manager from now on." I thought that was something.

Then in '47 we went to Havana, Cuba, for spring training. I was on a minor league all-star team of the Dodgers, and we would play the major league Dodgers every day.

We were fortunate enough to start winning a few games. Leo Durocher said he was managing the wrong team.

Though Campanella was thrilled to make it to the big leagues, he had the highest regard for some of the men he saw in the Negro leagues. Among them was Josh Gibson, who was credited with 89 home runs in one season, 75 in another, and more than 800 in his seventeen years with the Homestead Grays and the Pittsburgh Crawfords:

I played in the Negro National League with Baltimore, and Josh Gibson was a catcher for the Homestead Grays in the same league. He is by far the best hitter I have ever seen. He could lead the league in home runs and batting average. You'd hardly ever see him strike out.

In Campanella's ten years with the Dodgers, the team made it to the World Series five times:

In '47 they won the pennant. In '48 they finished second or third. In '49 we won. In '50 we lost the last day of the season. In '51, Bobby Thomson beat us in the playoffs. But we won in '52 and '53, finished second in '54, won everything in '55. That was the first World Series the Dodgers won. In '56 we won the pennant again but lost to the Yankees in the World Series. In '57, we finished second or third, and that was my last season. I played the last game at Ebbetts Field and then I had my–the Dodgers moved to L.A., but I had an automobile accident in January 1958 and never did get to play in L.A.

ROY CAMPANELLA • 85

*One of the key reasons for the Dodgers' success was Campanella's
ability to work with the pitchers:*

I could communicate with our whole pitching staff. I
think this is the most important part of catching. I caught
every pitcher on the Dodgers. It never shows in the box
score, but how a catcher can communicate with a pitcher and
the pitcher with his catcher means so much to a team. It
shows in winning, winning constantly. Because if you have
any friction and you're not communicating, you're not going
to be successful.

*When asked about being named MVP in 1951, 1953, and 1955,
Campanella displayed his typical modesty:*

Playing on a good team with so many good players, it
makes you a better player. I think any player on the Dodgers
could have been the most valuable player then, I really do.
Sure, I hit over .300 and I was the top-fielding catcher in the
league. I led all catchers in the league in fielding and
throwing.

But with my teammates—Snider, Furillo, Hodges,
Robinson, Reese—you could pick a most valuable player out
of every one of these fellas. It was just an honor to play with
them. They made me a better player just trying to keep up
and in line with these fellas.

*In the World Series of 1949, 1952, 1953, 1955, and 1956,
Campanella played against Yankee catcher Yogi Berra. Just as
Campanella was the National League MVP in 1951, 1953, and
1955, Berra was the American League MVP in 1951, 1954, and
1955. The Dodger catcher got to know his crosstown rival:*

We played a few exhibition games in Florida. Then,
before every season would open, we would play a three-game

series with the Yankees. Either two in Brooklyn and one in Yankee Stadium, or two at Yankee Stadium and one at Brooklyn. I was, I'd say, a friend of Yogi's; I talked to him. But when you get on the field to play, it's different. You're not friends then. You play to win.

Campanella was glad that the team that signed him was the Dodgers:

Brooklyn was the greatest place in the league. And the fans accepted Jackie Robinson, Don Newcombe, and myself, accepted the Dodgers being the first team to integrate the major leagues. We couldn't have done it in a better place than Brooklyn. We were accepted, rooted for, never got booed, and you can't ask for much more. But we were winning, and it's great to win.

JIMMY CONNORS

If there ever was a people's champion in recent American tennis, it was Jimmy Connors. Controversial, colorful, a man who seemed to go all out all the time, and a man who had little in common with the country-club set, Jimmy Connors became popular with tennis fans across America. Perhaps the only thing that exceeded his popularity was the quality of his tennis: whether measured by championships won, Grand Slam titles won, or number of years ranked number one in the world, Jimmy Connors is the greatest American tennis player since Bill Tilden. And the last year Bill Tilden was number one in the world was 1925.

In fact, there have been three Jimmy Connorses. First, there was the brash upstart who would angrily challenge tournament judges and umpires and break the delicate rules of tennis etiquette. Then there was the comeback kid, who beat the world's best long after his prime. Then there is the Jimmy Connors of today, an old master who can still rip a backhand and place a volley.

Jimmy Connors first became known on the American tennis scene in 1971, when, as a freshman, he led UCLA to the NCAA Division I championship and was the national collegiate champion. Connors was number one in the world five straight years, from 1974 through

1978, more years than any other player but Bill Tilden (six: 1920–25). He won Wimbledon (1974 and 1982), the Australian Open (1974), and the U.S. Open (1974, 1976, 1978, 1982, and 1983).

Connors is fifth on the all-time list for "Grand Slam" singles titles with eight—victories at Wimbledon, the French Open, the Australian Open, and the U.S. Open. Only Roy Emerson, Bjorn Borg, Rod Laver, and Bill Tilden have more. Though he began his career long before today's gigantic tournament purses, Connors still managed to win $8,513,840 from tournaments, seventh on the all-time list.

In addition to his five years as the top player in the world, Connors was second in 1979, 1982, and 1984 and third in 1973, 1980, 1981, and 1983. He was also fourth in 1985 and 1987, seventh in 1988, and eighth in 1986. In other words, he was in the top ten—generally at or near the top of the top ten—every year from 1973 through 1988, an amazing sixteen years. As such, he spans several eras of world tennis: in his first year in the rankings, the list included Rod Laver and Arthur Ashe; in his last year there, it included Andre Agassi and Boris Becker.

In the list of all-time tournament wins from the arrival of open tennis (tournaments admitting both pros and amateurs) in 1968 through the present, Jimmy Connors stands alone at the top, with 109 victories, followed by Ivan Lendl with 94, John McEnroe with 77, and Bjorn Borg with 62.

I know Jimmy pretty well, probably as well as anybody who broadcast tennis or was around the sport. He is very self-oriented. Part of that comes not from him but from his sport: I think to be a champion in tennis you have to build a little shell around yourself. You can't associate with the people you're trying to beat every day, and he never did.

He alienated a lot of people. Yes, he did capture the New York crowds, because he could be obnoxious. In his later years he got more subtle about it, but even then that word applied; even then he was obnoxious. He would unnecessarily bait officials who were only trying to do their best, and he rarely agreed to represent his country in the Davis Cup; as a result, the United States lost some matches it should have won. He was a brat from the beginning.

Nevertheless, Jimmy Connors helped his sport a lot. His greatest contribution was that he was the first to make the two-handed shot an accepted stroke. This happened especially in the classic battles he had with Bjorn Borg, who entered big-time tennis just after Jimmy did. The matches that Borg and Connors had, both of them hitting with two hands from the backhand side, encouraged smaller people to play tennis. These were people who otherwise never would have played because they didn't think they were strong enough. But then they started to play because they realized that you could keep both hands on the racket and still play.

Connors not only brought the two-hand technique to the game; he also brought a great gift of eyesight. His eyesight might have paralleled that of Ted Williams. Because of that, he had an extraordinary ability to return serve. He didn't have much of an overhead game, and he didn't have much of a serve himself, but what he did have was enough to win major championships.

Jimmy Connors grew up in a rough area of East St. Louis, Illinois. As a child, he won dozens of amateur tournaments:

Probably the only dream I had, like every young kid, was to just get involved in the game and be able to play it as well as you can. Then when you get to that point and you get a little bit older, you say, "Hey, wouldn't it be great to win a Wimbledon or a U.S. Open?"

But I played tennis at the beginning only for fun and to get me off the streets of East St. Louis and to give me something constructive to do so I wouldn't be out getting in trouble.

I never realized, and I don't know if my mother realized, once she started making the tennis available for me and teaching me the game, that it would ever turn into something like this.

Like many top athletes, Connors took awhile before concentrating exclusively on one sport:

I played everything. I played a lot of baseball and basketball and football, but once I was in school, I was happy to go do my schooling during the day and then try to get over and play some tennis in the evening, so that kind of cut into my team sports in school. But I did everything along the way.

When Connors entered the game, it was, even for the majority of top players, not much more than a way to win a college scholarship. It was no road to riches:

You played only because it was fun, and then if you could get your college education out of it, that was even better. And then even if you could go on and play among the pros and win a Wimbledon or a U.S. Open, what were you going to fall back on? After a certain age I would realize I made it or didn't, and then what was I going to do for the rest of my life to earn a living?

I never expected at any time that this amount of money would come into the game, that tennis would become a multi-million dollar game, leave the country club atmosphere, get into the streets, and bring every sports fan in the world into it.

Then when I was eighteen or nineteen, a bit of money came into the game, and I said, "Wow, what an opportunity for me to still play tennis and maybe make a bit of my own money so I don't have to ask my mom for it all the time." Then once that happened and tennis became more popular, Bobby Riggs played Billie Jean King, which got so many more people interested in the game. Man versus woman, husband versus wife, boss versus secretary. And then once that started, the snowball effect gathered with tennis, and tennis just jumped from level to level to level to where we are today.

Though Connors honed his career at UCLA, today's players rarely set foot in a college classroom:

If you go to college now, you're almost like a freak. Everybody's out there playing at fifteen, sixteen years old. They leave high school. They take their books on the road. When you're out there at fifteen and sixteen, you're a major player because you're playing in a man's game.

I left college at nineteen, and everybody said, "Oh man, watch out! You'd better get your college education. You're too young."

In reality, that was young at the time. All my peers finished college. Brian Gottfried finished college, and Dickie Stockton and Eddie Dibbs and Roscoe Tanner, but I left a little bit early, and it was like, "What's he doing? Is he crazy? Has he lost his mind?" And if I wouldn't have gone out there and been able to accomplish it at an early age, I would've probably drawn massive heat from that. And now—I left after my second year—now they don't even finish high school.

So that just goes to show that somebody's out there really pushing them to get out there; they see the major bucks out there and get out there and try to make it while they can. Because I don't think anybody fourteen, fifteen, sixteen years old is making his or her own decisions.

Connors realizes life could have been harder:

I've never gone to work. That's probably why I'm still playing today. I've done something my whole life that I really like and will continue to like. I just happened to earn a living at the same time. Not many people can say, "Hey, I'm going to work and it's fun."

I feel very fortunate that even though some things enter into the game that are a little bit tougher now with the travel and the living out of hotels and the suitcases, I still love the game now as much as when I first started.

One of the controversies surrounding Connors stemmed from the fact that he did not often represent his country in the Davis Cup:

I played Davis Cup sporadically over the course of my career, but not as much as John McEnroe has. He really dedicated himself to playing the Davis Cup. There's a lot of personal reasons why I didn't play. I feel that I've always been a loner, and even though I've played some team sports, I've always worked better individually. I didn't feel at any time that I should get on a team just to get on a team.

Even though I did play, I don't know if it was good for the overall picture for me to be a part of the team if it created controversy, if it created ill feelings, if there was tension at the time. I always felt it was better to get the best players and have the best atmosphere instead of having the best players and having a tension-filled atmosphere.

I don't play my best tennis like that. I don't think the team would get their best result like that. On the other hand, there's a lot of reasons that a lot of people don't know and probably won't know why I haven't played as much as I should have, and I'll keep those to myself.

During his years at the top of tennis, Connors had one gear when he was on the court: high. He brought an almost unique intensity to every shot, and to every disagreement:

I didn't build up any animosity toward my opponents. People pay their money and come first and foremost to see the tennis. If you don't play your best tennis, or at least try to, don't show up. Then whatever else the people get is even better.

For them to come down and to feel a part of what's happening there, to get involved, to beat on the signs, to do the wave, to yell, to scream, to really voice their opinion on what's happening, that's what's taking tennis to the boxing level, to the baseball level, the soccer and basketball level.

That's what tennis really needs. How much of it is planned? None. I've always gone out and been absolutely all natural. And if I'm out there and I feel I'm being wronged, I've got to let you know about it. Sometimes I'm going to step over that very thin line of what's right and what's wrong. But that's me. That's just the way I am, and I can only say that whatever happens out there, I guess it could always be worse.

Connors was the first player to develop a reputation of being extraordinarily tough on tournament judges and umpires, angrily and loudly challenging their calls and their decisions. John McEnroe was the second:

I wouldn't want their job, I'll say that right now. As long as I feel they're up there doing the best job they can, that's all you ask. Just let them watch the same match that I'm playing. That's all I can really ask. And pay attention and keep your mind on your business.

On the other hand, there's a lot of rules and regulations that have entered into the game that are no good. And that puts the umpire in a very difficult situation, and it takes an open-minded person, a fair person to look at a situation on the court and be able to make a quick decision, whether it's right for him to jump in or not. If a few rules were changed, that would outlaw a lot of things that happen, keep a lot of tempers from flaring, keep a lot of controversies from popping up, and make a lot of matches run a lot smoother.

Although he was often on top, Connors was not the only colorful player in tennis. With the advent of more and more TV coverage, the public suddenly became interested in the nontraditional players and the game they played:

They had a couple characters in there that created a lot of interest and played a lot of great tennis, too. Nastase was still around playing some great tennis. John McEnroe had just burst on the scene. Vitas Gerulaitis was playing. You still had some guys like Newcombe who were from the generation before but were still creating a lot of interest.

The popularity of the players plus television was a major part of that. Once television came in and started letting the viewers in on what was happening, at a minimum it created interest in the game and the players. It wasn't oversaturated; you were a specialty item. The Open was on TV, Wimbledon might have been on TV, one or two or three other tournaments over the course of a year.

So now we're walking down the street and all of a sudden, "I know him. Where'd I see him? Is that . . . ?" And then they'd turn on the TV for a tennis tournament and say, "I saw him on the street."

When television came in, it got the big companies involved. It got the people coming in more to sit in the stands. The whole thing just kind of streamrolled to the point where tennis jumped from—on the scale of a ten-story building where it was on level two—it jumped to an instant eight or nine.

Connors has a few comments to make about women's tennis, and these remarks test the border of political correctness:

Whether I like or I go along with the women's game and whether they're getting overpaid or not, or whether they get more money for endorsements or whatever, that's not my place to say. My place is to go about my business and work out what's good for me. I've never been one to quarrel. If I play an exhibition and I ask for five dollars and get it and the guy I'm playing gets seven dollars, I'm happy as hell for him.

That's really the way I feel about the women's game. We're playing for an awful lot of money in the men's game. We play a lot longer than they do, but I'm not going to say we put forth any more effort than they do, because for what they do and their makeup and what they have to work with, we're all putting forth the same energy per pound. So I'm not going to quarrel with that. Whether I like it or not, I'm going to keep that to myself. But I'm sure they're putting as much energy into their game, into their sport, into making their circuit a success as the men are, so good luck.

To become one of the most prominent players, you must win one of the Grand Slam tournaments:

The Grand Slams are where you really make your name. There's so much pressure on young players coming up that if you don't win a Grand Slam, you're really not considered a great player. Unfortunately, there's a lot of great players that aren't considered such. And I don't think that's really fair. But winning the Grand Slams are where your name is made and that makes it possible to play the exhibitions, to play the special events, to play the challenge matches, to really make the income necessary for you to keep up your lifestyle. Whatever else goes along with that—your personality or the way you go about things, the rapport with the crowd, your rapport with the companies, and so forth— is all incorporated in what happens after you win the Grand Slams. In my time there was no hype. You made your own hype by winning a Wimbledon or winning a U.S. Open. There was no company behind me pushing me or putting me up on a pedestal until I won.

Interviewed when his former rival Bjorn Borg was struggling in his attempted comeback, Jimmy Connors correctly predicted that Borg would never again rank among the world's top players. In so doing, he indirectly explained how rapidly tennis has changed:

He's been off for seven or eight years, so he's lost that seven or eight years, and everybody else has progressed eight years, and so he's really behind sixteen years in my book, which is a very difficult amount of time to make up.

Of course, over that period, the midsize and oversize rackets have come into play. The athletes are different. They're bigger, they're stronger, they're maybe better conditioned. They travel with their weight trainer, their coaches, their masseur, their guru, with everybody necessary to keep their mind on their tennis.

So for Borg to come back and to think he's going to all of a sudden fit in with the way it was when he stopped when he was twenty-six—it's an impossibility. He's not going to be able to cope. That's how much the game's changed and how much the players have changed. And if he wants to cope, he has to set a realistic goal for himself to start off and to break into the top two or three hundred. And then once he does that, set another goal for himself, then set another goal—reachable goals. He shouldn't overextend himself and put excess pressure on himself, because he's going to find enough pressure out there.

But I wish he'd make up his mind. To be honest with you, I wish he'd come back and either play or not play. You know, get back out there and grind it out with the boys or just continue to do what's he's been doing because, you know, it's his indecision that really is affecting him as much as anything. He has to make a decision to play or not to play and then be big enough to stick with that.

Borg and Connors, along with John McEnroe, formed perhaps the greatest three-way rivalry in the history of tennis:

We had a great thing, the three of us. We had a great rivalry because our attitudes fit each other. Borg was a very quiet, keep-your-emotions-in type of person, played the baseline with massive topspin, was a great athlete, moved well, but hardly ever came to the net. I liked playing him because I was always the aggressor. I was the one trying to get into the net. I was always forcing the play. I wasn't going to let him stay back and just run me ragged all day. So it was his very quiet and very subdued attitude, against my attitude of going berserk, going crazy, and playing the forceful game.

That's why he fit in with McEnroe in the same kind of clash. I fit with McEnroe because it was just the opposite. We had two personalities that were exactly the same, that weren't afraid to back off or run the other way from each other. And his game fit into my game. His serve and volley game was his forte. My return of serve was my game. And we kind of fit into each other, which produced our best tennis.

The rivalry we had among the three of us was something I don't think will ever be matched again in tennis because we had three guys who were the best at the same time. Borg was winning Wimbledon while I was winning the Open. McEnroe's winning Wimbledon while I was winning the Open. And everybody was chasing one another at the time, trying to get that little upper hand.

And frankly, if anybody deserves an explanation of why Borg got out of the game, it's myself and McEnroe, because of what the three of us had. It was very special, and I don't think that will ever happen again.

Connors's popularity soared as he continued playing, and playing well, long after most players had retired from tournament tennis:

I absolutely have to say that I don't think it could be any better than it is now. The transition that has happened to me in the last ten years or so is, I think, best said by when I was at the Open. I looked up into the stands and I saw a lot of familiar faces that were there twenty years ago watching me play Forest Hills. And that's the thirty-five-to-forty-five-year-old set. And they're still coming out and giving me the honor of still wanting to see me play. And watching me play and wanting me to go out and to continue to fall and scrape and bleed and yell and scream for them, and also produce the best tennis.

I feed off that, and that in turn enables me even now to try to lift my game to that level that pleases them. And my rapport with the people here in New York is something that has been so special that it's difficult for me to sit here and just tell you how special that is. They have won for me more than I can ever say, and in turn that has brought out the best in me so that I want to perform for them. And if I can keep that going for another year or two or three, then that would be great.

GEORGE FOREMAN

George Foreman presents a remarkable story. He came from one of the poorest areas of Houston. He became the Olympic heavyweight champion in Mexico City in 1968. Many still remember him carrying a small American flag in each hand, turning in each of four directions, and bowing to the crowd. Then came his pro career, a career that, against all odds, continues to this day.

I did George's first pro fight on June 23, 1969. It was against Don Waldheim at Madison Square Garden, the last undercard before Joe Frazier fought Jerry Quarry.

The Waldheim fight was scheduled for three rounds. But Waldheim was only supposed to be a heavyweight. He was lighter. The first time George hit him hard, he broke three ribs. A KO in the third—maybe a good thing, from the point of view of Waldheim's health.

On January 22, 1973, Foreman won the heavyweight championship of the world over Joe Frazier by TKO in the second round of a fight in Kingston, Jamaica. He defended successfully against José (King) Roman by KO in the first round in Tokyo in September of the same year and against Ken Norton by TKO in the second round in Caracas, Venezuela, in March 1974.

Then came the famous "Rumble in the Jungle," in Kinshasa, Zaire, on October 30, 1974. Foreman lost the heavyweight belt to the former champion, Muhammad Ali, who knocked out Foreman in the eighth round. In 1977 Foreman retired from boxing. He became an ordained preacher.

In 1986 Big George began training for a comeback. First he had to lose a little weight: he weighed 315 pounds. After switching from steak and salad to carbohydrates, he did, though nobody ever said he became skinny. His first fight was in March 1987 against an unknown, Steve Zouski.

After a dozen successful bouts against mostly weak competition, Foreman made it to an April 19, 1991, heavyweight championship bout against Evander Holyfield, who had won the title from Buster Douglas. Douglas himself had taken the crown from Mike Tyson. The six-foot-three-and-a-half Foreman, who had won the title in 1973 at 217½ pounds and had lost it in 1974 at 220, now weighed 257. Foreman lost to Holyfield by a unanimous decision in twelve rounds.

But Big George wasn't through. He had more fights, winning them all. Then, in June 1993, he lost a controversial twelve-round decision to Tommy Morrison. Finally, on November 5, 1994, George Foreman faced twenty-six-year-old Michael Moorer for the WBA and IBF heavyweight championships of the world. In April, Moorer had taken the title from Holyfield.

The fight was held at the MGM Grand Garden in Las Vegas. Foreman, now weighing 250, chose the old red trunks he had worn in Zaire two decades before. Some said he did so because it was time for Foreman to rid himself of the embarrassment he still felt from the loss to Ali. As the bout against Moorer unfolded, Foreman absorbed many punches with little damage and scored from time to time with both his left and his powerful right.

Still, entering the tenth round, Foreman was behind seven rounds to two on two judges' cards. But suddenly his left-right combination weakened Moorer. And a moment later, Foreman slammed Moorer's chin with a heavy right from the hip; the champion fell to the

mat. *The referee counted to ten, and at forty-five years of age George
Foreman became the oldest man ever to win the heavyweight crown.*

*After the fight, Foreman said, "Now I won't have to be introduced
as the former heavyweight champion of the world any longer."*

*Because of the fight, Foreman's commercial value increased dra-
matically. He placed sixth on the* Forbes *1995 list of highest-income
athletes, with $10 million from purses and $8 million from endorsements.*

*In March 1995 the WBA stripped Foreman of his title because he
refused to fight the number-one WBA contender, Tony Tucker. In
April Foreman defended his IBF championship in a controversial
twelve-round decision over Axel Schulz of Germany at the MGM
Grand. But only two months later he relinquished the IBF crown
rather than obey the federation's order that he give Schulz a rematch.*

*Foreman's overcoming his age was no more remarkable than his
overcoming his early poverty and early role models:*

I grew up in Houston, Texas. It was called the Bloody
Fifth Ward of Houston. All the role models I had were guys
on the street corner. Generally they had a scar on their face.
They had already spent years in prison. My greatest ambition
was to move up steadily to the corners, the big street corners
where the big thugs were and eventually get a scar on my
face and maybe go to prison and become famous on the
street corner.

My mother ruled. There was not always enough food,
and there was definitely not enough clothes to go around, so
there were some days I wasn't going to go to school looking
the way I did. And I figured as soon as I'd gotten big enough
and was able to provide better clothes, I would probably get
myself a better education. But having to go to school without
lunch and the proper clothes, I dropped out at maybe fifteen
years old, and I was running the streets and even started
robbing and stealing, and people told me I would never be
anything.

But then came the Job Corps:

I started to believe it, but in 1964 I heard a commercial by Jimmy Brown saying, "If you are looking for another chance, if you are a high school dropout with no hope, and if you are looking for that one extra chance, there is the Job Corps."

Lyndon Johnson started this program for high school dropouts, and I learned about the poverty program, and I joined the Job Corps and met up after a couple of years with Doc Broadus, my original coach, in the Job Corps in California. I had heard a boxing match between Muhammad Ali and Floyd Patterson on the radio. I kept picking fights. And Doc said, "You're so big, why don't you become a boxer?" And because of that radio show, I said, "O.K., I will become a boxer."

Doc looked me over and said, "You're big enough. You're ugly enough. Come on down to the gym."

I had my first amateur boxing match because I missed my family so much. You really think you're tough. Then at sixteen years old, you're homesick. You're in another state. I missed my mother, and it was embarrassing. Some nights I would cry and wake up.

So I decided I needed to do something in the evenings. I would go down to the gym and work out, and Doc Broadus told me to come down. I just wanted to learn how to hit the speed bag and maybe eventually become tough enough so when I got back to the streets of Houston, I could beat up everybody. But then he put me in the Silver Gloves tournament and then a Golden Gloves championship in 1967.

From then on, I thought I was a winner, and in 1968, I won a gold medal again. I went on. Became a member of the 1968 Olympic team in Mexico City, and it was a surprise to the whole world.

There was a lot of movement about possibly boycotting the Olympics. A lot of athletes wanted to show disgust with the system. Nobody bothered with me. Nobody ever gave me any lectures about the society and the evils of it. They just said, "He's not going to make it past the second round or the third round."

It just so happened that I was a product of a compassionate society, having been rescued from the gutter by Lyndon Johnson's program, the Job Corps, and literally under the gutter, hiding from the police, digging in the mud, just drinking and life going nowhere, but I was given another chance in life.

There's the solemn, religious side of George, and then there's the funny side of George. That side often has a lot to do with eating. I attended a banquet with him in Philadelphia in the spring of 1995. I told him I had done his first fight, the bout with Waldheim.

George remembered it well. He told me exactly what happened before and during the fight. He remembered he was just back from winning the Olympics. To promote the fight, there was an outdoor ring at Forty-second and Broadway. George carried an American flag in his hand, just as he had after winning the gold medal in Mexico City.

I was sitting between George and Herschel Walker. Herschel had a fruit plate and I had a salad. They were about to serve the main course, chicken, but we weren't planning to eat more than we had already. George had a different opinion; he had no interest in restraining himself. "I can't do it," he said. "If they bring it, I gotta eat it." He had his salad. Then George had our entrées—Herschel's and mine. That's a lot of chicken.

FRANK GIFFORD

One of my favorite members of the Pro Football Hall of Fame is my old teammate from the New York Giants, Frank Gifford. An all-around athlete, Frank was an All-American football player at USC. With the Giants he was a running back, defensive back, and place-kicker. Even that doesn't fully describe his versatility, because in most years he was among the team's leaders in not only rushing but pass receiving. In 1956, 1957, 1958, and 1959 he led the Giants in both categories.

Frank's versatility was illustrated especially by his statistics in his best year, 1956: he rushed 159 times for 819 yards (a 5.2-yard average) and five touchdowns; he caught 51 passes for 603 yards (a 11.8-yard average) and four touchdowns, and he even attempted five passes, connecting on two for a total of 35 yards, with both of his completions resulting in touchdowns. Even that wasn't all. He also made eight of nine extra point tries and one of two field goal attempts. It seemed like he did everything but launder the uniforms. That season, thanks in no small measure to Gifford, the Giants won the NFL championship, blowing out the Chicago Bears 47–7. At the end of the season, Frank was named the Most Valuable Player in the league.

With the Giants from 1952 to 1964, Gifford starred alongside *famed players like halfback Kyle Rote, quarterbacks Charlie Conerly and Y. A. Tittle, running back Alex Webster, linemen Roosevelt Grier and Andy Robustelli, linebacker Sam Huff, and safety Jim Patton; after I joined the team, I became the place-kicker and played end on offense and defense.*

Like most players of the era, Frank played both ways. In one streak of seven games, he played every single down on both offense and defense. Frank was physically gifted, but he didn't have a great feel for the game, and he wasn't graceful. He got the job done because he was a great competitor, a man with tremendous desire. Even though he was primarily a running back, he was also a good passer. He could throw it hard, but he couldn't throw it when it required any touch. He was a player who fit his era: he was less suited to today's age of specialization than to the 1950s, when many of the top players were men who could do many things well.

After retiring from the Giants in 1964, Gifford went on to a highly successful career in sportscasting with ABC. He is best known for his broadcasts of "Monday Night Football" with cohosts such as Howard Cosell, Don Meredith, Al Michaels, and Dan Dierdorf, but he has also distinguished himself in other sports, including the Olympic Games. His wife is also known to more than a few: her name is Kathie Lee Gifford.

Playing touch football with older kids gave Frank Gifford his first sense that he had talent as a football player:

I loved the ability to elude people. Long before high school, I was playing touch football on Hermosa Beach. I was smaller than most of the people because I hung out with my older brother a lot, and consequently I was playing with his crowd, and they were a couple of years older, and it's the first time I recognized I could do something better than they could. When we chose up, everybody wanted me on their team. And I usually was the one they threw the ball to or gave the ball to, because I was very elusive, very tricky. Oddly enough, that was never my style later on, but at the time I liked that. It was a very heady feeling to play with older kids and be able to elude them or beat them and, quite frankly, to be able to dominate the game that I played in.

When they were children, most famous football players dreamed of playing the sport professionally. Not Frank Gifford:

I really didn't ever dream of playing professional football, because I had never heard of professional football. I started playing football at Bakersfield [California] High School, and fortunately the football coach there, Homer Beatty, became a friend of mine. And he pointed out that if I wanted to and if I had a good year as a junior and senior, I probably could get a football scholarship.

That was my first thought, really, of ever going beyond high school. No one in my family had ever graduated from college, so there was no real incentive. Everybody usually worked in the oil fields. My brother dropped out of high school as a junior and went to work in the oil fields, and my father had dropped out of school and worked in the oil fields, and they were very successful.

I was recruited, but not very heavily. I think when they looked at my educational background—being a wood shop major until I was a junior in high school—there were a lot of schools I couldn't get into at the time. Maybe that wouldn't have made any difference today, but at the time I couldn't get into the University of California, which I thought of first; then later I wanted to go to Stanford. I changed my curriculum as a senior in high school, thanks to Homer Beatty.

I went one year to junior college, and I made junior college All-American, and there were a few people that came around and tried to recruit me at that point. But I had been so disappointed about Stanford and California that I decided that there's nothing wrong with USC; Homer Beatty had played there, so it was kind of an automatic transition for me just to go from Bakersfield Junior College to USC.

With the New York Giants, Gifford was known as an offensive threat. So his early history at USC will surprise some fans:

My first two years at USC, I played defense and I made honorable mention All-Coast, I think, as a defensive back my sophomore year and then again my junior year. And then in my senior year, we changed coaches and went to a wing-T, and I played the single-wing tailback in it, and we won our first seven games. We got a lot of attention—we beat the number one team in the nation at the time, the University of California.

All of a sudden I was being photographed by the various All-American selection committees, which I thought was rather amusing. We had played seven games, the season wasn't even over, and we came into New York to play Army at Yankee Stadium. Look magazine was there, and all the magazines were big in the All-American business in those days, and they were all there to take my photograph.

So in one year, everything in my entire world changed. I moved over and played offense and graduated as an All-American at USC, played in the East-West Shrine game, played in the Senior Bowl game. I was drafted number one by the Giants. So it really hit me all at once as a senior.

Though he had switched from defense to offense, Gifford was also a kicker:

I did all the place-kicking for USC for three years. And then when I went to the Giants, I fooled around with it a little bit. I was an All-American running back at USC, but the first two and a half years with the Giants I went back and played defense again. They had a pretty good football player ahead of me named Kyle Rote.

Then in 1953 I played a little bit of offense, too. Toward the end of that season, we ran out of football players, and in the last five games I never came out.

With the Giants, Gifford was not only surrounded by famous players, but he was also in the company of coaches who came to be regarded as the most prominent in the history of the game—not the head coach, but the assistant coaches:

Jim Lee Howell, the head coach, was very honest, a big good old boy from Arkansas, about six-six, a big shock of white hair and a very straight-out former Marine. And he literally didn't do any coaching at all. He really didn't.

In those days there were not the numbers of writers, and teams didn't have their own writers and people that cover them for local TV, and they really didn't know what was going on in the inner workings of different athletic franchises. Jim Lee Howell had Tom Landry coaching the defense and Vince Lombardi coaching the offense. So there was good reason not to coach, but to his credit, he didn't interfere with them.

Jim Lee, as far as I can recall, never had one bit of input into our offense and very little into our defense. But considering what happened to Vince Lombardi and Tom Landry, he didn't need to. He was a very strong disciplinarian. If you were late to practice you would hear about it, you would be fined.

I played both offense and defense. I didn't come out of the last five games in 1953, and the next year Vince Lombardi came in as offensive coach, and that was the end of it. He put me at halfback, and his first words ever spoken to me were "You are my halfback."

When I played pro football, it had to be fun or you didn't play it. When I came into pro football, my first contract was for $8,200, and that's not per game, that was for a year. And I was the number one draft pick. I thought if I didn't like it after the first year, I'd quit. I was working toward a degree. And I continued to do that, and I thought I'd just check it out. I had a lot of fun playing, I had a lot of fun being in New York. We had a lousy football team for the first three or four years.

I think Vince Lombardi's coming to the Giants made a world of difference. I was on the verge of quitting. I was tired of playing with a team that was down like the Giants were in those days. I was tired of not having a position. If somebody got hurt, I played that position one week, and then played another position. And besides that, it's embarrassing to think how much money I was making out of it. I could have done much better building homes for my brother-in-law in California. But I hung around long enough, and I think the reason I did was Vince Lombardi.

Until the mid–1950s, pro football was a weak second to major league baseball as the main national sport of the United States. Perhaps more than any other game, the 1956 NFL championship game, in which the Giants destroyed the Chicago Bears 47–7, changed things:

That game was not sold out, which is interesting. The following year Yankee Stadium was sold out for every game the Giants played. So I think pro football took a really giant stride in the season of 1956. The Giants had not won since 1936, and all of a sudden in 1956 here was a team in the media capital of the world. New York fell in love with the Giants and all of a sudden Sam Huff was on the cover of Time magazine. They wired him up, and he did a TV show. CBS did a documentary on the violent world of Sam Huff.

In 1956 I think there were 51,000 at Yankee Stadium. The stadium held 62,000. The following year, we had crowds of 65,000 and 67,000 when they sold standing room. And they stopped selling standing room after that, because we had some wild outbreaks up there.

Gifford remembers his teammates:

We had a lot of great players. It was a very unique collection of players that came together. Not only offensively— names that come to mind like Alex Webster and Charlie Conerly, Bob Schnelker, who went into coaching. I don't know how many of them went on to become head coaches, but many of them did—Dick Nolan, Harlan Svare. So many more went on to become assistant coaches. Jim Patton was a great pro. Andy Robustelli, Jim Katcavage, Sam Huff, Rosey Grier, Lindon Crow, Carl Karilivacz, and you can go on. Rosey Brown. Several in the Hall of Fame. A good tackle, Dickie Yelvington, Ray Wietecha. If you think about the offensive line, I can recall most of them, and I still keep in pretty good contact with a lot of them.

Another memorable game was the 1958 NFL championship, in which the Giants held a 17–14 lead over Johnny Unitas and the Baltimore Colts. There was one minute and fifty-six seconds to play:

That was the first sudden-death overtime in history. We had a chance late in the game even though I had almost fumbled the game away. I had three fumbles, two of which we lost and which resulted in scores both times by Baltimore. All we needed to do at the end of the game, however, was control the football, and there was a point at which I know on third and short I made a first down, but there was a tremendous pileup, and at the bottom of the pile there was a whole lot of screaming and yelling: Colts defensive end Gino Marchetti had broken his leg. And I think at the time the official was more concerned about the injury than he was about marking the football, and I had played the game long enough to know I had made the first down.

I only had about a foot to go, and yet when they marked the ball, they marked it short of the first down. So we decided to punt instead of going for it on fourth down. And then came the very famous drive by Johnny Unitas. He completed five or six passes, maybe in a row, to Ray Berry.

Even though he's never said so, I think Tom Landry would have loved to get out of his man-to-man defense and into some kind of a zone. As it was, it was Ray Berry who put himself into the Hall of Fame, I think, with this one series. And they went on and tied the game up, and then, of course, in sudden death overtime, they scored first and won, 23–17.

The Colts were the archrivals of the Giants, beating them in the NFL championship games of both 1958 and 1959, and they were formidable foes:

Johnny Unitas was a great quarterback. He also played on a great football team. Ray Berry is in the Hall of Fame. Lenny Moore is perhaps one of the greatest football players and perhaps one of the most underrated football players ever to play. Lenny Moore was a much more dangerous receiver than Ray Berry, and Ray Berry would be the first to tell you that.

When Lenny Moore came out of Penn State, he was a sprinter. He ran the 100-yard dash in about 9.7. He was about six-foot-three and could jump like a gazelle, and he was a very smart football player. They had Ray Berry on one side and Lenny Moore on the other, and they had a kid named Mutscheller at tight end, and they could all catch the football well, and they had people like Jim Barker blocking for Unitas.

Johnny was great and had a tremendous career, but when he left there, even though it was late in his career, he went out to San Diego, and it wasn't the same Johnny Unitas. I have always felt that so many of us—the numbers and the acclaim and all the awards—are only a reflection of the teams we played with. I think to some degree that was the case with Johnny Unitas, and he played with great football players, and I think Johnny would be one of the first people to tell you too, because whenever I hear him interviewed he's always talking about them.

But he played with a great collection of football players, and they were better than we were. I was really proud of what we did getting into two championship games against them, and certainly in 1958 I felt we should have won it. We lost it probably on a call but we lost to a team that I think quite honestly was better than we were.

In the 1970s, specialized defenses took over the NFL. The result was a less exciting game. This in turn resulted in new rules of play designed to improve the offensive game:

Even a subtle change makes a major difference once the coaches pick up on it. There have been many, many changes, but perhaps the most dramatic was when they started to allow a lot of different things for the offense. For instance, the defensive backs could only make contact at the line of scrimmage, and then they could use the bump-and-run, which I thought was a great part of football. I can remember the dramatic games of the Oakland Raiders defense with their bump-and-run tactics, and they really started using it first.

Then the rules changed, and they said you could only bump them once, and then you couldn't bump them after five yards, and that turned it into a different football game for receivers. And all of a sudden, you saw a proliferation of five-foot-nine, 175-pound All-Pro receivers who weren't getting hit at the line of scrimmage.

Yes, they are good athletes and they can go up in the air and come up with the football, but they can get off that line of scrimmage, and I guarantee they would have had a tough time against a Willie Brown or somebody who had perfected the bump-and-run. They were bumping you all the way down the field, and they were knocking you, too. And they changed that.

Perhaps the biggest change is how the offensive linemen can block. I don't know what blocking is anymore. I mean it's like Hulk Hogan: it looks like tag-team wrestling. And they call it holding every now and then, which is kind of strange because when they call holding they could have probably called it on the play before or they could have called it maybe on two or three players on the offensive line, and they happen to pick on one particular player. It's really hard to define, and I know a referee could tell me what holding is, but an offensive lineman today does just about anything and everything he can against the defensive player, and still they get to the quarterback, which is truly amazing to me.

Over the past quarter-century, football has become a game of specialization. Gifford would like to reverse the trend:

I came from an era when the football player was more versatile. He had to be involved in more plays, even at the same position. Today, when you look down at two teams on the sidelines, they sometimes have three or four different teams getting ready to come into the ballgame depending on what happens on a given play.

I think the fans are beginning to lose a little interest in it. They can't keep track of it anymore. Sometimes we can't do it in a broadcast booth; sometimes it is very difficult knowing exactly the unit that is going to come in on a given situation.

I would like to—and I don't know how you do it, but I think it would be good for the game—take it back a step, and I think by taking it back a step you might be taking two steps forward. You would make players play. If he plays quarterback, make him play. Don't have a defensive back that can't play the game of football. He's just a roving defensive back running around looking for the deep bomb. Make a wide receiver earn his right to get downfield and go for the football.

I don't know how you legislate that, and first of all you

would be fighting every coach in pro football, but I think the fans are getting to be a bit concerned: Who are these people? Where do they come from? They don't know the players. They can't look down there and rely on their favorite player being in on a given situation.

I would like football to get away from a lot of specialty units that play this game or try to play it. Get back to where the fans watching on television or watching in the stadium know who is going to be in the game on a given situation.

I think it might take away the tremendous focus we now have on the quarterback and the tremendous focus we have now on maybe one wide receiver. It might take it back to where there's recognition of offensive line play. Recognition of defensive line play. You don't know the names of the players like you used to, and I think that would be a big help. I would enjoy it a lot more than watching a fire drill on every changing situation. And it's almost like watching a war movie: everyone is walking around with a headset talking to somebody else wearing a headset. I would just like to cut those lines one day, just to see what would happen. I think we would have a lot better football games.

Frank Gifford sees another threat to football, but it has nothing to do with the rules of play:

I think there are some very real dangers to the game of pro football, as there are to every professional sport and sports in general. I'm talking about the number-one threat, and I think that is drugs. I'm talking about all of them, steroids right to the designer-types. The American public, the buying public, the consumer is getting totally turned off by this. They get their children involved, they're spending an awful lot of money to go to a football game, they're spending an awful lot of money on products that are sponsoring these football games, when all of a sudden they look up there and see a group of athletes that are associated with drug abuse rather than excellence on a football field or any field.

It's a turnoff, and it could be very subtle to begin with, and then it could have a tremendous snowballing effect. And it wouldn't take very long to where all of a sudden perhaps there was the boycotting of products, not to mention the attendance at games.

And the same people who, in their wisdom—and I'm not being facetious about it—decided they could pay $980 million for a product because there were that many people who were going to buy the products that sponsored the games, or the people were going to go to the game, or the interest would continue—all of a sudden the same people who paid the $980 million would see the interest change, and believe me, their interest would change much more quickly.

So what about more effective testing for drugs and for "masking agents"?

It would be an easy thing, I guess, if our society would do the same thing, but we don't. There are all kinds of issues involved; the players and their right to privacy and all of the things that come up when you sit down and you try to negotiate in certain areas. If the NFL wants to change its drug policy and they show an indication that they do—then they damn well should do it and then see what happens. There would be a tremendous outcry from some factions and justifiably so in some areas. You could take it too far, and it could be a basic violation of your privacy and personal rights. But the way I look at it, you wouldn't have to worry about it if it continues; there won't be anything to be private about.

Somewhere along the line, there has to be a total realization that drug use isn't the right way to go. And where it comes from, how it begins, I don't know. Maybe it's hard at the beginning, because in the beginning will be the backlash, when society says, "Hey, we've had enough of this. I don't want to raise my children in that kind of atmosphere. I don't want them to be even involved with this."

How many times do they look at an all-star pitcher and an all-star lineman and you're counting the days, holding your breath that he doesn't have a third test so he won't be kicked out of the game for good. What kind of a role model is this, what kind of an idol to hold up to your son? And when this gets to a certain point, I think there will be an enormous backlash, and we're damn close to it.

Looking back at all the players he's seen, Frank Gifford reserves his highest praise for Jim Brown:

As far as I'm concerned, Jim Brown is the greatest running back ever to play. He played for only nine years and put together a remarkable record. I don't think he ever missed a game because of an injury. He was their football team. He was their focal point. He was the only running back I knew of that when he was on the field and I was on the bench, I would go over and stand on the sidelines to watch. We beat him up a lot. But he always got up and always came back. Walter Payton was great. O. J. was great. But Jimmy Brown was very special—that's my opinion, and I have never hesitated to offer it, as I have to O. J. and Walter.

Gifford went on to a wide-ranging and successful career in sportscasting, but he didn't plan it out one move at a time:

I never really set out to do any one thing in particular. I mean I didn't set a goal. I've read all these books by people on setting goals and writing down ten things they want to do. I sort of took the Don Meredith philosophy: I just kind of chugged along and did the very best I could with every opportunity I had. And when I came to a crossroads, I took what I thought was the best way, and I did the best I could and never looked back and bemoaned not having done this or having done that.

I think if I ever was to offer any advice, and I've done it to my own kids, don't beat up on what is in the past, because you can't change that. Make the most of what you're doing and do the very best with what you have.

Of his many broadcasting assignments, the one for which Frank Gifford is best known is "Monday Night Football" on ABC:

"Monday Night Football" is so special. It's an entity unto itself. It really is a phenomenal thing that's grown up over the past twenty years. And I say "grown up" because there are a lot of people who keep saying "Monday Night Football" is not what it used to be. "Monday Night Football" is still football that is played Monday night; it's a great night to watch football. The players all know what it's about, they all know the other players are watching.

In terms of broadcasting, it's the biggest fishbowl anyone could ever be involved in. Something happens different on a Monday night. As a broadcaster, people hear what you say. I've done a lot of Sunday telecasts, and after one of those no one ever comments on what you say, it doesn't even matter. But boy, on a Monday night, you're going to make somebody very happy or you're going to make somebody very angry. There's an enormity to it when you're talking to 30 million, 40 million people, and they don't all agree on the same thing. So you just have to go in and basically enjoy the game yourself, and that's what I've done for nineteen years; we always seem to get good football games, and that makes sense, because they don't want to give us a bad football game.

WAYNE GRETZKY

When you talk about most sports and you say a particular athlete is the best in a particular category, you're in for an argument. Who's the greatest scorer in the history of basketball? It depends on what you mean (points per game, shooting percentage, ability to make the three-point shot, or some other factor), what era you're considering, and so on. Who's the greatest scorer in all the years of football? Same problem. But when you talk about hockey and you talk about scoring, you talk about only one man.

Wayne Gretzky.

Who has won the Art Ross Trophy, for being the National Hockey League's season scoring leader, the most times? Wayne Gretzky, ten seasons.

Who is the number one NHL player on the list of lifetime regular season points? Wayne Gretzky, 2,608.

What if you combine NHL and World Hockey Association (1972–79) experience? Wayne Gretzky, 2,718.

All-time regular season NHL goals? Gretzky, 837.

All-time regular season NHL assists? Gretzky, 1,771.

All-time regular season NHL points per game? Gretzky, 2.08.

Most points in a season? Gretzky, 215.

Most goals in a season? Gretzky, 92.

Most assists in a season? Gretzky, 163.

Most games in which scored three or more goals? Gretzky, 49.

Most consecutive games in which scored a point? Gretzky, 51.

All-time Stanley Cup leader for points, goals, and assists? Starts with a G.

In addition, "The Great One" has set or tied sixty-one league records. He has won the Hart Memorial Trophy as the NHL's most valuable player a record nine times.

He led the Edmonton Oilers to the Stanley Cup four times: in 1984, 1985, 1987, and 1988. Even in the 1995 season, his sixteenth, Gretzky, at age thirty-four, led the Los Angeles Kings in points (48) and assists (37). And he's still playing, now with the New York Rangers.

Gretzky has done almost as well at the bank as at the rink. Forbes's December 18, 1995, issue shows he is tenth in the world in income from sports, making $14.5 million a year, with $8.5 million in salary and $6.0 million in endorsements. His salary is the highest in the NHL.

Gretzky spent some time with John Madden and me in the TV production bus parked outside the stadium in Anaheim, before a game involving the then–Los Angeles Rams. Wayne is a good friend of our producer, Bob Stenner.

Wayne impressed me as being a very classy individual. Recently I heard he got a ten-minute penalty for abusing a referee, but that seems totally uncharacteristic to me. Wayne seems like a very gentle man. Modest, but with class.

On the ice, he makes difficult things seem easy. He reminds me of DiMaggio: he gets things done without the appearance of effort. When others strike the puck, you might say they hit *it. With Wayne, the puck just seems to* flow off *him.*

But before he became the greatest scorer ever, Wayne had to start somewhere. Wayne Gretzky began playing hockey at the age of five in his native Brantford, Ontario. Despite precocious skill, he was not allowed to play on a team whose members were all ten or eleven years old. A year later he joined them. At eight, at four-foot-four and 70 pounds, he outplayed fourteen-year-olds in the Bantam League.

By the time Gretzky was fourteen, his hockey skills were so extraordinary that he and his family decided he would move to Toronto in order to find adequate competition.

Many characteristics have distinguished his game. He is known for shooting against the flow and for setting up behind the net. Some skills came naturally, some came hard. He is aware of his strengths and weaknesses:

My puck sense was a positive. The ability to utilize everyone on the ice was my strength. The negative was probably my size. [The slender Gretzky is five-feet-eleven and weighs 170 pounds; many hockey players look like linebackers.] I always had to figure out a way to overcome my strength and my power and my size.

Fortunately for me, I had some good coaches along the way that always said, "Don't try to be something you're not. Utilize what you have, and that will make you a better player." I was able to carry that advice throughout my career.

Puck sense, Gretzky's other skills, and, especially, his communication with his teammates, were developed through practice:

We're always talking, we're always communicating. Practice is very important in our sport, and I think the biggest reason is that hockey is different from most sports, which have a lot of stopping and starting. In football you go into a huddle and you come out and you make your play. Basketball, unless you do a fast break, you go down and you kind of set up.

The sport of hockey is instinct. You're moving all the time, you're always going; sometimes a game gets pretty quick, and I think the sport is getting faster every year. So you don't have time to stop and say, "Now, where is this guy?"

or "Where is that guy going?" I mean the game is played at instinct, and the way to play the game at instinct is to practice every day.

When I get into a particular situation, I know where my defense partner should be, I know where my winger is going to be, and we have to communicate. Some of the rinks are loud, and we have this instinctive communication, as I call it, and for us that's been successful.

NHL hockey is known for its violence. Gretzky is an outspoken critic:

A lot fight at the younger levels. If you fight, you are ejected automatically. My big gripe, if you want to call it that, is that I really believe we need the United States of America in order for the sport of hockey to grow. We're not going to grow if we don't cater to the overall American crowd. There are a lot of people that like fighting. The East Coast in some cities. In Canada, fighting is probably accepted as part of the sport.

In my estimation people look at our sport as violent and a form of hooliganism because in the NHL we don't automatically eject people who fight. If you fight in baseball, you're ejected. You fight in basketball, you're ejected. In hockey, you get three tries and then you're ejected, and I think in order for us to have any possible chance of a national TV contract, we have to eliminate fighting.

Most exciting for the typical fan is the goal, not the assist. Gretzky sees it otherwise, taking more pride in setting up a teammate to score:

I guess it comes from the fact that when I was a kid, by my fifth year on the team that I started on when I was six, I had scored four hundred goals. And I can remember thinking some of those nights, it got to be not fun. I would score, let's say, my seventh goal of the game, and I look around and I'm supposed to be excited, but I'm not really. My teammates are supposed to be happy and their look is, "Well, another one, who cares? Now it's eight to one."

So I just started thinking, it's not going to benefit me to score six or seven goals. And from that point, I just felt that when I would see somebody else score, the excitement and the look on his face was extraordinary, and I just went from that. I love to score, don't get me wrong, but I think I also enjoy just as much watching one of my teammates score, and I don't think a lot of players can say that.

SCOTT HAMILTON

The United States has had more than its share of legendary figure skaters, both men and women. Among the men have been Olympic gold medalists Dick Button in 1948 and 1952, Hayes Alan Jenkins in 1956, David Jenkins in 1960, and Brian Boitano in 1988. But as good as any, perhaps the best, is Scott Hamilton, the winner of the gold medal in Sarajevo in 1984. In addition to his Olympics success, Hamilton also was the U.S. and World Champion every year from 1981 through 1984. Hamilton is now CBS's lead broadcaster on figure skating telecasts and remains a skilled skater, starring in professional exhibitions and competitions.

I've had an opportunity to sit down and talk with him, and I've found that far from being a narrow aficionado of only his own sport, he knows as much about sports trivia and football, baseball, basketball as anyone. He's a real sports authority.

For now, the demographics of the figure-skating TV audience are heavily female, though obviously some men watch the sport. Some men say they don't want to watch it; some men seem to think there are a lot of homosexuals in the sport and some men are bothered by that, but I think figure skating is becoming better accepted among men. After all, figure skaters, both men and women, are good athletes. They *can do some things that really require athletic talent, endurance, and strength, things that men supposedly admire.*

For young Scott Hamilton growing up in Ohio, skating was a salvation:

I know what I really liked about it was the fact that when I was younger, I was pretty sick and I didn't have a lot of physical development. Because of my small size and the fact that I was really underdeveloped, I wasn't competitive in a lot of sports and games that kids play. I had a malabsorption problem that caused me to not grow for several years and so not only was I going to be small anyway, but I was stunted in my growth.

So what skating really offered me was a way to challenge myself and to be involved in something that was active and physical, and it gave me a real good sense of self-esteem. Because of my size, my center of balance, I would pick things up quicker than kids who were much taller than I was. So it gave me a great deal. It was something I could do as well or better than all the other guys that I couldn't compete with in football or basketball. So it was physical and emotional.

Some who pointed toward the Winter Olympics had dreams of riches. Not Scott Hamilton:

I wasn't really goal-oriented or success-minded when I was younger. I was more into going out and having a good time and playing. I was the kind of kid that liked to be the center of attention, and I liked to show off and do a lot of things. That's the foundation, the basis for skating. It's whoever shows off the best that wins. I like that aspect of it. A lot of my motivation when I started was that it was something I liked to do, it was a lot of fun, and there were a lot of other kids there.

You'd race, play tag, play whip. You could play a lot of things, so for me, just to go out every Saturday morning and

skate with a bunch of kids my age and to learn new things was
pretty exciting. And I just sort of stuck with it, and one thing
led to another. And after a long period of time, I started
winning, and then my motivation changed, and I became more
of a goal-oriented person, where before it was just a lot of fun.

*It was a combination of watching the Olympics and the death of
his mother that inspired Scott Hamilton to think of pursuing the highest goals of his sport:*

You always watch the Olympics, especially if you're in a
sport that has Olympic connections. But I never really looked
at my career as something that would take me to the
Olympics. It was just something I did. In 1976 I won the
Junior National Championship and I thought, "Whoa, I might
get pretty good at this!" And then I'm thinking, "Well, four
years away, maybe the Olympics are possible."

That's because usually when you win the Junior Nationals
you end up in about the top seven the next year in the Senior
Nationals, so I thought maybe I've got a future in this. And
my mother, who was the biggest supporter of my skating,
passed away in '77, and she's the one that had set the highest
kind of goals for me. She was never really a "skating mother,"
but she always thought, "Hey, this kid could go and be in the
Olympics or win the world championship." I never felt that
way, but she did. She never expressed that to me as much as
she would to others. She was one of those who was proud
and all that stuff.

So when she passed away, I kind of absorbed a lot of her
Olympic aspirations for me. And when she died, a lot of my
lack of focus disappeared, because she really worked hard to
keep me in my skating. She did a lot of work and had a lot of
heartache and a lot of pain. She suffered a lot trying to get
more work and better work to pay for my skating when she
was suffering from cancer. I didn't want everything she went

through to be wasted because I was lazy or because I wasn't focused.

So her death really had a major impact on me, and I think the improvements I made rapidly after her passing really made the difference and set me up on a real discipline and a real focus to compete to make the '80 Olympics and then, after that, to win in '84.

Figure skating is extremely athletic, far more athletic than it appears:

A lot of figure skating has always been entertainment. You've got four and a half minutes to go out and prove yourself. And the sport has gone through a lot of changes.

You look at other sports, and I can be the most coordinated, strongest person in the world, pound-for-pound, but I'll never be able to compete with Michael Jordan. It's just physical size; a lot of what you are physically determines your success in your sport. I was always small for any other sport. Even hockey has turned into a big man's sport. Look at the guys out there now like Lindros. Hockey was always known as a kind of finesse thing, but now you look at some of these defensemen—they're six-three, six-four, two-fifty.

It's hard for a person of average size to compete in a lot of contact sports. Barry Sanders, five-eight; he's five inches taller than I am, and he's very competitive, but the guy's unique. He's special and he's awesome, but with my size and build, I was pretty much limited to gymnastics and figure skating.

In figure skating, you need a lot of fast-twitch muscle fiber in order to have quick reflexes and in order to react differently, because of a lot of the things you're doing—you're spinning three times in the air in less than one second. Usually, it's seven tenths of a second, so you're going from zero RPMs to massive RPMs to zero RPMs in less than one second. You've got to rotate three times in the air to land a triple jump, and it takes a lot of real quick reflexes and timing and, at the same time, you've got to last four and a half minutes doing these things. So you've probably got to be in the same physical condition as a mile runner.

So you've got to combine both these muscle types and fitness regimens into the same sport. It's physically demanding, and it's timing, strength, conditioning, there's a lot of things that go into it. The two sports you'd probably have to combine in order to come up with a figure skater are gymnastics and mile running.

Still, before he concentrated on figure skating, Hamilton gave hockey a serious try:

I played hockey for three years, and the skating wasn't my problem. It was the corners. If I were going to a puck in the corner and the defenseman, who was a head and a half taller than me, took me out, I mean he really took me out. I competed in hockey because of all the ribbing I took as a figure skater. Figure skating is not something that a kid from a small town in Ohio would pick up and not take any kind of ribbing—"Aw, ya big sissy, why don't you play hockey?"

Okay, come on out guys, let me see you do a double axel. Ain't gonna happen. It takes a lot of time and training, and I've given a part of my body to every jump I've ever accomplished. I had a hip operation from a triple lutz. I tore every ligament in my ankle doing triple toe loops. I had to relearn it a couple of times because of technique problems. Tailbone—triple salchow. Two years of falling hard to learn a double axel. There's a lot of failure involved in learning a lot of these tricks.

I played hockey for three years to get past all the peer pressure, and I realized I might someday be competitive in figure skating. I enjoyed it, and it was something where I didn't have to depend on the fat guy that couldn't skate backward getting me the puck so I could score a goal.

Your makeup limits you, and I'd never be competitive in hockey. Speed and agility would get me to a certain level, but once I got to high school, I'd never be able to compete with the big guys. My best friend took me out the last time. We played on opposite teams—he was a defenseman and I was a center and I went into a corner; I was trying to get the puck out, the winger was on the wrong side of the ice, and where was I supposed to be? In the middle, but it wasn't happening, and so I went into the corner, and he just dove and took me out, and I was in a neck brace for about two weeks. When one play puts you out for two weeks and you can't really move, I decided I'd just as soon do that to myself as have somebody else do it. So I started focusing on the figure skating, and I'm glad I did, because when I stopped doing gymnastics and stopped playing hockey and just put everything into figure skating, my skating improved rapidly.

Figure skating at the highest level—the Olympic and world championship events that are the only competitions that many people see—is so graceful that it seems almost effortless. But preceding it are years of hard and dangerous preparation:

A lot of the stuff that you do, mainly the jumps and real physical things you see in amateur competition—they have belts and harnesses for that, but they don't help. They hinder your preparation for the jumps because you have to go on one certain track to be lifted on this contraption. In professional skating, there's a lot of flipping. For that you need harnesses, you need spotters, you need a lot of off-the-ice training in order to learn. You're not going to learn how to twist or rotate off the ice in a lot of the triple jumps and things, because that's different. The whole idea of sliding into something with momentum is different from doing something off the floor, from being static to being in movement. So you don't really learn off the ice too much how to jump on the ice.

But with gymnastic moves like back-flips and things like that, you really can learn off the ice. And you're better to learn them off the ice and then take them on the ice, because of the danger involved in going heels over head. It gets kind of scary and dangerous, and even after you come off the harness after you learn those things, you're still going to make some mistakes and take some pretty bad falls.

America's first male figure skating gold medalist, Dick Button, perfected his craft through dance and ballet. Scott Hamilton went in a different direction:

Being from a small town in Ohio, one thing I did avoid was the bar and the mirror. I never really went to any dance classes. A lot of the movement I learned on the ice in order to connect a lot of the jumps and spins was done by choreographers. They took more of the angular movements, not so much based on any kind of dance but on positions that showed strength and continuity.

I tried to remain more of a skater than a dancer/performer in my competitive days, because a lot of what you're trying to accomplish you have to do with image and presentation. If I'm showing strength and angular positions, and if I'm connecting each step with positions that aren't really based on a ballet or jazz, it adds to the intensity and the drama of the performance as well as trying to create a masculine look.

A lot of positions that you can get into if you're a trained dancer get into more of a dance look or something that is not perceived by the lay audience to be athletic. I know that's a broad statement. I don't mean to be irresponsible in my words, but a lot of ballet positions don't offer the same kind of intensity and drama that I was trying to pull out of my skating. I wanted to be kind of a pure skater, to bring out the athletic side of the sport more because I didn't want to get lumped into what was previously perceived to be artistic skating. Robin Cousins, John Curry, Toller Cranston—a lot of those guys were artists, and I thought that really was limiting the participation and the interest in the sport by promoting artistry over athletics.

I wanted to present myself more like a David Jenkins. More like the way Dick Button changed the sport. Dick may have relied a lot on dance, but the man was an incredible athlete, and he was twenty years ahead of his time. He revolutionized the sport. He brought the excitement of risk into the jumping—triple jumps of high, exciting moves. The same with David Jenkins. When you watch David Jenkins— the guy was an awesome athlete! He could compete now. If you took his skating of 1960 and put it up against the guys now, it would stand up.

So that's the direction I wanted to put into my skating. I felt that was the side of skating that was ignored and that skating, especially male skating, was taking a bad rap. Men were artists, and women were athletes. I just thought that was a little bit out of whack because men were doing—at that time and even recently, except for skaters like Midori Ito and Tonya Harding—harder physical moves.

The physical maturation of young female skaters makes their improvement particularly challenging, as technique must conform to rapid physical change:

Men don't go through the same physical changes that women do. When the ladies are coming up, they're really strong—when they're twelve, thirteen, fourteen. When they get to fifteen, sixteen, they go through such drastic physical changes. Their hips grow; it's a natural, physical thing.

That doesn't happen with the men. They just get stronger. For the women, at a crucial time in their competitive careers, their bodies change drastically, and it's tough. You watch the differences, physically, with Katarina Witt, when she won her first Olympic championship to her second, and that's a lot of physical change to go through in a short time. And to keep your strength up and to keep you technical ability up, it's a lot harder to rotate a jump when your body has changed that drastically. That's one difference between the men and the women, the most important one.

Another thing is a sense of accomplishment. Once something has been done, it's accepted. Once a triple axel has been landed in international competition, more people are going to do it the next year. I think it went from one guy in '81 landing a triple axel to seven or eight the next. And then by the time you get to '81 to '88, you've got probably eight or nine guys doing it in the short program. So once something has been achieved, it becomes easier for everyone else.

The same with the quad. One guy did it, Kurt Browning. He and Brian Boitano were trying to be the first guys to land it. Kurt skated a group earlier than Brian and landed a quad. He was the first man to do it. Then you look down the line and, all of a sudden, there's like four guys that have a quad in their program, and one guy does it like inhaling and exhaling—it's amazing.

The same with the women: the triple axel's done by Midori Ito; the next one to come along, Tonya Harding. Bam! She had it in her short program at Skate America. Once something has been done, it becomes easier for everybody else.

Hamilton was a member of the U.S. Winter Olympics team in 1980 but didn't medal until 1984. But in some ways he enjoyed the earlier games more:

There's a big difference between going to the Olympics and going to the Olympics to win. Eric Heiden and I talked about this, and I was really curious because I knew what my Olympic experiences were, and I saw his and I still think what Eric did in 1980 is the greatest accomplishment in Olympic history.

The hockey team was a "miracle on ice," and that was great. They played the greatest hockey, and they just peaked, and it was wonderful to watch, and two guys from my home town were on the team, so we watched the whole thing. But what Eric Heiden did [at the 1980 Olympics in Lake Placid, Heiden won every men's speed skating event: the 500, 1,000, 1,500, 5,000, and 10,000], as an individual athlete, is the greatest accomplishment in Olympic history. From day one all the way through. I'll argue that.

Mark Spitz's seven gold medals was an awesome accomplishment, but to win every discipline from the 500 meter to the 10 [10,000 meter] is incredible. To win every medal available to you in your sport is a huge accomplishment. But he said he hated the '80 Olympics as an experience except obviously the medal-winning and the events themselves, because of all the distraction and all the stuff that went into it. To say "hated"—I'm probably putting words in his mouth. To say that he enjoyed the '76 a great deal more than he enjoyed the 1980 Olympics is more accurate.

I enjoyed the 1980 Olympics so much. Being the third guy—no pressure. Going out, just skating to skate and enjoying the pageantry and the village and the Olympics—all the stuff. The clothes, meeting all these great athletes from other sports, guys that you only watch on television.

That was a huge thrill, but '84 was difficult. I went to win, and there was a lot of media pressure put on me and a lot of distractions from the media. I was supposed to be the one sure gold medal, and I really felt fortunate to win those three world championships on the way to the Olympics and to have to repeat on that demand. It's hard to be the guy that everybody has on his or her list to interview. It's hard to know you've got to put your best stuff out there because it's expected.

Hamilton sees the Winter Olympics as an individual sport and a team sport all at once:

I think the majority of Winter Olympic sports are individual sports. You still go there as a team. I always felt the world championships are kind of for me. I felt not so much selfish about it, but I really felt the whole idea behind the world championships is to field the team from the United States and your best skaters, and whoever wins, wins.

But when it comes down to the Olympic championships, there you're representing the United States, and it's the world on common ground competing and celebrating their best, celebrating what makes people the best they can be. That's a whole different focus than a world championship. So the whole team idea comes out—not so much that you're competing on a figure-skating team, but you're competing for the United States, and you're representing several hundred million people. Your accomplishments you share. You don't share your failures, but you share your accomplishments.

A lot of people really get emotionally involved in the games, and I think it's to be shared. If I would've had a disastrous performance at the Olympic Games, it would've been really difficult for me to live with because I would've felt like I let down a lot of people.

But then, when I see what happens to people where they have a disappointing Olympics, I see how the entire country embraces them and says, "It's O.K., you're one of ours, and we love you and thanks for giving it your best try and we know you had a bad night."

I think what Debi Thomas went through touched a lot of people. "Hey, we all have days like that. We all have times and, gosh, we know how much that meant to you, but it's O.K. We're here for you, and we accept your evening, and we know that it was difficult." And I think that touches a lot of people more positively than even an Olympic gold medal because you can relate to that a lot easier than you can an athlete that just goes out and wins everything.

But again, when I won, it was like "Take the flag, this is for everyone." A lot of people contribute to your career, and a lot of people have an impact on what you do as an athlete and as a person, and you just want to go and represent your country as well as you can. Whether you have a great night or a horrible night, people are going to accept and support you.

On a bad night, I'm sure no athlete wants to share that with the world, but the world is ready to put their arm around you and say, "Go on, it's fine, it's okay. We accept you and we love you for it. Give it your best shot."

The rules of the International Olympic Committee have loosened and enabled figure skaters to make a good living and still remain eligible for Olympic competition. Still, Scott Hamilton believes that in Olympic figure skating competition there remains a certain purity:

You're never going to go out on the ice—never, I repeat, never—going to go out to compete and think about what comes from it and be successful. Even if you do walk away winning a medal, thinking that you're going to parlay it into something else, people are going to pick that up, and they're not going to like it too much. Some athletes, I think, have presented themselves as looking beyond the Olympics, going into the Olympics, and people really resent it.

The Olympics are pure competition. You go into the Olympics to compete and to represent your country. I hope and I pray that they let, and they are letting, professional athletes into the Olympics, but I hope it doesn't become a professional event. I think the Olympics should be a pure event where you go to test yourself against the best and to celebrate sports and the world on common ground, competing in a friendly way. No wars, no political, religious, race differences—you're just going out to compete. But to go out with commercial gain in mind is cheap and you're lessening the value of what makes the Olympics really fantastic for everyone.

For me, going in, I obviously knew there were things available afterwards, but my whole mind-set was that I have one opportunity in my life to win an Olympic gold medal—or an Olympic medal of any color would have been just fine with me—but to win a medal, and that's something I keep for the rest of my life, and that's something that will always be special to me. What comes of it afterwards, great. That's temporary, very temporary, and it goes away. If you're looking at making a lot of money, well, you spend money. An Olympic gold medal is yours for life.

I went to the world championships afterwards because I really wanted to complete that Olympic four years. I felt I'd won three. I won the Olympic title. I really wanted to go out at the world championships. If that was going to be my last competition, I wanted to go out completing that four years.

I was actually offered a lot between the Olympics and the world championships, but because of the rules and the way things were, I had to make a choice. Either I accept this endorsement, either I accept this amount of money, whatever it is, or I go to the world championships. I figured, that amount of money, or that endorsement, is fine. It's a huge honor and it's a thrill to be offered something like that, but that fourth world title is mine for life, and nobody can ever take that away.

Right off the top, the IRS is going to take half of whatever I make there and it's really kind of temporary and commercial. And that's nice and that's okay, but an accomplishment to go out and to compete on the world level, that's forever. And it's temporary that you'd be able to compete at that level, so take advantage of it, and then you have that for the rest of your life and it's pure and it's yours.

MICHAEL JOHNSON

The Man. The Machine. Michael Johnson. Three phrases, all synonymous.

Michael Johnson is The Man because this track and field champion dominates the world's competition in both the 400 meters and the 200 meters. Never was his preeminence more evident than in the 1996 Olympic Games in Atlanta.

Johnson won the gold medal in the 400 meters in 43.49 seconds, setting a new Olympic record. The second-placer, Roger Black of Great Britain, finished in 44.41, nearly a full second behind. But the climax to Johnson's Olympics was yet to come.

In the 200 meters, The Man came out of the blocks strongly, but at the halfway point was closely followed by Namibia's Frankie Fredericks and Trinidad-Tobago's Ato Bolden. About ten meters later, Johnson shifted into a gear only he possesses, bolting away from his very fast competition. Johnson rocketed across the finish line in a stunning 19.32, a new world record, breaking the old record (his own) by an amazing .34 second. By contrast, Canada's Donovan Bailey, the other men's sprint star of Atlanta, ran a 9.84 to set a world record in the 100 meters, but broke the old standard by merely a hundredth of a second.

Track & Field News, the "bible" of the sport, called Johnson's 200

MICHAEL JOHNSON • 137

performance "certainly the defining moment of Atlanta's Games." It timed Johnson's last 100 meters in 9.20 seconds (to Fredericks's 9.54 and Boldon's 9.62).

Johnson's margin of victory (.36 second over Fredericks, whose 19.68 was the third-fastest 200 ever run) was the largest in an Olympic men's 200 meters since Jesse Owens beat Mack Robinson 20.7 to 21.1 in 1936). Michael Johnson became the first man ever to win both the 200 and the 400 in the same Olympics (or in any Olympics).

Michael Johnson is also The Man because of his tough, masculine demeanor. Before races, he is all business, not one given to small talk, not one to smile.

Michael Johnson is The Machine because he runs with an unusually upright posture that makes him look more mechanical than other sprinters, with arms pumping like pistons. He is also The Machine because he performs with a consistency rarely seen in humans and commonly seen only in the mechanical world. So consistent is Michael Johnson that with the Olympic victory he had won 56 consecutive outdoor and indoor 400 finals.

Through his enormous ability in both the 200 and the 400, he almost singlehandedly changed the traditional schedule of track and field competition at the 1996 Olympics. Ordinarily, the 200 and 400—including their heats, quarterfinals, semifinals, and finals— are contested so closely together that it would be almost impossible to double. Michael Johnson petitioned the International Amateur Athletics Federation to change the Olympic track schedule to permit him to try for gold in both events. As noted, no one in Olympic history had ever won both events in a single Olympics. Nevertheless, such was Johnson's credibility—after all, he had just completed the same double in the 1995 World Championships—that the IAAF granted Johnson's request. In Atlanta, therefore, the 400 final was run on July 29, while the 200 did not conclude until three days later, on August 1.

I got to know Michael Johnson quite well in the months just before the Olympics. At the Dallas radio station from which "Pat Summerall's Sports in America" originates, Michael was doing a weekly, half-hour show just before ours. I had a chance to listen to him *respond to interview questions, and I simply had an opportunity to talk with him week after week.*

As I got to know him, I rapidly became an admirer. I learned that Michael Johnson is a very bright athlete who is enormously dedicated. His training routine is extremely demanding, but he sticks right to it. He had precise, well-thought-out plans on how to run the 400 meters one way and the 200 meters a different way, and on how to attack the unprecedented task of winning both events in the same Olympics.

Michael Johnson gives his parents a lot of credit for his success:

I think when I was growing up parents took a lot more responsibility for raising their kids than a lot of parents do today. There were myself, and my three sisters, and my brother. We all had the fortunate circumstances that both parents were around, and they both took a lot of responsibility in making sure that we were in school every day, and at home on time, and all those kinds of things. So I think that that definitely had a large part in the success I've had, as well as the success of my brother and my sisters.

My dad and I had a lot of talks about what I wanted to do when I got older. I think he had an instrumental part in setting my goals and career and accomplishing them.

Now the best in the world, Michael Johnson wasn't quite the best in the state in high school. Then again, the state was Texas:

I prefer to look at it this way: I had some success. I was the second-best sprinter in the state, and Texas is a pretty big state. But from some perspectives, if you're not the best in the state, or the best in the nation, you're not that good, and from another perspective, if you're second in the state of Texas, you're pretty good. So it depends on how you look at it.

Many top sprinters also play football. In high school and at Baylor University, Michael Johnson stayed focused on track:

When I was coming up, I was a track athlete, and I let it be known that I was going to be a track athlete and that I had no interest in playing football. So maybe because I put it out there like that, I really didn't run into as many people trying to convert me to a football player as most people think.

Track and field is no longer the amateur bastion that it once was, so Michael has probably done better financially in his chosen sport than if he had put on the pads:

Since I've become a professional track athlete, I haven't given any interest to football, and I made sure that my career has gone pretty well, and I've been pretty successful. I'm achieving my goals on the track, as well as achieving my goals financially in the sport.

Most people don't know this, but I wouldn't make as much money if I went over to football, because I don't have any experience there, and my talents don't lie there. I do have experience being the fastest man in the world, and that earns you a certain amount of financial status that can't be argued with. So from my perspective, I'm doing the right thing.

Johnson didn't read his tax return on the air, but he did give a sense of his income, as he compared it to that of stars of the NFL:

I'd say that since free agency has opened up a lot more now, I really don't know, maybe a couple of people on each team make as much.

It took a long time for the International Amateur Athletics Federation to decide whether to change the Olympic track schedule to accommodate Johnson's desire to double. The new schedule permitted Johnson to compete in all four rounds of the 400, have a day's rest, and then run in all four rounds of the 200. Michael's not entirely sure why the IAAF decided as it did:

It was a combination of things. I'm definitely happy that they finally did it. Trying to get those schedule changes is something I've been working on for about a year and a half now. At times it would look good and times it wouldn't, because the federation that we have is a very difficult organization to deal with.

I think they recognized from the beginning that it was something that would be advantageous for them, as well as for me, because it was what the fans wanted to see, and they would subject themselves to quite a bit of criticism if an athlete weren't allowed to participate in an event that he is ranked number one in the world in, because of a schedule conflict.

Really, changing the schedule didn't affect any other athletes, so I think this organization isn't used to change, and that's been one of the problems we've had. I'm just happy that we finally got it changed, and now I can just focus on training.

Here's what would have happened if the IAAF had not changed the schedule:

The problem with the schedule before was that I would start my series of 400s, and right in the middle of that series, I'd have to start a 200, and then, right when I got in the middle of the 200s, I'd have to go back to 400s, and finish up those races, and then come back to the 200, and finish up those races.

Even with the schedule now, with the day in between, it's still going to be tough, because I will have been running 400s for four days in a row, and then have a day's rest, and then, all of a sudden, I've got to switch my focus to the 200, which is a completely different race. You have to become, basically, a completely different athlete, because in the 200, it's fine to do things that you're trying not to do in the 400.

In the 200, you're trying to be aggressive. It's a skilled race, it's a technical race, and you're trying to be as aggressive as possible. In the 400, if you're being too aggressive, then you're working against yourself, because it's a much more relaxed race, a much more relaxed pace. Although you're still running extremely fast, the race is so long that you don't want to burn yourself out at the beginning. So you need to run fast, but at a relaxed pace for the first 200 of the 400; that's my particular strategy.

In 1988, a stress fracture ruined any chance of Johnson's making the Olympic team. In 1992, he was weakened by food poisoning. Some athletes might feel haunted by what might seem to be a pattern of bad luck:

Not at all. I look at the pattern and I figure, in 1988, I didn't make the team, and in 1992, I made the team, so this must be my year. If you look at the progression, I'm getting closer and closer! I think that those misfortunes have actually helped me, and hopefully, I've now had enough misfortunes to help me, I've gotten all the help I need, and now I can go out there and get some medals.

I think the experiences from 1988 and 1992 were out of my control, and that's nothing I can do anything about. Those things are going to happen; it could very well happen to me again. It's happened to athletes in the past. Some of the greatest athletes that ever participated in track and field finished their careers with no gold medals.

Greg Foster had bad luck every Olympics, but he's still known as one of the greatest hurdlers in the history of the sport. So those things happen, they're out of your control, and you just go out there. I just try and concentrate on the things I can control.

Although Johnson was pointing toward an unprecedented gold-medal double in Atlanta, he was not prepared to retire if he accomplished it:

Of course not. I'm twenty-eight now, and I think that it's a really good possibility—and I wouldn't have said this two years ago—I could very well be at the Sydney Olympics in 2000.

I'll be thirty-two years old at that time, and that's still prime age for sprinters. So I think that I'll be there. In the past, track and field was a sport where guys competed for four years or trained for four years and waited for the Olympics and then retired; now it's not all about the Olympics. Track and field is its own sport, with its own fans, apart from the Olympics.

DON KING

Don King is the most prominent boxing promoter of the modern era. He has promoted more heavyweight championship fights than anyone else and has been the center of more controversy. Once convicted of manslaughter in a case that many thought would end in a murder verdict, and often accused of taking too much of boxing purses and giving his fighters too little, King has risen to the top of the murky world of big-time boxing. He now controls the contracts of many of the world's top boxers, led by Mike Tyson.

After serving three years for rape, Tyson was released from an Indiana prison on March 25, 1995. Six days later, the former heavyweight champion announced he would continue to have King as his promoter. Shortly thereafter, Tyson signed two exclusive-service contracts with the MGM Grand Hotel and Showtime Entertainment Television. These deals guaranteed him and King a minimum $150 million for two and a half years or six fights, whichever came first.

A wild-haired man who will never use two words where ten will do and who has never met a hyperbole he didn't like, Don King makes political spin doctors sound as humble as Mother Teresa. In the August 19, 1995, postprison debut of Tyson, Iron Mike knocked down unknown Peter McNeeley at seven seconds of the first round and con-

tinued to batter him, knocking him to the canvas a second time. McNeeley rose again, but on unsteady legs. Then, at eighty-nine seconds of the first round, McNeeley's manager-trainer, Vinny Vecchione, suddenly scrambled into the ring to surrender. The result was a disqualification.

Some might think spectators—ringsiders who had paid up to $1,500 for a seat—should have felt shortchanged. But here's what King said: "It's not an outrage. The people might be disappointed that the manager jumped into the ring, but they can't say they didn't get their money's worth. We had quite a spectacle this evening. No one can say Peter McNeeley didn't come to fight. We saw a terrific altercation for the time that it lasted."

King scheduled Tyson's second fight for November 4, against Buster Mathis, Jr. But November 4 was also the date of the long-awaited bout between former heavyweight champions Riddick Bowe and Evander Holyfield. Both fights were to take place in the same city, Las Vegas. Everyone assumed there would be two pay-per-view fights the same night. Then King announced that the Tyson-Mathis fight would be on free TV on the Fox network.

It would have been the first major fight on over-the-air TV since 1978, when Muhammad Ali won back the heavyweight title from Leon Spinks. HBO had to proceed with Bowe-Holyfield as a pay-TV match. HBO's Seth Abraham said King wanted to create similar scheduling conflicts, and Abraham was ready to do battle, relying on HBO's stable of big-name heavyweight talent. [The Tyson-Mathis fight was postponed when Tyson broke his thumb. The two finally fought December 16, with Tyson knocking out Mathis at 2:32 of the third round.]

King had legal problems the same year, going to trial in September on charges of insurance fraud. Prosecutors alleged King had submitted a fake contract to Lloyd's of London to get $350,000 in nonrefundable training fees for a 1991 bout between Julio Cesar Chavez and Harold Brazier that was canceled when Chavez was injured. King faced up to five years in prison and a $250,000 fine on each of nine counts. When the jury could not reach a verdict, the judge declared a mistrial. It is not yet clear whether the case will be retried.

Although King has become a multimillionaire as a boxing promoter, he got his start in the sport by staging a charity event:

A black hospital in the state of Ohio, the only one at that particular time, named Forest City Hospital, was going broke, couldn't pay their pharmaceutical bills, couldn't pay for interns, so I initiated a fundraiser for the hospital to focus this plight nationwide, and I prevailed upon Muhammad Ali to come and to fight an exhibition, which he did. He fought four boxers and a local disk jockey, and it was a smashing success in bringing about what we wanted to do to focus the plight of this hospital and prove that Cleveland was the City with Heart, because industry began to chip in, so more or less funded the hospital to keep the doors open.

Muhammad Ali was a promoter's dream. He was really a delight. He came in to help me a week earlier because a lot of questions were going to the credibility of whether or not he would arrive and perform in Cleveland because of a guy like myself, Don King, just calling and asking him to do so. He not only came in a week earlier, but he worked tirelessly around the clock going to hospitals and homes for the aged and anyone that was sick and infirm, he was there, the retarded center, and he worked with the retarded kids. This was the first time of bringing sports and entertainment together. I had Wilson Pickett and I put on an extravaganza that was second to none and filled the arena up in its entirety, and we had a sensational event, and Muhammad Ali then prevailed upon me to come into boxing and just to think about it.

He said, "You are the best promoter I have ever seen," and he said, "We are the gladiators, the pawns, the bleeders in the center of the ring. We have no decision-making power in boxing." He said, "A promoter of your ilk, you can come in and really do some good for it. I am the only free fighter in the world. The rest of the fighters are getting the slave wages, and they can't make any decisions about their lives or their destiny."

And I said, "I don't know anything about boxing, Muhammad."

And he said, "You are the best promoter I have ever seen, and I wish you would come into the sport."

King took Ali up on his idea, and entered the new field:

Boxing is really not a dirty business, as everyone says it is. It's really not a sleazy business. There's a lot of sleazy people in the business and a lot of people that are very unsavory characters that seemingly take the offensive and people begin to believe what it is. The boxing history comes from a perception of sleaziness, the racketeer mob infiltration: you got to take a dive in five or your mother gets it. Cagney and Bogart in the movies, *Somebody Up There Likes Me*. All these different movies depicted fighters being used as pieces of meat.

When I came in through the boxing business, I brought a whole new refreshing concept that boxers were people and that people were boxers and that they should receive just compensation for the services they render to the promoter and to the public. And so I revolutionized the pay scale in boxing, and I brought in an approach that if you are fair and just with the fighters that you will be able to do more.

And so out of my career, it has proven to be so, because for nearly two decades—and I had the heavyweight division and the heavyweight champion and one time I had thirteen world champions at the same time—I was being criticized, vilified, character-assassinated, but it didn't work. But my promotional skills and my ability and capability to love people and to respect people—because people are my most important assets—is what has enabled me to take boxing by storm, so to speak. Even with the tumultuous background such that I have, and my love for the country—and I love this country because it's the greatest nation in the world—it has enabled me to overcome many impediments and many obstacles.

And so I put on my boxing show. Following the one in Cleveland, I put on another one and then I went to see, in 1973, Joe Frazier fight George Foreman. And in Kingston, Jamaica, the government there, the Honorable Michael Manley, the Prime Minister, had heard about my promotions in the city of Cleveland, and he asked me to help him to promote along with video techniques, the Sunshine Showdown, which was Frazier and Foreman. And I made good friends with Foreman, and Foreman bounced Joe Frazier around like a basketball, knocking him out in a couple of rounds.

And so then, George and I, we had a relationship established. So I worked with George. We went to Japan together to fight Joe "King" Roman, and then we came back from Japan and we fought Ken Norton in Caracas, Venezuela, and from there, we went to the big one with Muhammad Ali and the Rumble in the Jungle in Kinshasa, Zaire.

When Don King tells about his life, he describes a rags-to-riches drama:

My background was I came out of the hard-core ghetto of Cleveland, Ohio. Ex-numbers runner, ex-convict, got a full, unconditional pardon from the governor of the state, the Honorable James A. Rhodes. And my intellect and my stick-to-itiveness, my tenacity, my perseverance, has enabled me to deliver on everything I have ever promised, and this is what has given me an enviable record in the field of promotion.

I have done this through hard work, diligence, my faith in God, and perseverance. Because recognizing, in my country that I love, that it is very difficult for a black to be successful, and it is even more difficult for them to accept black success. However, I continue to work for the betterment of the country, looking at and extolling its virtues, rather than just decrying its inequities and injustices— which I do. But I look for ways and means to resolve them to make a better America for all Americans, black and white alike, because working together works.

And so I brought that approach to the field of boxing, which heretofore had been at the bottom rung of the ladder. It was the highest-profile sport, the lowest paid sport, and those who were not the few that became boxing champions were actually working for starvation wages in the sport of boxing and being treated and mistreated in any kind of way, shape, form, or fashion.

I felt that boxers were human beings and that they were people and that I myself, coming from the lowest rung of the ladder, could commiserate, identify, and relate to these people, that were underprivileged, downtrodden, and denied, and work with them in order to bring about that much-needed change in their psyche of dignity, pride, and being able to rise to the occasion and being able to deal with it forthrightly with candor, but taking the responsibilities of manhood and discharging them admirably, rather than sitting around and crying, sitting on your haunches, saying, you know, "If I wasn't black." Be black and proud.

Without economic independence, you are still nominally a slave. So you must be able to deal for yourself and create for yourself and to be self-reliant, self-determined, and to be able to deal with this type of self-assertiveness that will bring about the positiveness of a constructive situation, rather than one that is negative that has isolation and alienation.

So, with this approach coming into boxing—and no one wanted to be into boxing because it was like being in the trenches of the bottom of the ladder, so to speak, down in the gutter—you had an opportunity. It gave me an opportunity to come from the gutter to the upper. So I think it's something that I love. That's what I love about the country, giving me that opportunity. Now I can sit back and speak on it, and I can reflect nostalgically to the truth and point to the dips and pitfalls and the dip in high levels of my career, but all of them done with truth, justice, and fair play in the American way.

King says he revolutionized the way fighters were paid:

A boxer should really be paid by what he can bring to the table, public-wise to the ticket-buying public. He should be paid on a percentage, as it was in the earlier days in Madison Square Garden. So I think percentages sometimes were somewhat managerial or promotionally favorable to the Garden, rather than being equitable for the fighter and the manager and the Garden. However, I think that when a fighter can bring, let's say, an attraction, and that's where I come in. I revolutionized the pay schedules in boxing, because I put it back in its proper priority, so to speak. It was out of kilter.

They would talk about a hundred-thousand-dollar purse like it was the second coming, and in effect the fighter such as Joe Louis or Muhammad Ali or Sugar Ray Robinson would bring in a million-dollar gate. So the fighter really wasn't getting paid properly, but the media would jump on the hundred thousand because nobody had made a hundred thousand before, especially a black man making a hundred thousand dollars. They think that's more money than anything in the world.

Well, I felt the attraction is the most important. So, in an attraction, you get a super attraction, and then you make a sound, constructive business deal, which means recouping the investment and the bottom line profit, and then that profit is a profit-sharing position with a minimum guarantee to the fighter. Then, whatever comes in from wherever in the world, he has an opportunity to share this.

This automatically changed the whole scope in boxing when I brought this approach and concept in and seeing it through to its fulfillment in its culmination of what you see as being enjoyed today. Me, with Muhammad Ali in my time of promoting Muhammad Ali, the fights that I promoted him, I made him more money than all the fights he had collectively done together of the time he came with me. And so, usually two and two were four, became seven, and then I went into the geometric approach, where the money would grow geometrically, one, two, four, eight, sixteen, rather than going through the normal count, because I would promote to that extent, and I would take him around to different foreign countries in which I would make deals in order to promote the country.

And nothing in the world is more electrifying or dazzling than a heavyweight world title fight. And people would come from all walks of life and all parts of the world to the place where it'd be happening, and you have a dateline, any country that you would go into, Jamaica, and that means that reporters from all over the world would be there to focus on the culture of the city, of the country, the economic stability of the country, along with its culture and arts, along with the sport of boxing.

Say what you will about Don King; he has risen from the ghettos of Cleveland to become a wealthy, powerful man, and a man with great faith in what can be accomplished:

I am a very religious person, and I believe that God and I are a majority. And they say if you have the faith of a grain of a mustard seed, nothing will be impossible to you. You can tell yonder mountain to be removed in a twinkling of an eye, the mountain will be removed. I have been removing mountains out of my life consistently and continually.

SUGAR RAY
LEONARD

Once upon a time there was a boxer named Sugar Ray
Robinson. He was the world welterweight champion from
1946 to 1950 and then the world middleweight champion in 1951
and again in 1955–57 and 1958–59. I thought he was one of the
great artists of the ring. Many thought he was the greatest middleweight of all time.

Then, at the Montreal Olympics of 1976, along came another boxer
who dared to call himself Sugar Ray. His name was Sugar Ray Leonard.
Before they knew how good a fighter he would become, how quick and
effective he would be in the ring, boxing fans resented that this young
upstart would take on the name of the legend.

In fact, Leonard meant no disrespect. In fact, Sugar Ray
Robinson was one of Leonard's idols.

The end of the fairy tale is that Sugar Ray the Younger became an
even better boxer than Sugar Ray the Elder. He became the only boxer
in history to win the world championship in five weight divisions.
Here are the results of some of his most important title fights:

In 1979 he won the welterweight title over Wilfred Benitez.

In 1980 he lost it to Roberto Duran.

In 1981 he won it against Thomas Hearns.

In 1981 he won the junior middleweight championship against Ayub Kalule.

In 1987 he took the middleweight crown in a fight against Marvin Hagler.

In 1988 he won the championship of the newly created super middleweight division over Don Lalonde.

Later the same year, he won the light heavyweight title over the same fighter.

Upon his retirement, Leonard had higher winnings than any other boxer in history even though he never fought in the heavyweight division, which is traditionally the richest.

Though Sugar Ray Leonard the adult is known to the public exclusively as a boxer, Sugar Ray Leonard the child dreamed of other sports:

I think I had ambitions of being a basketball player, a baseball player, a gymnast, a football player; I've had all sorts of dreams. Boxing was one of those things that happened to come about. That's when I reached puberty. My three older brothers would at times tease me because I was never athletically inclined. I was pretty much a mama's boy, so it became one of those things where it was like I was forced into doing it to kind of prove my manhood.

My introduction to boxing, if you want to call it that, was actually a street fight. I moved from Wilmington, North Carolina, to Washington, D.C. And being a young country boy, I was not used to the street-smart kids. I recall vividly going to a barbershop one weekend and some young kid challenged me, and he kind of punched my lights out. I ran home and cried, and my parents told me to stand up, never to back down. That actually was my introduction to fisticuffs.

But what took place as a kid had no bearing on my decision to become a boxer. My older brother, Roger, was already involved in boxing, and I kind of wanted to be like him. That's what lured me into getting involved in boxing. Then, once you get involved, you understand that the more you win, the chances are greater that you will eventually participate in national and international competitions, endorsements, and opportunities to travel the world.

I am very competitive, and I always felt that I could beat anyone. And from the first day I put the gloves on, they didn't feel too comfortable, but it was great just holding my own. As years went past, I really progressed very rapidly as far as displaying my talent, and my confidence grew along with it.

As an amateur, Sugar Ray Leonard had 150 fights and lost just 5. But even when he lost, he won:

Each loss I suffered was always a valuable experience. I don't think it made me better, but it made me understand that there are so many other guys that are just as talented as you are and even better. And those five losses that I suffered in my amateur career were very, very important ones.

I tried to qualify for the '72 Olympic team although I was still too young to qualify. I was sixteen. I lost in the nationals. I remember those fights, very vivid memories. It's like when I lost to Roberto Duran: I came back stronger and a lot more smarter.

Leonard's early idols were two of the greatest fighters of all time:

I tried to emulate Muhammad Ali and Sugar Ray Robinson. I would watch tapes of Joe Louis, and I would tend to incorporate those great fighters into my own ability.

Though Leonard took on the same nickname as Sugar Ray Robinson, his mother had named him Ray in honor of another famous man:

The name Sugar Ray derived from Sergeant Thomas Johnson back in 1972. He gave me that name after I lost in the quarterfinals of the Olympic trials. Actually my name is Ray Charles. My mother named me after Ray Charles, the singer. I felt there was no economic feasibility in me trying a singing career, so boxing became the natural thing for me to get involved in.

The loss in the Olympic trials of 1972 set Sugar Ray on the road to the Olympic Games of 1976:

I'd never known the significance of wearing a gold medal, never knew the significance of being in the Olympics until I lost in the quarterfinals in 1972 and people talked about how great the Olympics is. Now, this is after I lost. Then I saw the guys on television in the Olympics, and it dawned on me, "Wow, I could have been there!" It even bothered me more; it really motivated me more, became much more of a force. I was driven to win in the 1976 Olympics.

Despite Sugar Ray's talent, his parents didn't take him seriously as a boxer until the Olympic trials:

They never took me serious until I guess I actually tried to qualify for the Olympics. My father was a hardworking man, he still is, never could envision his son in boxing because I just didn't have that personality. I was not a rough, violent kid, and it just didn't seem the natural thing for me. But once they saw that my heart was tuned to boxing and that I was dedicated and motivated, they came to see me a few times.

As a fighter in the 139-pound light welterweight division, Sugar Ray was named captain of the 1976 United States boxing team:

The camaraderie was incredible. It was a very familylike atmosphere. I had the pleasure of being captain of the team, and the Spinks brothers [Leon and Michael, each of whom became heavyweight champion], Leon Randolph, Howard Davis, we were some incredible individuals, and we stuck together. We always respected each other, and we gave each other support. [All four of the fighters would win gold medals.]

I had beaten all of the opponents of all the countries up until the finals five-nothing. I beat them outright until I fought the Cuban guy, Andrès Aldama, who had knocked out everyone. The odds were that I couldn't beat him, and the general consensus in the Olympic village was that I would get my clock cleaned. But I was so driven by beating the odds that I felt no way could I lose.

Sugar Ray won the gold medal. Andrès Aldama went on to win in the Olympics of 1980 in the welterweight division. Sugar Ray went on, at least temporarily, to give up boxing:

Having the gold medal placed around my neck brought about sadness and happiness. It was like, "I'm glad it's over, my dream has been fulfilled," yet there was a part of me that said, "Hey, this is it, it's over now, no more competing."

Both of my hands were badly injured because I had bad hands throughout my amateur career. But to have that gold medal placed around my neck and have the national anthem playing, all the American fans and supporters there in Montreal, words cannot describe the feeling that I got from that, but I just wanted to go home. I wanted to go home to my family, that's all I wanted to do.

He intended to earn an undergraduate degree at the University of Maryland, but family needs dictated a different decision:

The deciding factors for me to becoming a professional were that my parents were very ill, financially we were in the slumps, it just was a necessity. It was a reality I came home to. The glory of the Olympic medal is neat, but the reality sets in weeks later, that you need to put food on your table, you need clothes, you need a better home, and it just boiled down to taking advantage of the exposure or go to school.

The transition to professional boxing was a transition to a different world:

As an amateur, it was fun, carefree, no pressure other than your opponents. You don't worry about anything, and it was a wonderful, wonderful experience. All you had to do was get in shape and compete. But as a professional, you had just so much more that's right on the line: from making sure that you win, making sure that you're paid for your services, maintaining a certain outlook on your management of your future. It was just much more to be concerned about as a professional.

In professional boxing, because of the nature and because of the people involved, because of the emotion that's involved to enhance the ticket sales, you've got to have that night-and-day contrast that has the villain, the good guy, the white, the black. You have that mixture to create some excitement, to create dark and light, and that's the way it works. But as I've reached a certain point in life, there is not that kind of scenario anymore. It's not necessary anymore.

I think there's racism everywhere, all over the world. I think in certain places it's very subtle and in some places very bold. I think promoters have a tendency to use it to the extreme to create that kind of controversy. It sells tickets, and that's human nature.

Early in his pro career, Sugar Ray made an ally of the man who had been the cornerman of a boxer named Muhammad Ali. His name was Angelo Dundee:

I put Angelo Dundee in and took the advice of Muhammad Ali. I asked Ali if I did decide to turn professional, who should I bring in as trainer, and he right away said Angelo Dundee. Muhammad had a great impact on me; I looked at him as being a mentor. He was more than an idol; he was like an adviser, indirectly. But Angelo Dundee is one of the top trainers and most intelligent trainers out there.

Sugar Ray's training regimen stayed the same throughout his career:

I do three or four miles a day, going to the gym and working about an hour, hour and a half—speed bag, big bag, a variation of exercises and calisthenics, sparring. So basic, but it's just so intense, and my training relies heavily upon my concentration, so you couldn't go by my own regimen. I don't go by the books. I walk to my own drummer.

Unlike many fighters, Leonard didn't concoct a hatred for his opponents in order to motivate himself:

I don't ever create an aggression to defeat my opponent. For me, it's just an intention of defeating the opposition. I never had to hate or say anything derogatory about anyone I fought, but it's a winning attitude. It's focusing on what needs to be done to be effective and turn it out. You execute it.

Leonard turned professional in 1977 and won twenty-five consecutive victories. But then he met Wilfred Benitez for the WBC welterweight title on November 30, 1979. Benitez's record was even bet-

ter: thirty-nine wins, no losses, one draw, and he was the champ. The fight was in Las Vegas:

Benitez was the epitome of a champion. Here is a young man who had all the talent in the world, but I just felt that I was better, without being too overconfident. But I just felt that I could win. He had more talent, I just had more desire, and that enabled me to win the fight.

Sugar Ray knocked down the champion in the third round and was narrowly ahead on all cards going into the fifteenth. There, he won on a TKO:

It was a very emotional fight for me. Talk about butterflies, I had so many of those I could have sold them, but I just fought. Even in the later rounds, I was so exhausted, so tired from missing so many punches because he was so elusive, but I just kept pouring it on. I can visualize the fight so easily because I recall I gave it everything I had and much more.

Leonard's next title fight was a 1980 defense in Montreal, this time against the man whose Spanish nickname was "Manos de Piedra": Hands of Stone. His name was Roberto Duran, and before retiring, he would hold four divisional championships:

I went in there with just the thought of beating Duran. I trained specifically to box him, outmaneuver him, but I think during that period of my career, I actually learned the value of the advantage of psychological warfare. He used it on me, and he challenged my manhood. He did a few gestures, unkind gestures, and it just took control of me. I succumbed to it. I fought my heart out and I didn't win, but I learned a very valuable lesson: to maintain composure at all times.

Later the same year, the two fighters would meet again, this time in New Orleans. And because of a single phrase uttered by Duran, this nontitle fight became more famous than perhaps any championship bout in which Leonard fought. In the eighth round, Duran refused to continue, saying, "No más." The fight was stopped on a TKO:

If anything I had more confidence facing Roberto Duran the second time around, because I knew that I had lost the first fight because I elected to fight him the way I did: toe-to-toe, his fight. I just felt that if I boxed him, if I utilized what I had, speed and know-how, intelligence, I would be far more effective and victorious.

Was I surprised at "No más"? I think the world was. I think he was, too. I think it was just a matter of all the frustration and humiliation that succumbed Duran to quitting.

Leonard moved up a division and fought Ayub Kalule for the WBA junior middleweight championships in 1981. He won, retired, and then came back to face undisputed middleweight champion Marvin Hagler in 1987:

I went to those divisions not because I thought I was neat, but that's a little contradiction, because it was fascinating for me to move up in weight and challenge the heavier champions, because they were marked names: Marvin Hagler, Thomas Hearns. But I was competing against these bigger men, and I would have to find a way to totally beat them with a much more scientific approach as opposed to just being physical. So that's what I did. I went to the higher weight categories and found ways to beat the bigger man. Tough, but worthwhile.

The guys punch harder, the guys are bigger and stronger, they're taller, and it just requires much more of my ability to beat them. Their arms are longer and their punch is stronger, and it just requires much more of a physical aspect as opposed to just mental.

Uniquely successful and at the same time shattering the image of the brutal, inarticulate fighter, Sugar Ray Leonard rapidly developed into a media star. He appeared in commercials for companies such as Ford, Carnation, Seven-Up, and Nabisco and did commentary for ABC, NBC, ESPN, and HBO. I worked a couple of fights with him, and he was just a delightful guy:

I think that the perception of boxers is that they are illiterate and basically inner-city and people with low self-esteem and character. But that has changed. It has evolved to the fact that you see more fighters endorsing major, major products. But what happens is that one person can pretty much kill it for the rest of the guys because if he should do something that's somewhat inconsistent and outright mean, it takes away from the other guys.

JOHN MADDEN

John Madden has been a major national success as three different people. There was John Madden, coach of the Oakland Raiders from 1969 through 1978. With 112 wins and just 39 losses, John has the second highest winning percentage in NFL history among coaches with a hundred or more victories; his .731 is exceeded only by Vince Lombardi's .740. Along the way, John's 1976 Raiders went 15–1 and won the Super Bowl 32–14 over the Minnesota Vikings.

There is John Madden, sportscaster—and my colleague. Because of our work over the years, probably no one knows John Madden better than I do. In his broadcasting role, first with CBS and now with Fox, he has had success that can truly be called unique. He has won eleven Emmy Awards. His insight, his humor, and his larger-than-life personality (BOOM!) have made him one of America's best-loved personalities. His popularity has helped promote many services and products, including Madden NFL, the all-time best-selling interactive sports game (the updated Madden NFL '97 has just been released).

Football isn't just a seasonal job to John; it's a year- round job. I've been amazed at John's dedication to improving his work in the *broadcasting business and his willingness to do whatever homework it takes to present the product as well as it can be presented.*

He and I have an understanding, a working relationship, that I think comes out of respect for each other and out of admiration, certainly from me for him and for how hard he works to get ready. He won't leave a production meeting, or a meeting with players or coaches at a practice that we might go to, until he has satisfied his own curiosity, and he won't leave a stone unturned to get himself prepared.

There's probably nobody in the history of sports who has ever done a better job as a broadcast analyst. In broadcasting in the beginning, the executives looked for somebody who looked good and maybe sounded good, and the substance of what they said didn't really make any difference. Then they started hiring a player who had played baseball or basketball or football or whatever, but the viewers came to realize that the players were familiar with their own positions but not necessarily the entire scope of the game.

Then people like John, who had been coaches, who saw the whole picture, just took the education of the fans to another level. I think John's presentation, broadcast techniques, and awareness of what's happening on the field have not even been scratched yet. There's so much more that he wants to and can tell the football fan. The amount of information that the man has in his mind, and how he wants to get it done, is just staggering. He'll continue to improve until he decides to retire, which I don't see happening anytime soon.

And there is John Madden, author. All three of his books published in previous years have been New York Times *best-sellers:* Hey, Wait a Minute (I Wrote a Book!) *(1984),* One Knee Equals Two Feet (And Everything Else You Need to Know About Football) *(1986), and* One Size Doesn't Fit All (And Other Thoughts from the Road) *(1988). His just-published fourth book,* All Madden, *is already selling strongly.*

John Madden grew up in the San Francisco Bay Area with another famous coach, John Robinson of USC and the then-Los Angeles Rams. As kids, they played sports, but not just football:

I don't think you jump things. When it was baseball
season we played baseball, and football we played football,
and basketball we played basketball. At that time television
wasn't as big as it is, so you didn't get to see the major league
sports, and we didn't have an NBA team and we didn't have
major-league baseball. We had the triple-A San Francisco
Seals, and we had college basketball. USF was great at that
time. And football, the Forty-Niners were the one major
league thing we had.

I think as a kid you would copy those guys. I mean, we
would go to Forty-Niner football games and sneak into San
Francisco Seal games, and you would copy the way they
played. You know, "I'm this guy, I'm that guy," and that's the
way we would play.

Then you would go in high school, and when you were in
high school, you would think of playing in college, and you
really didn't think of playing pros, or at least I didn't, until I
got to college, which would be the next step.

*There was an unusual "home run" involving the young Madden,
who was a catcher:*

I played baseball in high school and junior college. We
were playing Sequoia High School in Redwood City, and a
guy struck out, and I was going to throw him out at first, so I
kept it in front of me, so I waited and waited, and I was going
to throw, so I threw it so hard it went over the first baseman's
head, down the right field line and out of the stadium, and the
guy ran all the way around the bases and scored, and John
Robinson says I "threw a home run."

*Before there was John Madden the football coach, there was John
Madden the football player. He played at Cal Poly-San Luis Obispo
and was drafted by the Philadelphia Eagles. The player's career
ended in the Eagles' training camp in his NFL rookie season, 1959:*

When you're playing, you never think of the day that you can't play. I never did. People never realize that if a person is a ten-year pro, that doesn't just mean he's been playing the sport for ten years. If it's football, it means that he has probably four or five years of college, four years of high school, and a couple years before.

So by the time you get to the pros, you've been playing football ten years of your life, and you don't see any end to it. You think that things like retirement and pensions and stuff like that are for old people. So you don't think about what you're going to do after that until it comes to a point, and in my case, I got injured in my first year.

In those days they didn't have the surgery like they do today. Now, with that same knee injury, I'd probably be back playing the next year. But the way it was then, they would just put you back together, and you would never play again.

So when you know you can never play again, then you start deciding. You're twenty-two years old or whatever and you start deciding, "What am I going to do?" And I thought I better get back to school and finish up some of those things and get on with coaching.

It was a different era in sports:

Professional sports weren't big nationally. Professional sports were just like college, and the difference between college sports now and professional sports is that college is really a regional thing. If you're from Nebraska, you're a Nebraska fan, and you don't care about South Carolina. If you're from Miami, you could be a University of Miami fan, and you don't care about the University of California. That's the way pro sports were.

I think in 1960 is when it started, when the AFL came into being. So that brought in two television networks. Now we had NBC doing the AFL, and then we had CBS doing the

NFL, so there started to be more exposure. But it still wasn't really big. Then I think the first step to being big was when the Jets signed Joe Namath and he got four hundred thousand dollars or something. That was the thing, and Broadway Joe and then football became a national thing.

Then they merged, and probably the single best thing for the merger, of course, was when the Jets beat the Colts in that Super Bowl. Then, after that, I think the next big thing was "Monday Night Football" with Howard Cosell. Whatever anyone thinks about Howard Cosell, I think that when he came in—and I was a coach at that time—that made it big. Then when it was on all three networks, it was on Sunday with national games and on Monday night with national games, that's when pro football came to be what it is today.

But before that time, it was a very regional thing. I remember my contract that first year was like seven thousand or seventy-five hundred, and that's about what most people were being paid. Then you were just playing it for the love of the game, because you could go out and get a job and make the same amount of money. I made more money my next year teaching than I did playing for the Eagles, and I didn't have to move back East to do it.

John's pro football heritage is the AFL:

I was a coach in the AFL. I coached the Oakland Raiders. So I love that football, the AFL. We started opening it up, making it more of a passing game and a pass-defensive game, and the thing Lamar Hunt always wanted was a two-point rule, which I always believed in too. After the merger, it never came to pass, because that was an AFL thing. But I think that every year the game gets better. I'm not one of those old guys that say, "When I played, or when I coached, it used to be better."

It was not better. There are more players, they start at a

younger age, their diets are better, their training habits are
better, the coaching is probably better. Everything is better
today. Anyone that says that the good ol' days were better is
living in the past, in a fantasy.

*John's coaching career began at San Luis Obispo High School in
California:*

When I first went back to Cal Poly, after I found out I
couldn't play any more, I was going to get my teaching
credential. At that time, San Luis Obispo High School had
fired their coach, so it was in the spring, and the new coach
was at another school, so he was going to come the next fall.
So they didn't have a coach to run spring football. So Phil
Prijatel, the athletic director at the high school, asked me if I
would coach the team in spring football. And I said yeah, so I
didn't know any better. So I coached the whole team; I was
the only coach.

Phil used to come out there and watch me, and I coached
everyone, and the guy who was going to be the new coach
would send me plays and defenses, and I would work his
plays and defenses, but I was the offensive coach, the
defensive coach, the kicking coach, the coordinator and
everything, and I did all this for nothing, there was no pay. I
just did it. I really loved it. So that was that. Then I was the
coach of the alumni in the alumni game.

Al Baldoch, the coach at Allan Hancock Junior College in
Santa Maria, needed a line coach, and Phil Prijatel
recommended me. So my first real, paying coaching job was
at junior college. I was the defensive coach and the line
coach for Hancock College in Santa Maria, and in those days
I still wanted to play. I used to go out there and wear arm
pads and hit sleds and everything with the players. I was an
assistant there for two years, and then I became the head
coach.

*John went to a coaching clinic, and a contact he made changed
his career:*

I used to go to all these coaching clinics, and I was a young
coach, and this was in the early sixties, when the I-formation
was a big thing. So I went to this clinic, and John McKay was
the USC coach, and he was speaking at this clinic about the I-
formation. Everyone copied everything. That's the way you
learn and you coach. Someone does something, he does it well,
then you go and you listen to him and then you do it. During
his talk, John said he learned the I-formation from Don Coryell.

Don Coryell was the guy who started the I-formation at a
junior college in Washington, and then he worked at USC as
an assistant for John McKay, and the two of them worked
together and they put in the I-formation. So he said he
learned it from Don, and Don was there, and John introduced
Don and Don stood up.

So after this lecture, when McKay is finished, all these
guys run up to the podium to talk to John McKay. And I
looked over, and Don Coryell was standing all by himself. So
I said to myself, "Well, if this is the guy who John McKay
learned it from, I'll go talk to him." So that was my first
meeting with Don Coryell.

When I was coaching at Hancock College, Don was the
head coach at San Diego State, and he came to recruit, and
San Diego State didn't have a lot of money, so I said, "Don't
get a hotel, stay at my house." So he spent a couple days at my
house, and that's how I got to know him.

Then Tom Bass left San Diego State and went to the San
Diego Chargers, and Don offered me the job as an assistant
there. That's when things really took off. Don knew the I-
formation in the running game and then learned the passing
game from Sid Gillman of the Chargers. So we used to go to
their camp and learn defense and the passing game from
them, and he incorporated that into his system.

What we did is we recruited junior college guys. Once we got a passer and had a passing game, it was easy to recruit junior college kids, because there weren't that many passing colleges in America. So if you were a quarterback or a receiver or a defensive player who wanted to be a pro and work on pass rush and defensive backs and stuff, you'd go to San Diego State, because there weren't any other colleges. Stanford used to throw then, Washington State threw there for a few years, but in those days there were very few passing college teams.

When we became a passing team, we were recruiting players that wanted to be NFL players. So when scouts would come and stuff, we would encourage that, and then that got the most out of the players. That was our whole thing, and that's how we were able to get players to come to San Diego State, because they knew that they were going to be exposed to the NFL, and that's what they wanted. I think that was a pretty good system.

In those days, the guys still had to go to school, and they did all that thing. I mean, we didn't just go out and get bums, we got students. We had tougher entrance requirements than a lot of schools, but we got people who wanted a college education and wanted to play football and hoped to play in the NFL some day.

When I went there, we didn't have a lot of money, so I was a defensive coordinator, and Sid Hall was my defensive backfield coach, and I could hire one graduate assistant, and the guy I hired was Joe Gibbs. Joe had played at San Diego State as a guard. So when I would coach the defensive line, I'd have him coach the linebackers. Then, at the end of the first year, we got into an argument, so Joe became an offensive coach, and I was a genius.

Then my next step, what I really wanted to be, was a head college coach. I applied for a couple jobs and never got one in the three years I was an assistant at San Diego State. Then Al

JOHN MADDEN • 169

Davis came down to look at some of our players, and I met Al Davis, and we were playing North Dakota State, and I remember I was sitting out on the bench, and I was diagramming defenses and stuff, and he came out there and sat with me and we just talked football. We didn't talk anything about players or jobs or anything, we talked about defense, because they used a full house backfield at that time.

So I was going through ideas, and Al gave me some ideas, and I tried some things, and that was the end of our conversation. Then after the season, I got a call from the Raiders, and they wanted me to come up to interview for a job, and they hired me as an assistant in 1967. I mean really, I was enjoying what I was doing as an assistant at San Diego State, thinking my next step would be a head college coach, and then, boom, this thing came and I became an assistant with the Raiders.

Even when I first went there, I didn't know if I would maybe come back and be a college head coach. But I went there in 1967, and the first year we won the AFL and went to the Super Bowl, Super Bowl II. In fact, we lost to Vince Lombardi and his Green Bay Packers, and that was the last game Vince Lombardi coached for the Packers.

The Raiders of John Madden and Al Davis developed a reputation for winning and for aggressive play:

None of those things work if you don't win. We had good players. Daryle Lamonica was a quarterback, and we had George Blanda, Kenny Stabler, Jim Otto, Willie Brown, Gene Upshaw, Art Shell, and Fred Biletnikoff. I mean, these guys are hall of famers.

Then I think part of that thing was the uniform, the silver and black. We were an easy team to dislike. Everyplace we'd go, we were that team's rival. We played San Diego, that was their big game. Kansas City, we were their rivalry. New York

Jets, Denver Broncos, we were their rivalry. Every place we'd go, we'd lead the league in boos.

Then you kind of get stuck with that, and then Al had this thing that he was this or that, and rather than fighting it and saying, "No, no, no, we have a good image, we're good," we said, "Okay, if that's what we are, then that's what we'll be, and let them worry about that."

John has found that what's needed to win in college and what's needed to win in the NFL are two different things:

In college, the most pivotal guy is the running back. If you look at the college teams that win championships, it's usually a running back. For example, just take Herschel Walker. When Herschel Walker was at Georgia, they can win a championship. When Herschel Walker goes to the pros, whether it was the USFL, the Dallas Cowboys, or the Minnesota Vikings, he can't win a championship.

O. J. Simpson, one of the greatest running backs of all time, a Heisman Trophy winner, can win championships at USC, but he goes to the Buffalo Bills, and that's one thing that they can't do.

In the pros, a great running back can't win for you, but a great quarterback can. So it changes as you go up. In the pros you have to have the great quarterback and in college the great running back, and that's assuming you don't need anyone else. You better have those guys blocking for him. Then you better have guys that can catch the ball and run and do all those things.

The Forty-Niners won those Super Bowls with Joe Montana, but he also had a pretty good offensive line, and he had a great receiver in Jerry Rice, and John Taylor was also a heck of a receiver. And then they had good defense. But Joe Montana was the guy. If they didn't have Joe Montana, they wouldn't have won those Super Bowls.

Another difference between college ball and the pro game is that the NFL does no recruiting:

In the pros, you had the players longer, and you didn't have to recruit and worry about school and grades, so you could devote more time to football. But you were playing teams that were also devoting more time to football, so you didn't get any advantage there. I think pro sports are good for someone who just wants to work on the sport, but in college sports, recruiting is even bigger than coaching. It's still getting the players there, and they have to go through that process. In the NFL we had the draft, so we never had to go through a recruiting process.

Guys like Bear Bryant and Woody Hayes were great college football coaches, and those guys were college guys who would never be in the pros. I could never see Bobby Knight being an NBA coach, like I could never see Bear Bryant or Woody Hayes being NFL coaches. Then there are some guys that are pro coaches that just wouldn't work in college.

Many of the players on Madden's Oakland Raiders were colorful nonconformists:

Kind of wild. I have always believed that athletes were kind of like artists, that if you put too many restrictions on them, you could coach them or restrict them all the way down to robots, and I see that. You have to let them have some freedom within a system. A defensive player, you have to have discipline to get him started, to get him his reads, to get him to go to a direction, but after he goes at them, he has to play on his own. You think of Lawrence Taylor, one of the best defensive players I have ever seen, and he's been best when he's been unrestricted. If you tried to restrict a Lawrence Taylor and tell him he has to do this and do this step and that step and everything, he wouldn't be anything.

I only had a few rules and kind of let them go, and they better play. That was the thing. I was never as interested in how they looked or how they talked or what they said during the week. I only had three rules, and that was to be on time, to pay attention, and to play like hell when I tell you to. That was all. It doesn't sound like much, but if you have that, you can't lose.

Some people say you gotta wear a coat and tie and you gotta cut your hair and you can't have any beard, and all those things have nothing to do with winning and losing. If you get caught up in all those things, then you say that this is important. Well, is it more important in the fourth quarter that everyone gets off at the same time and knock the line back, is that more important than wearing your necktie on the plane trip? Some guys on some teams think it is more important to wear the necktie on the airplane trip and look good in the lobby, and then they forget to play on the goal line. If you narrow down the things that are important and just do those things and don't worry about all those other things and put things in order for them, then I think you have a chance at being successful.

Coach John Madden knew how to be successful. One example was the way he told his players to approach Super Bowl XI:

The Super Bowl is the ultimate. I mean that's what everyone goes for and that's what you're measured as— who's the champion? I realized well before we got there that getting there didn't mean anything. That was the first thing I told my players after we beat the Pittsburgh Steelers in the championship game.

I said: "Look, we haven't done anything yet. This doesn't mean anything. All we do now is get to go play in it, but if we don't win it, then we haven't done anything, we're no different than the rest of them." Because the biggest gap in sports is the difference between the win of the Super Bowl and the lose of the Super Bowl. I mean, they give the winner parades, they throw confetti out of windows, they do everything. The loser, he goes home and takes a lot more abuse than the other teams that didn't even get there.

So before we got there, we knew that getting there is nothing. I mean, this doesn't mean anything. Don't get excited that you're in the Super Bowl, because if you don't win it, then it doesn't mean anything.

Then we went on and we won it, and then, when you win it, you can have the whoopees, then it's great. I mean, then it's everything. And you know that that year, you won, and you'll always be the champion of that year, and they can never take it away from you.

MICKEY MANTLE

I met Mickey Mantle in 1950, when we were both playing minor league ball in the Sooner State League. At first we were just passing friends. The number one thing that impressed me was his speed. Number two was that at that point he wasn't very big but he generated a lot of power. And then he got bigger. He was far better than anyone else in the league.

When I was with the New York Giants and he was with the Yankees, we developed a casual friendship. Our team was pretty much in its heyday, and so were the Yankees. I remember the competition between him and Maris in 1961, when it looked like either or both might break Babe Ruth's single season home run record.

After his playing days were over, he moved to Dallas, and I stayed in New York. I'd see him at banquets, at dinners. I could see he was struggling with alcoholism. I had great empathy for him. I had gone through the same thing.

When I moved to Dallas, we began to see each other a lot more. He joined my club, the Preston Trail Golf Club. We became close friends. We'd play golf a couple of times a week. We'd go to dinner a couple of times a week.

When we were both in New York, we'd see each other at the

Regency and at some of our favorite restaurants—Capriccio's, the Post House, or, of course, Mickey Mantle's on Central Park South.

As we would play more and more golf in Dallas, he would ask more and more questions about alcoholism and what to do about it. He knew I'd been to the Betty Ford Center, and he wanted to ask what it was like there, but it was hard for him to say the words. Everybody who's an alcoholic is embarrassed to talk about it. You have to admit it to yourself. You have to admit it to others.

But then we did begin to talk about it. After many conversations, after many tearful lunches—and it wasn't just Mickey who was crying—he finally asked if he could get in. I said he could, and I got him in. He went there in 1993.

After he finished with the Ford Center, Mickey was different. You never recover from alcoholism, but you can stop drinking. I had. He did.

He was different because he wasn't drinking. He was a different kind of human being. When he had been a drinker he sometimes could be surly, caustic. After he stopped he was more warm. More tolerant. Kinder. More giving.

After Betty Ford, he enjoyed life for the first time. This is hard for some people to believe, because to many people, being a sports star sounds like the ideal life. For some it is. For Mickey, it wasn't. Even when he was young, he didn't realize why he was idolized.

He would forever say, "Why would people pay me for an autograph? I've done that all my life for free. Now I make my living doing it." He was just a modest guy with rural roots. There was absolutely nothing phony about him.

One day we were getting ready to play golf. He knew something was wrong. I could tell. I asked, "What's the matter?" He showed me that his abdomen was swollen.

I told him, "You've got to see a doctor."

So he had the liver transplant. When he came out of surgery, he told me he had cancer. He felt it was terminal.

His death was a blow for me. They say a man's lucky if, when he dies, he has five close friends. Mickey was one of my five. I was one of his.

It was a great personal loss for me, but I felt glad I had helped him make the trip to Betty Ford. He died much more at peace with himself than he had ever been before he went there.

His death has made my life different: there's a missing element. His locker was right next to mine. I still go to the course, and I still go to the locker room, but he won't ever open that locker again.

Mickey Mantle may have been the most exciting baseball player of the last half of the century. He truly could do everything and do it superbly. He could hit for average, for power. Before his knee injury, he may have been the fastest base runner in history; his time to first base was faster than Bo Jackson's. He could field balls that most players never would have reached. He could hit strongly from both sides of the plate.

Mickey could help a team to do its best, and his Yankees were among the most successful teams in the history of sport. With Mickey, they won the American League pennant twelve times in fourteen years, winning the World Series seven times. Mickey holds many World Series records, including most lifetime home runs—eighteen.

So when Mickey Mantle walked up to the plate, there was excitement, a sense of anticipation: astounding things were likely to happen. You might see the longest home run in the stadium's history. You might see a groundout turned into a single or a single turned into a sliding double. A little while later you might see a stolen base or another kind of theft: a "sure" base hit that Mickey somehow would catch in center field.

"The Mick" had a special hold on the fans of New York and the fans of the nation. Part of it was skill, part of it was just the way he looked. As baseball historian Donald Honig put it:

> *He was tough, he was inspirational, and he was a winner. Blond, built like a halfback, with the smile and boyish good looks of an American small-time beau ideal, Mantle put together a glittering 18-year career that elevated him into the Ruth-Gehrig-DiMaggio pantheon of Yankee untouchables.*

Mickey Mantle was a high school star in Commerce, Oklahoma (hence the name "the Commerce Comet"). A scout saw him and signed him to the Yankees organization. He went on to play more than 2,400 games, more than any other Yankee. But at the beginning, there were moments when it looked like Mickey would be a minor league washout instead of a major league superstar. Mickey's road to New York started in Kansas:

I was playing in Baxter Springs, Kansas, for the Whiz Kids, and Tom Greenwade, a Yankee scout, came through there. I was playing shortstop, and he saw me play. I hit three home runs, two right-handed and one left-handed, and they all went into the river.

After high school, I went up to play in Coffeyille, Kansas. The first thing that Tom said to me before I signed was, "I'm not sure that you can be a major leaguer." He said, "I think you'll be a good minor league player but you're probably not big enough to play in the major leagues." I was really pretty small then. I think Greenwade gave me a five-hundred-dollar bonus and twelve hundred for the rest of the year in 1949.

Anyway, just as soon as I signed, he said, "You just get out there and gain some weight and get a little bit bigger, and you're gonna be one of the greatest ballplayers that ever lived."

I finished up in Independence, Kansas, and then I went to Joplin in 1950, and after the end of the season I came to the Yankees, in 1951. Casey Stengel moved me from shortstop to the outfield because they figured that was going to be DiMaggio's last year, and they wanted me to be the next DiMaggio.

That's a pretty big load on a nineteen-year-old kid: coming to New York and Casey was saying I could outrun everybody, I could hit a ball right-handed and left-handed farther than anybody. He said, "This kid's phenomenal."

He said that so much that the ballplayers, Hank Bauer

and Woodling and Allie Reynolds and all the older guys, Yogi, everybody, started calling me "Phenom."

But of course I didn't do that good when I first got up there. The fans were booing me quite a bit, and I was getting uptight, and I lost all my confidence. We went to Boston, and I struck out four or five straight times. I had struck out the last time I had been up the game before, and four times the next day, too. I was breaking bats and kicking the water cooler and hitting my hands on the dugout.

When we got to Detroit, Casey said he wanted to talk to me. He told me I'd lost all my confidence and he was going to send me back to the minor leagues. He started crying and I started crying. Being sent back down about broke my heart.

Casey told me that just as soon as I started hitting they'd bring me right back. He was gonna keep an eye on me. But down in the minors I went 0 for twenty-two.

Now we're in Kansas City and I call my Dad.

My Dad had been a miner. They tell me he was a great semipro baseball player in Oklahoma. A lot of people say that if a scout would have seen him, he could have been a major league baseball player, which I believe. He was a switch-hitter, and he taught me to switch-hit. He would pitch to me right-handed. Then he'd make me hit left-handed against my grandfather; he'd have my grandfather, who was left-handed, pitch to me.

I said, "Dad, I don't think I can play baseball. I don't think I can play even triple-A."

He said, "Where are you?"

And I said, "The LaSalle Hotel here in Kansas City." And he said, "I'll be up there." He didn't say when or anything, he just said he'd be there, and he hung up.

It's about a hundred and fifty miles from Whitebird, Oklahoma, where he was living at the time, to Kansas City. About four hours after the call, there's a knock on my door. It was my Dad. He come walking in the room, and he didn't say a word. Just grabbed my suitcase and started throwing my clothes in it. I didn't have very many clothes then, a couple pair of Levis and penny loafers.

I said, "What are you doing, Dad?"

And he said, "I'm taking you back to the mines. You can be a miner like me. I thought I raised a man. Hell, you're nothin' but a coward."

And he's packin' my stuff, and he's got tears in his eyes. I thought he would come up there and pat me on the back and say, "God, hang in there, Mick, you know you're gonna make it."

But he just really let me have it pretty good. I talked him into giving me another chance. And from that time on, I ended up hitting about .365 and had about fifteen homers and fifty RBIs in a short time. It was unbelievable how I turned around. And Casey brought me back to the Yankees, and they kept me from then on.

Mickey acknowledged that major league baseball had changed since his time:

Everybody on the whole Yankees team seemed like more of a family than baseball teams are now. I don't think the guys now know each other that well. I was broadcasting games at Yankee Stadium, and I'd go down to the clubhouse, and everybody had a briefcase and an agent. Everybody had their own radio. When I was playing, we all listened to one radio. It doesn't seem like a family anymore.

My first game back from the minors was in New York against the Red Sox. There were sixty-five thousand people in Yankee Stadium, and I started in right field. The first guy that hit me a fly ball was Ted Williams. It seemed to me like the ball must have gone two thousand feet high, and I thought it was never gonna come down. I did catch it, and I felt very lucky that I caught it.

The Yankees had already won in '49 and '50. I came up, and we won '51, '52, and '53. That's five straight World Series. In '54, the year Cleveland beat us for the pennant, we still won a hundred and four games out of a hundred and fifty-four.

In those days, the World Series check was probably five thousand dollars. Now it's ninety-five thousand or a hundred thousand or something like that, and there are a lot of bonuses. You didn't have to give us bonuses. There was so much pride, we felt like we were gonna win every game. Casey used to even say, "If we can stay close to 'em to the seventh, eighth, and ninth, I guarantee you we'll win the game." So we felt like we were that much better than everybody else.

After we lost in '54, then we won in '55 and '56. I think Milwaukee beat us in '57, then we won '58. Then the White Sox won in '59, and then I think we won five more. So my first fourteen years we won twelve pennants.

We never knew how much each other was making. I finally got up to a hundred thousand dollars, but I didn't get a raise after I got to a hundred thousand because they said that's the most DiMaggio ever made.

I have a lot of people ask me do I feel bad about the players that are making two or three million dollars. But I really did feel like I was overpaid because there was Whitey Ford, who was a great pitcher, a Hall of Fame pitcher, and there was Yogi Berra. Moose Skowron never made over thirty-five thousand, I don't think. There were guys on our team who didn't make half as much as I did, and I felt like they were just as good. The salaries really didn't mean that much to us. It was the winning I think that meant more than anything else.

Mickey Mantle had many close friends on the Yankees, but the two closest were Whitey Ford and Billy Martin:

Billy Martin and Whitey Ford were like brothers to me. One of my toughest times as a ballplayer was in '57, when George Weiss, the Yankees' general manager, traded Billy to Kansas City. There were a lot of things that led up to it. But first of all, Mr. Weiss said Billy was a bad influence on me.

But in '56 I won the Triple Crown. And the year they traded Billy I was hitting almost .400. I was the Most Valuable Player in '56 and '57. So Billy's comment was, "How good could you have been if I hadn't've been a bad influence on you?" Of course he was joking.

When I came to the Yankees, Casey was saying I was gonna be the next Babe Ruth and Lou Gehrig and Joe DiMaggio rolled into one, and of course it didn't work out like that. But I started hitting .300 in '53 and '54. In '55 I had a pretty good year.

In '56 I won the home run title and the batting title and the RBI title. I think I started believing a little more in myself, and the fans were not quite as bad as they were for me at first when I wasn't doing that good. So they got behind me. And the players were all behind me, and I was getting older. I was twenty-five by then, and I had a little more confidence, and I think that's what really pushed me over—I think the turning point in my career was winning the Triple Crown.

Mickey was one of the greatest home run hitters of all time. He had 536 lifetime home runs, eighth on the all-time list. He was the American League home run leader in 1955, with 37; in 1956, with 52; in 1960, with 40. In 1961, he and Roger Maris were challenging Ruth's great record of 60 home runs in a season (Ruth's season was 154 games). Mickey hit 53 before being sidelined for sixteen games with a staph infection (Maris went on to hit 61 in a 162-game season; Mickey finished with 54). But what could Mickey have done in a "normal" stadium, not Yankee Stadium, where the left-center-field and right-center-field fences were farther from the plate than in almost any other park?

Whitey and I figured it out one time. I hit at least ten balls a year—now this is a low number I think—on the track in center field that were caught. Those would have been home runs in left center and right center, where it's 461 and 457. I played eighteen years, and if you figure ten times eighteen, it'd be a hundred eighty more, but I know I hit a lot more than ten that were caught.

Those numbers are plausible. Mickey Mantle had big shoulders and muscular forearms. He always seemed a size too big for his uniform. Today, home runs of 425 feet make headlines; people still talk about the 565-foot homer Mickey hit in 1953 at Griffith Stadium in Washington, D.C. Ten more home runs a year would have given Mickey 716 lifetime home runs, even in Yankee Stadium.

During his career Mickey had many injuries. These too cut into his home run production. George Will has said, "Take the tape off and the pain out of his legs, Mickey Mantle could have done anything in baseball. I mean he's just one of the top ten players who ever put on a uniform—period." Mickey's teammate Elston Howard estimated that if Mickey had been healthy, he would have hit seventy home runs a year.

More food for thought is that Mickey Mantle retired at thirty-six, early for a superstar. If he had been in better health, Mickey would likely have played three to five more years. If everything had gone right—shorter fences, fewer injuries, longer career—The Mick might well be the lifetime home run leader, and by a big margin.

Despite the great achievements he had at Yankee Stadium, Mickey remained in awe of the most famous ballpark in baseball:

I still feel funny when I go to Yankee Stadium. They refurbished it, and it doesn't look the same anymore. But I still get a feeling. When I'd come back for old-timer games, I used to feel like maybe Lou Gehrig and Babe Ruth were still hanging around out there somewhere. I mean I'd get goosebumps. I still do. And the fans, they give you a big hand, it makes you feel good, and I still feel like a Yankee.

But not all of Mickey's memories were so pleasant:

I don't know what Hitler was really like, but I would say that George Weiss was probably pretty close to it. He was great in one way; he kept the team intact.

In the '56 season I led the league in everything, but I was only making thirty-two thousand five hundred dollars. The next year the first contract I got was for like a five-thousand-dollar raise. Well, I knew that Ted Williams and Willie and some of the other guys were making pretty good money, and I had a better year than they did, so I told Mr. Weiss I wanted to double my contract. I wanted sixty-five thousand dollars. And, well, he went crazy. Finally Del Webb and Dan Topping, the owners, had to tell him to go ahead and give me what I wanted.

In '57 I hit .365, I had about forty home runs and a hundred RBIs. I was the Most Valuable Player again. But the first contract I got in 1958 was for a cut because Mr. Weiss said I didn't do as good in '57 as I did in '56. He felt like he was the führer or something.

One time I tossed a ball underhanded to a kid in batting practice at the stadium, a batting practice ball. Nowadays, every time somebody gets close to the stands, they give them a ball. But after batting practice I was called up to the office, and Mr. Weiss took fifteen minutes telling me about how much that ball cost and it wasn't my ball to give away and if I'd have hit somebody in the face with it, the Yankees could have got sued, I could have got sued.

Mickey Mantle's statistics put him among baseball's all-time leaders. But he was never fully satisfied. After retiring, he used to have a recurring dream: He would pull up to Yankee Stadium in a cab, and he would be wearing his uniform. There was a wall separating him from the field. On the field were manager Casey Stengel plus Whitey Ford, Billy Martin, and Mickey's other teammates.

Mickey tried to crawl through a hole in the fence. He was supposed to be on the field. But he just couldn't squeeze through; he got stuck. The public address system would blare, "At bat . . . number seven . . . Mickey Mantle." At that point Mickey would awake, drenched in sweat.

Mickey looked back on his career with a mixture of pride and sadness, a sadness about what might have been. He believed his disappointment over what might have been contributed to his admitted drinking problem. His drinking was a major cause of his 1995 liver failure, subsequent transplant, and untimely death. If he could have, he would have done some things differently:

If I could do it all over again, I would change a lot of things. I would have taken better care of myself. I retired when I was thirty-six years old. Willie played till he was over forty. Peter Rose played till he was over forty. All those guys that took good care of themselves are the guys up at the top of the lifetime statistics, and I was a little bit dumb, I didn't realize what was going on.

At twenty-five on up till I retired, I was young enough that I didn't think it was gonna ever end. I wasn't smart enough to see that my legs were getting worse. I should have been doing my exercises and stuff. I just like to tell kids, don't do drugs. I didn't do that; we didn't have drugs when I played, but I had a few too many beers once in a while, and I didn't listen to my doctors and my elders, I guess you'd call 'em. I can remember Allie Reynolds and Vic Raschi, even Yogi, the big brothers of the ball team, saying, "You guys better cool it, you're burning the candle at both ends, and if you don't slow down, you're gonna have to retire before your time." And it really happened to me.

In 1969, the year after I retired, the Yankees had Mickey Mantle Day at Yankee Stadium and like seventy-one thousand fans showed up, and they retired my number seven that day. And I said during my speech that I didn't know how a guy like Lou Gehrig could stand there, and he knew he was going to die, and they had Lou Gehrig Day, and he stood at home plate and said he felt like he was the luckiest man on the face of the earth. And that day, when they retired number seven along with three, four, and five, I think I knew how Lou Gehrig felt.

JOE MONTANA

Many observers think Joe Montana is the greatest quarter-back ever to play the game of football. I think the thing that most separated him from other quarterbacks who have played in the NFL is that he saw so much more than did most anybody else. I remember riding to the 1990 Super Bowl with Mike Holmgren, then the offensive coordinator of the 49ers. We were in New Orleans for the game in which San Francisco beat Denver.

We were talking about the fact that most quarterbacks will look for the primary receiver, then look for the secondary receiver, and then, if they can't find either one, will dump the ball off. But Holmgren said Montana could almost simultaneously look at all five receivers as well as at the defense and tell who was open. He didn't have a great arm, but he had incredible peripheral vision plus an incredible sense of timing. So Holmgren said, "My guy sees all five, and if Denver stays in the defense we've been seeing, he'll cut 'em to pieces." And Montana did cut 'em to pieces: the final score was 55–10; no team in Super Bowl history had ever scored so many points or had such a margin of victory.

I don't think any quarterback in the history of the game has seen more than Montana did. In addition, Montana had an unusual capacity for anticipation. He would throw the ball before a receiver *ever broke: he knew where the receiver was going to be.*

Bill Walsh, who coached Montana to his first three Super Bowl wins, designed what became known as the West Coast Offense, an offense in which passing, not running, became the means of controlling the ball. Joe Montana executed Walsh's design.

But scores, statistics, and techniques don't tell the whole story. Much of the story of Joe Montana was his heart and his gut. At Notre Dame and then with the 49ers, Montana became the best come-from-behind quarterback in the history of football. When a Montana team was down by six points with two minutes to go, you didn't think he had just a chance to win; you thought the opposing team had little chance to hold onto its lead. And most of the time you were right.

The Montana-led San Francisco 49ers won four Super Bowls, in 1982 (26–21 over Cincinnati), 1985 (38–16 against Miami), 1989 (20–16 over Cincinnati), and 1990 (55–10 against Denver in the game just mentioned).

Joe Montana was the MVP of the Super Bowls of 1982, 1985, and 1990. He is the all-time Super Bowl leader in passing completions (83) and passing yards (1,142). He holds the Super Bowl record for most yards in a game, with 357 in 1989.

Joe Montana five times was the top-rated passer in the NFC. Over his career, he was the second-highest-rated passer in the history of the league, second only to his former teammate Steve Young. He is fourth all-time in touchdown passes, with 273, and fourth all-time in passing yards, with 40,551. Montana was named MVP of the NFL in 1989 and 1990.

In 1993, the 49ers traded him to the Kansas City Chiefs, where he played out his career in style, completing more than 60 percent of his passes in his two seasons and leading the Chiefs to the playoffs in both 1993–94 and 1994–95; in the first of those seasons, he took the team all the way to the AFC championship game. Joe Montana retired after the 1994–95 season.

I've never seen a better quarterback.

Despite his unique accomplishments, Montana takes a balanced view when asked about the importance of the quarterback:

People always look at the quarterback. It all starts there, but you have ten other guys on the field at the same time who have the same type of feeling and confidence. Otherwise, all your efforts are for naught.

I think a lot of the success I've had has been associated with the people around me and the fact that they have confidence in me and I have confidence in them. And because of that mutual confidence, we are able to get things done, whether it's the first quarter or last minutes of the fourth quarter. I think you have to have those kinds of people around you or you are not going to have that kind of success, no matter how determined you can be.

Once Montana joined the 49ers, the team rapidly became the best in all of football:

When I first got here, things were changing, and even though my first year we didn't play very well and even the second year, you could see the changes taking form, and you knew things were going to turn around for the organization. For it to turn around that big right away was somewhat of a shock. I think in essence we went from basically nowhere to a Super Bowl win, but I think the thing that says the most is that we were able to hang on and continue the winning pattern. We could have easily said, "Oh great, we got where we wanted," and then drop back down, but that didn't happen. There was a big winning tradition and a lot of pride.

Presumably football was Joe Montana's first love:

Not really. Actually, basketball was. I had more fun with it, and it was one of those things that you could do by yourself; you could go to the playground and there would be only two guys and you could play. It was just fun for me to play, to practice.

I liked football a lot, but the main reason I concentrated on it was that I wanted to go to Notre Dame, and the only way I could was to play football. It turned out good for me in the end, but initially I would have rather played basketball. It's nice and warm inside, too. You don't have to play in those cold games.

Did Montana ever think about playing two professional sports?

Not really. You saw Bo Jackson doing it. It's difficult in football. You need the time. It would have to be a non-contact type of game, maybe baseball; you could get away with it because you don't play all the time or you're on the road and it's not a very physically demanding sport other than to travel. Otherwise, your body needs the time to rest. You need those six months.

Some football players see their sport as a war. Montana used a different word:

I think it's more of a fight than it is a war. They use the term "war" a lot, but I think, in essence, it's more of a street fight where you know you're going to get hit, and you know it's not a life-or-death situation. But it's a physically demanding sport, and when you go out there, you know it's going to happen. It's just part of the game, and you do your best to put it out of your mind, but you know it's going to happen. The earlier it happens in the game to the quarterback, I think the better mentally. Once you get hit, you're back to normal.

JOE NAMATH

Joe Willie Namath was the man who bridged the gap between the American Football League and the National Football League, the man who made the AFL legitimate in the eyes of the fan. It was January 1969, Super Bowl III in Miami. Super Bowl I had been won by the Green Bay Packers, 35–10 over the Kansas City Chiefs. In Super Bowl II, Green Bay had beaten the Oakland Raiders, 33–14. Conventional wisdom, the longer history of the NFL, and the outcome of these Super Bowls told the fan that the AFL could not compete with the NFL.

But then came Joe Namath, who had learned about football growing up in Beaver Falls, Pennsylvania, and then under the tutelage of Bear Bryant at Alabama. He had made his professional debut with the New York Jets and had been named 1965 Rookie of the Year. So stylish and such a ladies' man that he was called "Broadway Joe," Namath wouldn't subordinate himself to any man or any league.

Namath's Jets, under Weeb Ewbank, had won the AFL, beating the Raiders 27–23 in the championship game. The Baltimore Colts, coached by Don Shula, had won the NFL, on a 34–0 shutout of the Cleveland Browns. On the eve of the Super Bowl, Namath did the unthinkable: he not only predicted his team would win, he said, "I

*guarantee it." And he made good on the guarantee: the Jets beat the
Colts, 16–7. Namath was named AFL Player of the Year.*

*The power structure of football was forever changed. That was
1969. The 1969 season was the last year of two separate leagues: in
1970, the leagues merged, so that there no longer was an AFL and an
NFL, but rather an American Football Conference and a National
Football Conference, both within the expanded National Football
League.*

*Eventually Namath would be enshrined in the Pro Football Hall
of Fame. But even in his early days, he was more interested in the success of the team than of the individual:*

When I was a kid, I always had sports on my mind:
football, basketball, baseball. I guess up until college I really
didn't have any specific dreams of a professional
championship.

When I got to college, our goal, under coach Paul "Bear"
Bryant, was to win the national championship, and that was
wonderful. Every dream I have ever had in sports has come
true.

My family and the guys that I hung out with and the
teachers that I had always put the team ahead of the
individual. Even though we know the individual is very
important to the individual, and you've got to satisfy your ego
in some way, you have to realize you don't do much on this
earth totally alone.

The last fifteen to twenty years at least, every shooting
star I've seen, I've made the same wish. I've been happy,
healthy, feeling great, my dreams came true in sports by
winning a championship on each level, and I've wished for
myself and my family only good health and happiness.

High school was a very critical stage for me because I
was the youngest in the family and my three brothers, all
older than me, had left. My mother and father had some
medical problems, and I had been with my mother since the

sixth grade, and I guess I was pretty hard to discipline.

I had a lot of freedom, and I had a high school coach named Larry Bruno, who turned out to be one of the most fortunate friends I ever developed. He came to our high school my junior year, and by my senior year, thirteen of us went to college on scholarship. Larry Bruno did the honors at my induction into the Pro Football Hall of Fame.

I went from Larry Bruno to Bear Bryant. Now, you talk about a couple of wonderful teachers. They kept me out of a lot of trouble I could have gotten myself into. I did get into some, being that mischievous kind of a guy, being a Gemini.

I believe everything starts at home, how your parents treat you, how your brothers and sisters treat you, what you infer from them, and I was very fortunate to have the kind of family I had. But if it wasn't for Larry Bruno and Bear Bryant, I'd have been a career man in the service, because those were my goals.

When I was coming out of high school, I wanted to go into the Air Force. I went for a physical, I took the papers back, I wanted my parents to sign them, because I was going to join the Air Force, like my big brother, who was a career man in the Army. And my parents wouldn't sign the papers. They said, "We want you to go to school." And I ended up winning a scholarship to Alabama and the rest worked out.

Even in college, I wasn't planning on playing pro football. I wanted to be a coach, and when these pro football teams started showing interest, that's when it evolved into possibly playing pro football and, of course, the goal of making the team win the championship.

Namath's coaches did more than keep him out of trouble:

I'm a gifted athlete, I had a lot of ability, but being able to use that ability correctly is something you need help with. It's like a golf swing; you can't see yourself swing the golf club, you need somebody else to look at it and see what you're doing technically correct or incorrect.

The mind part of the game was taught to me early on and continued with Larry Bruno in Arrow Falls High School. That's back when quarterbacks called their own plays in high school and college.

Coach Bryant made his quarterbacks call their own plays. One time Coach Bryant said he'd called a play for me and, don't you know, it was a bad play; he was trying to take the heat off of me. It was a play that didn't work, and he said he'd called it. That's the kind of leader he was. But those coaches, Coach Bryant and Coach Bruno and their staffs, taught me the importance of the mind game, being prepared.

I was leaving a hotel along with two other quarterbacks prior to my first collegiate game, against the University of Georgia. It was kind of an historical game: a magazine dubbed it the story of a college football fix. They said Paul "Bear" Bryant and Wally Butz at Georgia had fixed the game, which was totally untrue because I was a sophomore and I called every play. I didn't know anything was fixed, and there wasn't anything fixed.

But we were walking out of the hotel to take our pregame walk with Coach Bryant, and Coach Bryant looked at me and he said, "Joe, you got the game plan?"

I said, "Yes, sir, I think so."

"You think so? Boy, it's time for you to know." And he jumped on me with both feet with that. "It's not time to think so, you got to know, you got to convince yourself you know what you're doing."

And that was one of the best lessons I ever had because there wasn't but one game in the rest of my athletic career that I wasn't convinced that I was totally prepared. Ironically, that one game that I wasn't prepared, I was sitting in front of a locker jamming in a short play, a short yardage play. I was a wreck, playing Baltimore at Baltimore. Johnny Unitas had a wonderful day. They scored thirty-four points, he threw forty-some passes, our defense didn't touch one of them.

However, our team scored six touchdowns through the air, and we beat 'em forty-four to thirty-four that day, and I was lucky. I was purely undeserving of what happened there, but I figured my team deserved it more than I did and the good Lord was looking after my team that time.

That was the only game I wasn't totally convinced I was prepared. So probably the biggest lesson Coach Bryant had given me came in that little chat right there, "Are you ready, Joe?" And from that time on, I knew and it helped me every game. The Super Bowl game we played the Colts, I was ready and so was the rest of our team.

When Joe Namath came to the Jets in 1965, he had company— the team signed Namath for a then-gigantic $400,000 but spent another $200,000 on Heisman Trophy winner John Huarte from Notre Dame:

John Huarte was drafted by the Jets along with myself and Bob Schweickert from, I believe, Virginia, three pretty good quarterbacks. And I was a little surprised that the Jets had drafted a couple of other quarterbacks after they had drafted me.

The most important thing in the whole episode or transition going from college to pro ball was what Coach Bryant had told me prior to signing. He said, "Joe, get to know the people you're going to work for. Visit with them, see what kind of people they are, see what their goals are, because you're going to be with them in close quarters and a good working relationship is critical."

Well, after getting to know [Jets owner] David A. [Sonny] Werblin and [Jets coach] Weeb Ewbank, there was no question in my mind where I wanted to play, and with what team. I had met with the Cardinals' representatives earlier, and then I met with the Jets, and I was very excited about playing football for the Jets. At the time, I wasn't concerned with NFL-AFL battles. I wasn't concerned with the level of the game. I had been watching the AFL play football on television since 1960, and there were some awful good football players out there.

I went to the New York Jets because of Weeb Ewbank and Sonny Werblin, not because of New York City, not because of the AFL, not because of the money *per se*, because the money ended up being matched and bettered by the NFL. But my decision had been made because Weeb Ewbank had already worked with Johnny Unitas, had already won a world championship with the Baltimore Colts. Here I was, the luckiest player around, I thought. I played for Larry Bruno, I played for Paul "Bear" Bryant, and now I was going to get a chance to play for Weeb Ewbank. That's how I ended up with the New York Jets.

When he paid $400,000, Sonny Werblin got more than Namath. He also got star power:

Sonny Werblin was brilliant in that he believed in the star system when football didn't want the star system. They wanted to treat everybody alike. That's why Mr. Werblin offered me that much money. It was wonderful publicity. It was the star system: put a star in the system, sell out the tickets. He did the same thing with Matt Snell the year before, and then he did it with me, and we had a great response from the New York area and our season tickets.

When Namath joined the Jets, he also joined a league that was different from the NFL in more than name:

The AFL may not have had the quality defenses that the NFL had, so there was a more wide-open style of play or higher scoring–I don't know the statistics, but it looked that way. The AFL also implemented defensive blitzing on a level that hadn't been used much in the NFL, safety blitzing, strong-side safeties, weak-side safeties. The multiple defenses the AFL used really helped prepare us for the Baltimore Colts in the Super Bowl, because throughout the wonderful season they had, they annihilated people defensively. They could put pressure on them from their safeties, their linebackers, their front, their blitzing, but hey, we were ready for that, because we had played against it in the AFL.

Our offensive linemen and offensive backs and wide receivers all needed to make adjustments, and all of them were all very capable of doing that. We were able to read defenses, not just old Joe–it's not just the quarterback reading a defense, it has to come from everyone involved.

The year we played the Colts, they were so dominant they were kind of in that Catch–22 situation: "We're so good, why change anything for this team, the Jets? We don't need to change anything for this team; let's just keep going with what got us here." And ironically, those are the same words that Weeb Ewbank used to me the day before the game, because I went to the coaches and said, "Let's open up the game with the two-minute offense."

I wanted to just get up to the line and let it roll, because I knew we could attack these guys, and Weeb said, "Geez, that's interesting." But then he said, "You know, Joe, we've been very successful with what we're doing; let's stick with what got us here."

The Colts approached the game with the same philosophy defensively. And before the snap of the ball on nearly every play, I had a good idea of what that defense was going to do, and we must have run seventy, seventy-five percent of our plays right at the line of scrimmage. We were able to operate from the line of scrimmage, anticipating their defenses, and took advantage of them that way. But if

Baltimore had it to do over again, I'll betcha they'd play the same way, because they just felt like that wasn't their day.

In New York, the competition was the NFL's New York Giants:

We weren't accepted in New York except by the New York Jet fans, and we were always angry about that. We had guys that had been in the AFL since 1960: Larry Grantham, our linebacker, Don Maynard, Billy Mathis, our halfback, and when they went on a speaking engagement, banquets, they'd get fifty to a hundred dollars, and the Giants would get two or three hundred.

You'd go to restaurants and there were some restaurants that were New York Giant hangouts, and the Jets weren't welcome there. It was like you were second-rate until we beat the Giants following the Super Bowl; we weren't accepted. Even after the Super Bowl, the old hard-core NFL Giant fans still felt like they were better, and then we got a chance to play them and we beat them real good, and I think that solidified our position in New York.

The Jets' offense was more famous, but first Namath wants to credit the defense:

We had the best defense in the AFL the year we won the championship, and they grew beautifully. And without the defense you're not going to do much.

But our offensive unit, you can't go very far without saying [wide receiver] Don Maynard's name first, because he was the game-breaker, the knockout punch. He was the guy that every defense we played against said, "Hey, we got to stop him. You got to stop him first."

Despite having to face the fearsome rush of AFL and NFL defenders, Namath never had the mobility he had displayed at Alabama.

When he was well, he had a shotgun arm. But he played much of his career when he couldn't perform at 100 percent. In that respect, he was like Mantle.

One is tempted to put Namath on the list of all-time greats, but I think that before you start putting athletes on that list, you have to look at how long they lasted. Unfortunately, because of his injured knee, Namath didn't last very long. Namath's physical decline was a major reason that the Jets rapidly declined; if Namath had remained healthy, the team might have created a dynasty:

Before I played my first dime of football with the Jets, I had torn cruciate ligaments in my right knee, torn cartilage, and I had hurt my knee my senior year in college. In January of '65, the Jets signed me to a contract without even looking at my knee. Then Dr. Jim Nicholas, the Jets' head orthopedist, looked at it. We were in the men's room of 21 or somewhere else, and he said, "My goodness, we need to fix this."

He took me to the hospital the next day, operated on me, and when Dr. Nicholas came to visit me that first day, he said, "Joe, the operation went well. Your knee will be fine. We think you can play four years."

And I was the happiest boy you could imagine. I'm laying in bed saying, "Thank you, God. I get to play four years of pro football."

I don't know whether that influenced me or not. We won the Super Bowl in my fourth year. Maybe it was an urgent thing to get done, but I fully expected only to play four years because of my physical condition and because of my knee, and I ended up playing thirteen. So I got a better shake than I ever dreamed of, but I played hurt from day one.

Never being the athlete I was in college or prior to that because of knee injuries was a bit frustrating. Maybe it helped me as a passer, because it helped me get rid of the ball more quickly to avoid the losses.

*Namath traces the progress of the Jets toward that championship
season:*

There was no real success or happiness my first few
years, because the goal was to win the championship. My
rookie year I performed reasonably well for a rookie, and
then my next year was the old sophomore slump or whatever;
it wasn't as good. And then the third year, our team set a
record for fourteen games, against defenses that could beat
up receivers, that could head-slap offensive linemen.

We threw the ball for over four thousand yards in
fourteen games when it just wasn't being done; no one had
ever done it. We came together as a team with the passing
game, and after that our running game came to life. And '68,
the year we won the championship [the Jets won the Super
Bowl in January 1969], we went, I believe, a streak of six
games without having a touchdown pass. But we won all of
them, which was a real tribute to our running game and our
defense. So our passing game helped develop our running
game and vice-versa, and by that fourth year, we were hot
offensively, and we played a game that allowed our defense to
control things.

Coach Ewbank schooled his quarterbacks to the point
that when game time was there he trusted us. Coach Bryant
at Alabama, same philosophy. We were taught what plays to
call, when to call them, versus what defenses, and there was
no signaling plays in.

Today, I don't know if there are any quarterbacks playing
that had to even call their plays in high school, because once
the coaches on an elementary level, prep level, and collegiate
level see what the pros are doing, they figure, "That's right,
so let's start calling 'em for the kid." And I think that's awful,
because how do you learn leadership, how do you learn to be
a field general by always taking orders out there?

I believed in having the opportunity, and I still believe to this day that a quarterback can look at his team, his offensive linemen, his receivers, his running backs and see who wants it right now. And he can look across the line and see a defensive lineman who is so angry you know that a sucker play is going to work right now on him. Or a defensive back with a slight limp; you go right after him. Now you can only do that stuff from the field, you can't do that from the sideline. And the way these guys do it today I think is lousy, I hate it.

I watch games on television, and most of the time I'm sitting there watching the quarterback staring to the sidelines, waiting on a play, and the rest of the team is standing out there looking at each other waiting for something to happen.

I don't believe in that; I don't like that philosophy. I like the philosophy of jumping on the defense, never giving them a chance to breathe or a chance to rest, and to do that, you've got to have the man on the field doing it.

If they really want to improve the National Football League—and they talk about protecting quarterbacks from injury, especially young quarterbacks, guys that can't get out of bad plays—they gotta let these guys have more time when they get to the line of scrimmage, and the only place they're using up time is waiting on the coaches on the sidelines and the press box to decide what play is right.

When you're calling plays, you're often setting plays up in advance or you're going back and thinking what you had called in a similar situation. The key is being able to call that play in the huddle quickly enough to get up to the line of scrimmage and still have enough time to call a better play if need be.

What's happening today is the teams are breaking the huddle and getting up to the line of scrimmage without enough time to call audibles, and they're locked into a bad play, and the quarterback gets clobbered because he couldn't get out of that bad play.

Before the game against the Colts, Namath made the guarantee heard round the world:

I was at the Touchdown Club of Miami accepting an award, and it was my turn to speak. I got up and approached the podium, and one of the guys in the background, it was a Colt fan, said, "Namath, we're going to kick your what-what."

And I said, "Wait a minute, now, you guys have been talking for the last couple of weeks about how good you are, everybody's talking about how good Baltimore is and all. It's my turn to talk now. I'm up here at the podium and I've got news for you: we're going to win the game, I guarantee it."

That was purely out of anger, purely out of frustration. You've heard how guys want respect, we want respect, we get no respect. Well, that's what happened to me at that time. Our team that had just beaten the Oakland Raiders, wasn't getting the respect that I thought we were due, and it was out of anger that I said, "We're going to win the game, I guarantee it."

I don't recall extra pressure because of that statement. There was already enough pressure on us to win the Super Bowl. To win a championship, to be so close to that goal, to have that dream come true, plus we're playing my favorite team, the Baltimore Colts. This was a dream I had. As I mentioned earlier, every dream I ever had came true in sports. This was a dream I had—wouldn't it be something to play against the Baltimore Colts? It came about, and I still get excited thinking about it. I can remember nearly every play like it was yesterday. It's wonderful, it's still a wonderful feeling.

In that storied Super Bowl game, Joe Namath was to play against his boyhood hero, Johnny Unitas:

When I was in Beaver Falls, Pennsylvania, we had a kid from Beaver Falls playing for the Baltimore Colts, Jim

Mutscheller, tight end. Because of him I was a Colt fan and because of Johnny Unitas my nickname at Beaver Falls was Joey U., and I wore number nineteen for home games on my jersey; for away games, we didn't have a nineteen, so I wore twenty-nine. Johnny Unitas was my idol as a football player.

Prior to the Super Bowl, the Colts, without Johnny Unitas playing, continued to annihilate teams because Earl Morrall was just an outstanding quarterback. Of course, in the Super Bowl game that we played them, Earl had an off day, Johnny came in and Johnny wasn't himself; he had a bad arm, wasn't a hundred percent. Our defense knew it, and we played accordingly, gave up the short stuff and didn't allow 'em to get the quick score on us and ended up winning the game.

The Jets did more than win; they controlled nearly the whole game:

The Colts threatened early, but our defense got tight. Al Atkinson, our middle linebacker, made a wonderful play deflecting a pass that was intended for Mitchell, their tight end, and Randy Beverly came up with the interception. Our defense kept making the big plays, and then our offense put it together in the second quarter, and then we kept adding the field goals with Jim Turner.

We got up to sixteen-nothing. We went into our conservative game. We really did play a conservative second half there, once we got ahead sixteen-nothing, because we had that confidence in our defense. This team had to score three times on us and we felt like we could score again, but let's not take any chances.

When Johnny Unitas came in, there was some apprehension, some nervousness. I looked up at that clock, and to this day I can remember seeing six minutes and eleven seconds left, and I said, "Please, Lord, run the clock." That was the first time I got real nervous. We were ahead, it was so close to victory, I got a little scared.

Namath was a magical figure, one of those guys who didn't just make a lot of money (and he made a lot before practically anyone else in football), but had an aura about him that attracted people. Like Michael Jordan today, Namath had a high profile not only on the football field but also in the social life of the nation's biggest city:

I had a lot of freedom in New York, afforded me, first of all, by the team president, Sonny Werblin. He says, "Joe, this is the greatest city in the world with the greatest team in the world. I want you to get out there and know 'em; get to know the New Yorkers." He said, "I don't care if you spend your whole paycheck getting to know New Yorkers here, get out there and know 'em."

He didn't have to tell me twice, 'cause I got out and enjoyed New York. Coach Ewbank believed in practicing as close to game time as possible, so we didn't have to be at the stadium until noon each day. Well, we would practice from noon until about four, go home, look at the films, do the homework, and everything's finished; and then you could go out and visit a while, and even if you got in at two in the morning and got eight hours' sleep, that meant you didn't have to get up till ten o'clock. So I did move around New York quite a bit.

My responsibility as a football player always came first. I knew that, my teammates knew that, and my coaches knew that. As much as I liked to play around in the evenings and at night, I was always ready for work, and my teammates recognized that. Otherwise they don't make you offensive captain. They just don't do that to a guy they don't trust.

GREG NORMAN

Australia's Greg Norman is the most charismatic player in golf today. A shark fisherman, an aggressive player, and a man with hair so blond it's almost white, Norman is called the "Great White Shark." Tall and tanned, sporting a trademark straw hat, and walking with a confident swagger, Norman is a magnet for the crowds that follow PGA tournaments.

I first saw Norman when I was broadcasting the Masters for CBS. It was Greg's first Masters and I didn't know who he was. Another announcer told me he thought Greg had a good chance to win, and I said, "No way." We made a bet.

But three and a half rounds into the tournament, on the tenth tee on Sunday, Greg was in the lead. I couldn't believe it was happening. I couldn't believe this guy, in his first time at Augusta, was hanging in there. Eventually he lost, but it was a memorable first impression.

Since then I've seen him in social situations, and, of course, I've seen him play. I've seen what a competitor he is and what a gentleman he is. He's never out of line, never loud.

His self-control was certainly tested at the 1996 Masters, where he entered the final day six strokes up but then lost by five to Nick Faldo. Despite a collapse that would have made most any other *player explode in anger or shrink in depression, Norman maintained his sportsmanship throughout and expressed his sincere congratulations to the champion.*

He's a gentleman, but a gentleman who works very hard. Even with the enormous success he's had, he trains every day, especially aerobics. Plus all his practice out on the course. This helps to explain why he has endured and why he will continue to endure.

Jack Nicklaus calls the Shark "the longest straight hitter ever." One of his drives was measured at 483 yards. Norman won the British Open in 1986 and 1993. For years he has been "in the hunt" in almost every major golf tournament in which he has played.

He is the PGA tour money leader for 1995, having won $1,654,959. He held the same distinction in 1986 and 1990, with $653,296 and $1,165,477, respectively. In 1994 he won the richest event on the PGA tour, the Players Championship, earning $450,000 and recording a 264, the lowest score in any PGA tournament of the year. In 1995 he won four tournaments: the Memorial (his prize money was $306,000), the Canon Greater Hartford ($216,000), the NEC World Series of Golf ($360,000), and the Australian Open ($114,750).

In 1989, 1990, and 1994 Norman won the Vardon Trophy, which is awarded to the PGA Tour regular with the lowest scoring average. In 1995 his scoring average was 69.06 per round, the lowest of all time. This would have won him the Vardon again had it not been for a back injury that prevented him from starting one round of one tournament (Vardon rules permit no missed or incomplete rounds).

Norman's popularity among golf fans is perhaps best illustrated by the fact that his income from endorsements far exceeds even his prize money: in Forbes's year-end 1995 survey of athlete income, Norman ranked seventeenth in the world and number one among non-senior golfers, with a total income of $9.7 million on $1.7 million in winnings and $8.0 million in endorsements.

Norman is first on the PGA's all-time list of total winnings, with $9,592,829. He finished the 1995 season in first place in the Sony

World Rankings, which rate performance on the combination of the U.S. PGA and the European PGA tours.

The Great White Shark was not a man who depended much on coaches:

> I was basically self-taught. When I had a twenty-seven handicap, which was the highest handicap you could get, I went to a few junior clinics that the local pro gives on Saturday mornings. There were about twenty or thirty kids around.
>
> I went to those, but I was self-taught. I read Jack Nicklaus's golf books: *My 55 Ways to Lower Your Golf Score* and *Golf My Way.* I read those books every nighttime, and I wanted to because I never saw the Palmers in full flight or the Hogans or the Nelsons or the Sneads. I only saw Nicklaus because of how old I was, and he was right at the peak, just winning everything.
>
> So when I was focusing on golf, the guy who was hot at the time was Nicklaus, and he is the greatest player of all time. So I gravitated toward his ideas about how to get around on a golf course and how to play the game and the physical latitude of swinging a golf club.

Norman sees particular differences between prominent amateur golfers and the top professionals:

> An outstanding professional golfer can keep a good round going. He can't do it every time, but he has a tendency to do that. A good amateur plays by feel and just goes and plays because he loves the game, he's good at it, and he just goes and hits it and doesn't worry about the consequences. So he approaches it in a kind of athletic mode. The better you become, the more analytical you become, because you don't want to go and just hit the ball, you don't want to get too aggressive on a certain hole and travel around it and wipe out a good round.

SCOTT HAMILTON

DON KING

DON KING WITH JOE FRAZIER AND MUHAMMAD ALI

SUGAR RAY LEONARD WITH TRAINER ANGELO DUNDEE

MICKEY MANTLE

ARNOLD PALMER

PETE ROSE

FRANK SHORTER

O.J. SIMPSON

JOHN WOODEN

Now the amateur might get up there and see it hitting the water and take six, and instead of shooting sixty-six, he shoots sixty-eight, whereas the pro might lay back a little bit and make sure he doesn't make a major mistake. And I think all top pros, when they're really in their zone and playing well, are capable of doing that.

So we play with that athletic flair, but, on the other hand, you use a bit of maturity and growth that you've developed through the game not to make that major mistake. And, yes, it's hard when you're a kid. I know when I was a kid, all I wanted to do was just hit it as hard as I could, go find it, hit it again, which is not a bad way to play, but sometimes you pay the price for that, too.

Even the Great White Shark had to pay his dues:

When I turned pro, I had to go through a different routine than anybody else, because in Australia at that time, the only way you could become a professional golfer playing in tournaments was to go through a three-year apprenticeship course with the PGA of Australia, not the PGA Tour. So I had to go to a pro shop and spend time in there and do exams and sell and buff golf clubs and pick up range balls and stuff like that. And I did the three-year course in two years.

I requested to be able to do all my exams because all I wanted to do was play golf; I didn't want to be a club professional. And when I came out of there, my golfing skills were rewarded. Instead of waiting another year, they said, "Well, you're good enough. You've won so many assistants' championships, you've shown your performance factor is pretty good, we'll give you a special tournament exemption."

I went out and won the third tournament I played in, and that was a big enough incentive to tell me that, "Hey, I can win and I know how to win," because at that time I played against the David Grahams and the Bruce Devlins and the Bruce Cramptons and the Peter Thomsons back in '76 as well as a few American players that were over there at the time.

So I took it from there. I said, "O.K., you've proven you can do that, now what do you want to do? Do you want to be the best you can be? You've already gone up one rung in the ladder, now you've got to keep going up the ladder, you can't stay stagnant." So I refocused my attention into the game of golf probably fifty percent more, and that was enough.

People ask me to this day, "What was the most important win of your career?" I've won some good tournaments, but that first one was enough to prove to me that I was good enough to be a professional golfer—not to prove to everybody else that they were wrong, but to show me that I did make the right decision, that I did trust my internal instincts.

ARNOLD PALMER

Every golfer on the PGA men's tour today should get down on his knees and face wherever Arnold Palmer stands that day, because Arnold has done so much for the golf game. He might not technically have been the equal of Jack Nicklaus, but he did for the game of golf what no other player was able to do: attract the crowds, increase the television rights, make golf a household sport, and make himself a household name.

I was at the Masters in April 1996, and I went to the Riverwalk in downtown Augusta to watch as they dedicated a life-size statue to Arnold Palmer. Arnold is no Augusta hometown hero; he's from Latrobe, Pennsylvania. Yet the whole population of Augusta must have been there for the ceremony.

I watched Arnold in the practice round he took, and he still has such a big following that he would walk from one side of the fairway to the other, shaking hands, walking with the people. They still adore him. His career peaked more than thirty years ago, and he hasn't won a seniors tournament since 1988, yet nobody gets bigger galleries to this day. He still is the magnet that brings people to the game. He's got so much more—I hate to use the word charisma—but that's what it is, than most any other golfer. He relates to the people better *than anybody else on the tour ever has or, I guess, ever will.*

He changed the game not only in the amount of attention the public gives it but in commercial value. He was the leading money winner in 1958 with $42,608; now, of course, the winner of almost any single PGA tournament makes more than $200,000; in two tournaments, the first-prize money is $540,000. The 1995 money leader, Greg Norman, earned $1,654,959, almost forty times *what Palmer received in 1958.*

Part of the financial success of the game stems from the agencies that have grown up to represent golfers, but Palmer played a key role even there. Mark McCormack is the founder of International Management Group (IMG), the largest sports agency in the world, and McCormack started out as the agent for a man named Arnold Palmer.

Cutting a handsome figure on the course, a man at ease with presidents and the common man, he was and is the greatest ambassador the game of golf has ever known. He is to golf what Muhammad Ali is to boxing. In the late 1950s and early 1960s, Palmer captured the public's imagination not only with his many victories but also with the way he won them.

Arnold first came to major public attention when he won the U.S. Amateur in 1954. He dominated the Masters, winning in 1958, 1960, 1962, and 1964 and tying for second in 1961 and 1965.

At the U.S. Open he was the champion in 1960, the runner-up in 1962, the co-runner-up in 1963, and the runner-up in 1966 (each time tied at the end of four rounds, he lost in a playoff) and 1967.

In the PGA, he was tied for runner-up in 1964, 1968, and 1970.

He won the British Open in 1961 and 1962 and was second in 1960.

When he won, he often won from way back. He would be many strokes off the pace at the end of three rounds, but would steadily cut the leader's margin until he passed him on the final holes. His exciting finishes drew the tournament's largest crowds, and the fans who would follow him on the course became known as "Arnie's Army."

Palmer was named player of the year by the PGA in 1960 and 1962.

Since 1937, the PGA has awarded the Vardon Trophy to the PGA tour regular with the lowest scoring average. Arnold Palmer won the Vardon in 1961 with a 69.85 average and won it again in 1962 (70.27), 1964 (70.01), and 1967 (70.18). He is one of only four players to win it more than three times.

He was the PGA money leader in 1958 with $42,608, 1960 with $75,263, 1962 with $81,448, and 1963 with $128,230.

Palmer ranks seventh on the list of all-time winners of major championships (the U.S. Open, the British Open, the PGA, the Masters, the U.S. Amateur, and the British Amateur), with seven victories. On the list of all-time winners of PGA tournaments, Palmer ranks fourth with sixty championships.

After moving to the Seniors tour, Palmer won the PGA Seniors' Championship in 1980 and 1984, the U.S. Senior Open in 1981, and the Senior Players Championship in 1984 and 1985. He won the Senior Skins Game in 1990, 1991, 1992, and 1993; going into the 1996 season, he was the all-time Skins leader in total winnings, with $855,000. Forbes placed him eleventh in the world for 1995 sports income with $14.1 million, $14.0 million of it from endorsements.

Some golfers do not begin the game until well into their teens, but Arnold Palmer was born into it:

I was born and raised on a golf course. My father was a golf professional, and I spent a great deal of my time playing cowboys and playing golf at the same time. And from the time I was aware of golf and all the aspects of the game, Jones and Hagen and Sarazen and Nelson and Snead and those people were the big names in the game of golf. And of course I followed that religiously, and I started playing golf at a very early age and thoroughly enjoyed it even though I played other sports and enjoyed them. I played baseball and football and basketball, but golf had a mystique for me that was one that I thoroughly enjoyed. The challenge was constantly there.

I started playing junior tournaments when I was about twelve years old. I played my first junior tournament, and I enjoyed the competition. I enjoyed competing against the other guys and I enjoyed all that was happening, and I knew that there was going to be some sort of an affair between myself and the game of golf. I didn't know how serious it would be, but as time went on and I got into high school and started playing on the high school team, the thrill and the excitement of playing competition was very evident.

My father was a golf professional, and he was very helpful with my golf game and giving me little tips about competition and how I would fare in competition. And it was something that I was fortunate to have, the fact that my father was a golf professional who had an interest in what I was doing and chose to help me in all ways, not just in actually playing the game but in learning the etiquette and learning to conduct myself as a gentleman, which was part of the game.

After winning the U.S. Amateur in 1954, Arnold Palmer joined the PGA tour the same year:

After having won the Amateur, I gave serious thought to being a businessman, not pursuing golf as a career. But shortly after winning the Amateur and continuing to work as a manufacturer's rep, I found that the desire and the drive to be on the golf course was greater than anything else. And shortly after that, I made the decision to turn pro and start playing on the tour.

In his second year, Palmer captured the first of his five dozen PGA championships when he won the Canadian Open with a dramatic finish:

I spent the first eight months playing professional golf not doing particularly well, although at times seeing a ray of light and seeing that the opportunity was there for me to do pretty well. And then, of course, one year almost to the day after having won the Amateur I won the Canadian Open, and that was a tremendous lift and boost that helped me to get started and really start winning a lot of golf tournaments.

In Palmer's rookie season of 1954, the PGA Tour was still in its infancy:

When I started on the tour, the largest tournament on the regular tour was about twelve or fifteen thousand dollars, and maybe there was one exception to that; that was the Tam O'Shanter George S. May event, which was a fifty-thousand-dollar tournament. So we played constantly on the tour, and for a number of years through the fifties where the biggest tournaments were fifteen-to-twenty-thousand-dollar tournaments and first prize was maybe, if you were fortunate, a couple thousand dollars. Today there are tournaments where the last place money is as large as the entire tournament purse was in the fifties.

An alumnus of Wake Forest University, Arnold Palmer is an impassioned advocate of NCAA golf, which has become a major source of PGA talent:

I have always felt, in my era and even before, that college golf was going to be the big thing in prepping young people to become professional golfers, and today it's becoming more and more the case. Most of the people who are playing professional golf today are going to college. It's almost like an apprenticeship. The guys going through college are spending a great deal of time practicing their golf and getting ready for the professional tour. And I don't think there's any question about it: a man who doesn't do the college tour bit is not as apt to step onto the tour and do as well.

From 1957 through 1964, Palmer ignited extensive interest in pro golf, not just in his native country, but internationally. He was the dominant golfer of the period, winning thirty-nine PGA Tour championships and more than a dozen foreign titles. His victories included four Masters green jackets, back-to-back British Open titles in 1961–62, and a U.S. Open championship in 1960. At the same time, suddenly most everyone in the United States had a TV set, and network TV brought prominent tournaments into the American living room. And golf achieved a special prominence because President Dwight Eisenhower, who held office from 1953 until 1961, was an avid golfer. Arnold Palmer was the right man at the right place at the right time:

I guess television, Eisenhower, all of those things came along with me at the same time, and I guess maybe again I was fortunate to be in that position to be able to enjoy the fact that golf was something that the people of the world were discovering. We can't really tell too much about what has happened because it's still happening and it's going to continue to happen. I think golf is a game that will revolutionize the world as far as the sports scene is concerned in the near future.

An all-around athlete with impressive physical strength, Arnold Palmer appreciates the athletic skills required to play championship golf:

Golf is just like any other sport. The guy that's most physically fit is the guy that's going to have the best chance to win. You can play any sport in the world, and if you're not physically fit, it's going to take its toll on you. So I don't have a question in my mind that golf certainly is number one, a sport, and a sport as tough as any other sport. The fact that you don't get beat in the head and you don't get legs broken and arms broken has nothing to do with the fact that it is a game that is played under some very extreme conditions. We see those conditions when we see tournaments such as the Masters, where the guys are under very heavy pressure. I have no question in my mind that the most fit guys are the guys who are going to win.

At his peak, Palmer was the greatest player in golf. His success came from an intense will to win:

I had a great determination to win, and I took that determination with me when I went on the golf course, and I think that is very important. Golf was my business. But I never failed to think of playing golf as a game. I hope I can continue to feel that it is a game and that you've got to get after it. You've got to attack it, and you've got to play it for all you're worth.

I've played reasonably well in major championships. The Open is one that I've been a little disappointed in. But I've won once and I've lost three times, I think, in playoffs, finished second once or twice on other occasions. I would like to have won it a couple of more times.

But in the Masters I've played very well in over the years, in the early years particularly. Not so much in the recent years, but I have a reasonable record there. The one tournament that of course has been fleeting to me is the PGA Championship. And of course I'm sorry that I haven't won that championship.

I think that major championships are suited for some people, and for some people they're not. And of course we've seen people who were really great players on the tour but were never fortunate enough to win any major championship, so you never know how that is going to react.

There is one thing about major championships that I suppose I have a quarrel with—I'm not sure who has decided what are or are not major championships. But the one tournament that I won and a few other players have won that I think is a major championship that is never announced as such and never carried as such is the U.S. Amateur Championship. And of all the golf tournaments I ever won, I think that one was probably the most difficult.

Palmer is best known for his victories in his home country, but he has also had enormous success abroad. In addition to winning many foreign championships, Palmer was a six-time member of the U.S. Ryder Cup team and a seven-time member of its World Cup team:

One of the things that is growing and is going to continue to grow very rapidly is international golf, and I think that a lot of the American players who have not experienced international competition are really missing one of the great excitements in the game of golf. I think that to be a well-rounded champion you really have to play internationally, and I think that it not only gives you a better point of view as far as the game is concerned, but it also makes you much more competitive. And if the American professional today is having a problem competing with the Europeans or the Japanese or whoever else it might be, they probably have not competed enough against those people on their own terms.

We play individually week in and week out, and I think that team play is fun for the players. I think it's interesting from an international competition point of view, and I think that it does take a little bit of monotony away from playing individual seventy-two-hole competitions every week. So the Ryder Cup, the Chrysler Cup, the America's Cup, the World Cup, whatever the team competition, I think they are very good and I think we should continue to have those championships.

Palmer has won ten Senior PGA Tour events, and he predicts that the senior tour will continue to be a big success:

I think that people enjoy seeing the competition, and I think that the Senior Tour is very competitive. I feel that if that competition was slowed to more of a pastime, the Senior Tour would have problems succeeding. But as long as the competition is there and you have the kind of names coming into it that we've had over the years, I don't see anything but continued success for the Senior Tour. It's very enjoyable, and of course, you start comparing ages and you start looking at people coming along and I enjoy very much that I'm competing with people that I've competed with for, in some cases, almost fifty years.

Arnie's Army has cheered Palmer to victory after victory, first on the regular PGA Tour and now on the Senior PGA Tour, and Palmer is grateful for their support:

It's been vitally important, because without that backing and without that support that the fans gave me, I suppose that my enthusiasm for traveling and playing wouldn't have been as great. Certainly I'm playing today partly because of the support the fans gave me. I love the competition, and I love what I do, but I also enjoy very much seeing the people who are following me and supporting the program as much as they do. And that certainly has encouraged me to continue to play.

JERRY RICE

It's hard to get a consensus about the best player ever to play a particular position in any sport. But you could get a consensus for the best wide receiver in the history of football. The name would be Jerry Rice. In statistics or talent or winning, Jerry Rice is the all-time leader. If you combine statistics, talent, and winning, Rice only increases his margin of victory.

Jerry Rice, at least in short bursts, is the fastest player in the NFL. If Rice has his man beat, the man stays beat. Rice has moves that shake him free from the best defensive backs in the NFL. And he can take a hit. At six-foot-two and 200 pounds, a little bigger and stronger than most receivers, and just maybe tougher, he can take multiple hard hits in the same game, get up, and gracefully grab the next ball for a touchdown.

Though he was NFL Rookie of the Year in 1985 and Most Valuable Player in 1987, Jerry Rice has never been even the most famous member of his team. That honor has always gone to the quarterback, first Joe Montana and now Steve Young. But taking nothing away from those two Hall of Fame-bound QBs, one must wonder just how successful they would have been if they could not have thrown to number eighty.

Jerry Rice has led the NFC in receptions in 1986 and 1990 (when his 100 catches also led the NFL). His 1,570 yards in 1986 remain an NFL record. He led the NFL in scoring in 1987 with 138 points.

Rice is a leader in many single-season categories. His twenty-two receptions for touchdowns in 1987 are still the most ever. Rice also ranks seventh, and is tied (with himself) for ninth with seventeen TDs in 1989 and fifteen in both 1986 and 1993. His 112 receptions in 1994 tie him for second. In touchdowns by rushing, passing, or returns, his twenty-three in 1987 tie him with O. J. Simpson for second in that category, behind only John Riggins's twenty-four in 1983.

What about a single game? With thirty points at Atlanta in 1990, Rice is tied for fifth on the list for most points. In the same game, he tied for first on the list for most touchdowns receiving.

Here are Jerry Rice's rankings in the all-time NFL statistics: In receiving yardage he's number one, with 15,123. In receptions he's number one, with 942. In TD receptions he's number one, with 146. In touchdowns he's first, with 156. All these statistics are over only eleven years.

How about winning? Jerry Rice's San Francisco 49ers won the Super Bowl in 1989, 1990, and 1995 and made it to the NFC championship games following the 1990, 1992, and 1993 seasons.

His three Super Bowl appearances gave Rice a chance at the Super Bowl record book, and he wrote his name all over it:

All-time leader in points, at forty-two. Tied for second place are Roger Craig, Franco Harris, and Thurman Thomas, at twenty-four.

All-time leader in touchdowns, with seven. Second place is four.

First in receptions, with twenty-eight. First in reception yardage, with 512; second place is 323. First in all-purpose running, adding fifteen rushing yards for a total of 527.

Single-game Super Bowl records? Here we go:

Tied for first in receptions, with eleven in 1989. On the same list, he's also fourth with ten in 1995. All alone in reception yardage, at 215 in 1989 (and fifth with 149 in 1995 and sixth with 148 in 1990). Third in all-purpose running, with 220 in 1989. Tied for first in scoring, with eighteen points in both 1990 and 1995 (the men tied with him are also from San Francisco: Roger Craig, 1985 and Ricky

Watters, 1995). Tied for first in touchdowns, with three in both of those years (again, with Craig and Watters).

Perhaps most impressive about Rice's amazing statistics: after his 1985 rookie season, Rice hasn't been able to sneak up on anybody. He regularly draws the opposing team's best defensive back, and he's often double-teamed.

I think there are important similarities between a great receiver and a great basketball rebounder and that those similarities explain why Jerry Rice is the ultimate receiver in football. You've got to go up, you've got to figure, "That ball belongs to me, and I'm gonna get it." If the ball comes down and there are two or three defenders around, or if somebody hits the quarterback's arm and the pass is fluttering, a Jerry Rice will decide, "That ball's mine," just like a great rebounder will.

Plus, Jerry Rice has an unbelievable workout ethic, not just during the season but in the off-season. There are people who go to work out with him. Ricky Watters told me about working out with Jerry Rice. Roger Craig worked out with Jerry Rice. Other athletes have, too, but nobody can ever stay with Jerry, especially when Jerry starts running up hills. Walter Payton was famous for the hard workouts he designed for himself, but when he worked out with Jerry Rice, even he couldn't keep up.

Jerry Rice made his name at a small black college, Mississippi Valley State in Itta Bena:

I think my collegian days really got me ready for the pros. For one thing, we had a tough work ethic at Mississippi Valley State University, and it made me into a better football player, because I knew what to expect when I came into the NFL, and everything fell into place for me.

No defensive back intimidates Jerry Rice:

If they feel they can intimidate you, they can take you away from your game. But also, I've been around for a long time. I feel I'm a veteran now, and I can't get intimidated. I know exactly what my role is. They pay me to go out and make catches and help this ball club to win, so I try not to think about intimidation. When I go up against a good defensive back, I know my work is cut out for me. For one thing, he's not going to play cornerback if he's not the best athlete on the field. So I go in with a lot of intensity and just try to get the job done.

Jerry Rice set records at Mississippi Valley State, where he was a Division II All-American. Even so, he was concerned that in the NFL draft he might be overlooked:

I think there is doubt in every player that he might not get drafted. You never know what's going to happen in a draft. You might get chosen and you might not. But I had it down in my mind just in case I didn't get drafted, that I would do something else. But everything worked out for me, and once the 49ers called my name, I said to myself, "I'm going to get me a Super Bowl ring." It didn't work out that way because my first year, we went to the playoffs and we lost to the Giants, but everything is working out now. I'm having fun here with the 49ers, and I feel a big part of this football team.

On some teams, there is an unfriendly rivalry between star wide receivers. The 49ers have had many talented players play that position during Rice's tenure, most obviously John Taylor. But Rice says there has never been any unpleasant competition:

We don't really compete against each other. Maybe during training camp, because we feel we have to work for this job. Once we achieve this job, then we can focus in on our football, but we try not to compete against each other. It's just the opposing team when we go out every week. Just to see if we can come up with the big plays. If we can win the football game, that's the most important factor.

Jerry Rice seemingly has done it all, but even he has a dream he hasn't yet achieved:

My dream catch is catching the ball on the five-yard line, bouncing off guys, and going ninety-five yards. That's my dream catch, but I don't know when that might happen. If we can catch the football underneath, we could make something happen. We make the defense miss and make a big play. We are not the type to catch the football and just fall down.

Rice had a close football relationship, but not a close social relationship, with Joe Montana:

We had a great working relationship. But once we left that place, certain players hung out together, but I'm the type that I like to be by myself. I spend a lot of time by myself. But I felt Joe and I had the best chemistry in football because I knew exactly what Joe was thinking at all times and vice versa.

During practice, we talked about so many situations. If I ran a pattern and it didn't work out like we drew it up on paper, we'd come back together and talk about it. And in a game situation, everything was going to work out because we practiced all week long on that particular pattern, and it worked.

In high school, Jerry Rice was an all-around athlete. Does he fantasize about playing another sport?

I love tennis, I love basketball, but I think basketball. I might fit in with the Golden State Warriors. I've got a pretty good outside jumper, and I consider myself as being the next Michael Jordan. So that's my dream fantasy: to play NBA basketball.

CAL RIPKEN, JR.

Baltimore Orioles shortstop/third baseman Cal Ripken, Jr., was the biggest story in baseball in 1995.

Records are made to be broken. With one or two exceptions. One exception was the record for most consecutive games played, 2,130. After all, it was set back in 1939 by the immortal Lou Gehrig. After all, Gehrig was called the Iron Horse. After all, Gehrig played with Babe Ruth on the most legendary teams in the history of baseball. After all, on July 4, 1941, a plaque was placed at Yankee Stadium that referred to Lou Gehrig as "a man, a gentleman and a great ballplayer, whose amazing record of 2,130 consecutive games should stand for all time."

As the 1995 season approached, only one big hurdle loomed between Ripken and the record. Because of the conflict between major league players and owners, "replacement players" had already played many exhibition games. If the replacement players played in regular season games, Ripken's consecutive game streak would come to a halt. Ripken was a union man and had vowed not to cross a picket line.

Fortunately, the conflict was settled in time for the regular season, and Ripken's streak remained unbroken. Not incidentally,

Ripken's humble and earnest pursuit of the record restored some of the luster to the game that had been lost in the strife between owners and players.

On September 6, 1995, came the game in which—assuming he played and assuming the game went long enough to become official—Ripken would break Gehrig's record. A sellout crowd of 46,272 fans packed Baltimore's Camden Yards for the game between the Baltimore Orioles and the California Angels. Among those in attendance were President Bill Clinton, Vice President Al Gore, and Baseball Hall of Fame members Joe DiMaggio and Brooks Robinson.

As the top of the fifth inning ended and the game became official, the crowd erupted in a roar and a banner proclaiming "2,131" dropped on the B&O Railroad building behind right field.

The game was delayed for twenty-two minutes, fifteen seconds. The crowd brought Ripken out for eight "curtain calls." He took a victory lap, in which he shook the hands of children, teenagers, security guards, pitchers in the Oriole bullpen, and members of the opposing team.

Ripken spoke to the crowd:

> Tonight, I stand here overwhelmed, as my name is linked with the great and courageous Lou Gehrig. I'm truly humbled to have our names spoken in the same breath. I know that if Lou Gehrig is looking down on tonight's activities, he isn't concerned about someone playing one more consecutive game than he did. Instead, he's viewing tonight as just another example of what is good and right about the great American game.

One footnote to the consecutive game record shows just how extraordinary it is: yes, Gehrig played 2,130 straight games. But next on the list after Ripken and Gehrig is not a player who played two thousand games or even nineteen hundred. Third place goes to Everett Scott, who played in Boston and New York and didn't miss a game from 1916 to 1925; he held the record before Gehrig, but his streak was "only" 1,307 games. In fact, only six players in major league history have ever played more than a thousand consecutive games. By the end of the 1996 regular season, Ripken's record stood at 2,316.

But Ripken is remarkable for more than longevity. He was voted Most Valuable Player of the American League in 1983 and 1991. In the former year, he batted .318, with twenty-seven home runs and 102 runs batted in, and his team won the World Series four games to one over the Philadelphia Phillies. In the latter year, Ripken hit .323 with thirty-four homers and 114 RBIs.

At the start of the 1996 season, Ripken was fourth on the list of active players with the most RBIs, with 1,267 in 2,218 games, for an average of .57 per game. He was eighth on the list for most hits, with 2,371 in 8,577 at-bats, giving him a lifetime batting average of .276 over fifteen years. Forbes ranked Ripken sixteenth in the world in sports income for 1995: $6.3 million from salary and $4.0 million from endorsements, for a total of $10.3 million.

I have not had the good fortune to spend much time with Cal Ripken, though I have met him a couple of times. But to know what kind of man he is, all you'd have to do is watch him the night he broke Gehrig's record. You could see his character in the way he conducted himself. This is obviously not a man who thirsted for fame: if renown had not been thrust upon him by the pursuit of the Gehrig record, Cal Ripken would just seem like the guy next door, the guy sitting in the next booth at a coffee shop. And I mean that as a high compliment.

Growing up in Aberdeen, Maryland, Ripken was an all-around athlete:

All the sports really interested me. I tried all of them. A lot of them came easy. I seemed to understand the sports pretty well—basketball, soccer. I didn't have the opportunity to play organized football only because of my dad being in the minor leagues, and we never got back in time for me to join the football league.

But it was evident really early that compared to the other kids I was much better at baseball than I was in basketball or some of the other sports. It just came so easy, and I understood it, and it wasn't a matter of physical size. All of a sudden you could be the smallest person, and you could still be one of the dominating players in baseball. I'd say probably at around ten or eleven I knew that I had a special talent and I thought I could be a professional baseball player.

Cal Ripken, Sr., was a coach and manager in the minor leagues and major leagues; he would eventually manage his own son with the Orioles. Cal Sr.'s work—especially in the minor leagues, where he coached when Cal Jr. was a child—did not provide the advantages to his son that people might think:

Other parents of other Little League kids would tell their kids after a loss, "Well, that's all right. His dad's in professional baseball, and he works with him every single day."

And people thought my dad was out there throwing me ground balls and throwing batting practice to me and showing me how to hit and showing me how to steal from morning till night. But that's farthest from the truth because my dad, being in professional baseball, had a great deal of responsibility. If you're a minor league manager, you're also the hitting coach, the pitching coach. You throw batting practice. So that took up most of my dad's time.

Where I really learned to play baseball was going to the ballpark with my dad and listening to him instruct the infielders and instruct the pitchers and going to clinics with him when he would talk about baseball and the basic fundamentals. He never really worked with me personally one-on-one. I seemed to have to be around it and listen.

And when I went out and played the game, I actually tried some of those things he said. So the biggest advantage that I had that most kids don't have is that if I needed an answer to something, I had someplace to go to get that answer: "How do you field a ground ball here?" "How do you back-end a ball there?" "What do you do when the pitch is inside?" "What happens when the pitch is outside?" And not only could I ask my dad, but I had the opportunity to ask any of the baseball players that were in the minor leagues.

I asked Don Baylor, Al Bumbry, Doug DeCinces. There was a system that I quickly developed. I would go to these certain players and get information from them. They would say, "You catch a fly ball with two hands on the right side of your body."

I would say, "O.K." And I would go back to my dad at the end of the day, and I'd say, "I talked to Don Baylor today, and he said I should catch a fly ball like this, with two hands," and I'd show him what he told me. And my dad would say, "That's right." And when he said that, I knew Don Baylor was O.K. to talk to.

But if I went to an outfielder and he said, "You catch a fly ball with one hand on your left side," and I went to ask my dad and he would say, "That's not right," I would "X" that guy off my list.

So I quickly learned who I should talk to and who I shouldn't talk to. And I could talk to pitchers, outfielders, infielders, catchers, and then go back and bounce it off my father to make sure I was getting accurate advice.

At Aberdeen High School, Cal Ripken, Jr. played shortstop and third base and was a pitching ace. He won the Harford County batting title with a .492 average and led all pitchers with an amazing earned run average of just 0.70. He struck out a hundred batters in only sixty innings:

I enjoyed all aspects of the game, but a lot of times in Little League or high school, most of the action is pitching. You're in every single play. I like the positions where you're in the most action. And I picked shortstop because when you're not pitching, that seems to be the second position with the most action, besides maybe the catcher, which I tried a couple of times and didn't like a whole lot.

Again, I got to learn some of the inside things about pitching. At an early age I knew how to throw a curveball, and I knew how to throw a change-up, and how to throw a different type of change-up. So I really enjoyed pitching, but I also knew that at a professional level, in order to play every single day, you can't be a pitcher. I couldn't get over the fact that if I was drafted as a pitcher, I would only get to play one out of every four or five days. And fortunately enough I had a choice.

Earl Weaver was the manager of the Orioles, and he had the opportunity to see me take batting practice at Memorial Stadium, and when I was drafted, I think a lot of people wanted me to go to rookie league as a pitcher. And Earl spoke out and said, "I've seen him hit, and I think we should give him the opportunity to be a regular player." He gave me the opportunity to see if I could be a regular player first, and if that didn't work out, then I could always go back and try to be a pitcher after that.

It was at shortstop that Ripken made his career. He is the tallest man ever to play the position regularly in the majors. His agility may derive partly from the basketball and soccer he played as a child:

I would highly recommend at an early age to learn other sports. It hasn't been proven that some of the movements in other sports can make you a better baseball player, but I think for reasons of agility and coordination, if you learn to play other sports, they can be useful in your main sport.

I still play a lot of basketball in the off-season. It gives an explosive kind of training—quick movements that I think can help you in baseball and keep you having your legs underneath you. I think when you get older you start to get the Rubber Legs Syndrome. So I play basketball to stay in shape.

Ripken hit only eight home runs in his first two years in the minor leagues. In 1980 at Charlotte, however, he hit twenty-five homers, drove in seventy-eight runs, and earned a quick promotion to AAA Rochester:

When I was drafted, I was six-two, one eighty. So physically I was a late bloomer. I'm now six-four and about two twenty-five. And there's a lot to power. When you go to the minor leagues and you try to hit a ball far, you tend not to hit it so far. The more you play, the more at bats you have, the more you realize that power really comes from waiting longer and generating a quicker swing and having everything come together at one time.

A lot of people make the mistake of thinking they've got to start their body real soon and swing real hard with their whole body. And to me, learning to wait a little bit longer and let the fastball get a little closer to you before you explode on it translated into power. Maybe that's the kind of hitter I am.

Then actually getting stronger physically and putting on a little bit more weight helped me hit the ball over the fence, whereas before maybe I was just reaching the warning track. So I think it was a combination of learning how to hit, learning how to wait on the ball, and gaining some physical strength, and all of a sudden the home runs came.

Ripken thoroughly enjoyed his four years in the Orioles' farm system:

When I look back on my career, some of the best memories come from the minor leagues or winter ball, where everyone is really in the same boat and you spend a lot of time together.

In the minor leagues everybody's fighting to get to the big leagues, but it's not a cutthroat type of fighting. Everyone's in their own individual position, and you're trying to get to the next level. But while you're at the level, you spend all that time with the group of players that have been assembled and put on that one team. You spend a lot of time on the field, but you spend a lot of time off the field, in bus rides and just hanging out with each other, because you go to a new city where you don't know a whole lot of people.

Most guys aren't married, and you rely on each other for companionship as well as you rely on them on the field as teammates. You make some really good friends and you learn a lot about baseball, so there's some really good moments, when I think back. Probably the best moments are the minor league days.

But Ripken soon graduated to the majors, where he became the American League's 1982 Rookie of the Year:

I didn't know what to expect. Most of my experiences in professional baseball as a child all centered on the minor leagues. I very rarely got a chance to hang around the big leagues, and it wasn't until I guess my dad got to the big leagues when I was sixteen and I had one opportunity, one season to take batting practice down there and hang around it. But it seemed so strange. It seemed so different from the minor leagues.

And when I went to the minor leagues, I felt kind of comfortable being drafted and going down. I was very scared at first, but once I started to play a little bit more, I felt comfortable with the whole situation, being away from home, and I was able to develop, and my skills were able to come along, and I was able to move up.

But once I got to the big leagues it was a whole different ball game. You went from small stadiums and small media coverage to, all of a sudden, these huge stadiums where the stands were sold out, and it was just a crazier and different atmosphere. So coming into the big leagues, I wasn't really prepared for it. It was new, and it took a long time to adjust to playing in front of a lot of people and knowing that if you made a mistake you would be all over the newspapers all over the country or that people would be able to read about it or see you on TV. Those kinds of things I hadn't thought about before.

But now the big leagues have become enjoyable:

It's a lot of fun. The stakes are a little bit higher. It's a little bit more serious. I'm blessed with the talent to be able to play, and I thoroughly enjoy it. I enjoy myself in practice. I enjoy myself in the game.

But sometimes it gets serious. Every single day you have to do it. You have to develop a professional and serious approach to what you do, because the bottom line is that you're trying to win. And that's the real difference between the amateur and pro ranks. In the amateur leagues, if you have a bad day or you lose, it's really not the end of the world. But in the professional ranks, it seems like the end of the world. It seems like you're a professional now and you should go out and take care of your job and not have bad days.

As a two-time winner of a Golden Glove, and the shortstop on the Sports Illustrated *all-time team unveiled in the October 1992 issue, Ripken is strong in the field as well as at the plate:*

There are two parts to the game. There's the offensive part and there's the defensive part. And the better you are at separating the two, the better you're gonna be defensively and offensively. If you make an error in the field and then you come in and you're thinking about the error when you go up to the plate, it's going to affect your hitting, and you're not going to be as good a hitter. And when you're not hitting real well, it usually affects your fielding, because while you're in the field, you're thinking about why you're not hitting real well.

So I've always been able to separate the two, and a lot of times I take the approach, if I'm not hitting well, then I'm going to do a little better in the field. I'm going to concentrate a little bit better, or maybe I can make the key play of the game. Maybe I can turn a double play in the eighth inning that helps us win. And I might be 0-for-5, but as long as you make that key play, you've had a good day. So I turn it around. If you're not fielding well then you're going to try to hit a little better or contribute to your team's success with the bat.

In the minors, because of an injury to another player, Ripken moved from shortstop to third base, and he excelled there. But after Ripken joined the Orioles, manager Earl Weaver had a surprise for him:

Earl one day decided to move me to shortstop without even really telling me. One day, there was a "6" next to my name in the lineup as opposed to a "5," "5" meaning third, "6" meaning short. I thought it was just a mistake, that he wrote the wrong number down. But it turned out he wanted me to play short. And he asked me just to go out and make the routine plays. If the ball came to me, just catch it, take your time, and throw the ball to first base.

And so I had to learn the position all over again— shortstop— at the big-league level. It was a struggle at first, but I think once I learned I could play third base, when I went back to short, it was a whole lot easier. I was ready for the longer throws. I was ready for playing a little deeper. And I was ready for the double plays and all the things that are required at shortstop.

And maybe because I had grown physically and my arm strength had come up a little bit, it was much easier going back to shortstop. They're similar positions, but they're very different. You're on the same side of the infield. At third, it's the hot corner. You have to react very quickly to balls to your left and right, maybe one or two steps. At shortstop all of a sudden you have all this ground to cover. You're responsible for four to five steps to your right, four or five steps to your left. And you have to come in. You have to go back. The responsibilities are so much greater at shortstop, and it took me awhile to be comfortable and deal with that. But I was glad I had the opportunity to go back to shortstop.

The most difficult play is probably the ball that goes deep in the hole, because it's a longer throw and, with a fast runner, you don't have any time. You just have to catch it, and you might not have a good grip on the ball, and you have to let it go and just hope it's on-line.

Most of it is preparation. You have to think about what's going to happen and what the situation is. You run over all the possibilities in your mind. If the ball's hit slowly, if the ball's hit hard, if it's hit to my right, if it's hit to my left, what am I going to do with it? Then you come up with answers. Then, when the ball is hit to your right and to your left, you instinctively react, and you know what to do with it.

If you don't know what's going on and all of a sudden a ball's hit to your right and you react naturally to catch the ball but you don't know where you're going to throw it or how you're going to make the play, then you're going to mess the play up.

Ripken is consistent not just in suiting up for a record number of consecutive games and not just in the field; he's also consistent as a hitter. As of the start of the 1996 season, he was one of only eight players in major league history to hit more than twenty home runs in ten consecutive seasons:

A lot of the problems in hitting are mental. You might feel a little bit tired physically, so you sit there and analyze. You say, "Well, I'm a little tired today, so I have to change something in my swing. I have to start a little faster." And then your brain kind of gets in the way of your skills.

You practice it over and over and over again, where it's a reaction. You see the ball and you react to it and you hit it. And that's muscle memory.

Sometimes I think the mind or the brain interferes with that. Sometimes you can psych yourself out. You go against a pitcher like Roger Clemens and you say, "He's throwing really well, I can't hit him." And that can be part of a slump. If you can just take the mental aspect of it and keep a real easy feel and allow your physical skills and your reactions to take place, I think you're much better off.

Ripken hits with power, but he doesn't swing for the fences:

I think the key to my success is that if I hit for a pretty good average, that means I'm going to be consistent. The power numbers will take care of themselves. The RBI numbers—everything else will fall in line. So you've got to convince yourself that you want to have a successful at-bat every time. And a successful at-bat, at least by my definition, is you want to see the ball and then put a good swing on it and hit the ball on the good part of the bat. You're not always going to hit a line drive. You're not always going to get a hit.

But if you can consistently go up there and have successful at-bats, then over the course of a long season, six hundred fifty at-bats later, you're going to have pretty good numbers. And you put too much pressure on yourself if you just look at that one at-bat, knowing the situation dictates different things for different players.

If you're a player that moves the guy over from second to third with a bunt or hits the ball to right field or you're a hit-

and-run guy, then you have specific things you have to try to do with the bat. If you're an RBI guy or a guy that can hit the ball out of the ballpark, your job relatively stays the same regardless of who's on base.

A lot of times, if you're able to put out of your mind the people on base in a bases-loaded situation or an RBI situation or a team-winning situation, you can say to yourself, "O.K., I'm going to have a successful at-bat. I'm going to see the ball. I'm going to make sure the ball's in this area. I'm going to get a good look at it, put a good swing on it." If you can do that, you're going to be successful driving in the runs just like you're going to be successful hitting the ball with nobody on base.

When you get to a big part of a game and you start thinking to yourself, it goes back to the mental part of the game. Really, your at-bat is no different with people on base than it is with nobody on base. You just have to convince yourself the guy's going to throw the ball, and I can see it and I have to hit it. The crowd thinks it's a bigger at-bat. And everyone watching the game on TV thinks this is a huge at-bat. And if you think in those terms—you're the player at home plate and you're saying, "Golly, fifty thousand people are screaming, and I've got to get this hit"—then you're starting to work yourself up and getting outside your means to be successful.

If you're able to go back and really simplify it and say, "O.K., you've still got to throw the ball, and this situation is no different than any other situation; he'll throw it up there, I'll get a good look at it, I'll put a good swing on it"—you're going to approach it the right way and you're going to be successful one more time. All hitters react to pressure a little bit differently. But if I start thinking about it—"I gotta do it, I gotta do it"—then I won't do it.

As he approached Lou Gehrig's record, Cal Ripken said his own streak had come from his enjoyment of the game:

I haven't allowed myself to sit down and really analyze it, trying to understand the streak. To me, it's just something that's happened. It's something that has developed over a period of time because of the fact that I like to play.

I want to play every single game. I've always been someone, even with other sports, who's wanted to be in the action. You can't do anything if you're sitting on the bench watching, and you can't do anything if you're on the sidelines. So I always want to be in the middle of the action and that's how I've always approached it. But now that I'm in the streak, everyone makes a big deal out of it. Everyone has an opinion about it. Then you really have to sit back and say, "I realize there's a streak," and I have to manage that situation as best I can, not to let it interfere with my focus. And so I accept it, but at the same time I don't try to change my approach or my focus one bit.

My goal is to approach the game the same way I did my first or second year, before there was a streak. I play just to be successful in this particular game. And then when they begin tomorrow I want to be in that game, and I want to play that game. And when that game's over, I want to be in the next game. That's how I got to this point, and that's how I want to continue to play.

PETE ROSE

Pete Rose is the greatest baseball player never elected to the Hall of Fame. In that single sentence are the two elements that make up the unique story that is Pete Rose. On the one hand, he is a remarkable ballplayer, a record-setter, a winner, a man who tried as hard as anyone ever has. On the other hand, he is a man victimized by his own mistakes and by the judgments rendered on those errors.

Pete Rose holds the all-time major league records in three categories: most hits (4,256), most at-bats (14,053), and most games played (3,562). He is fourth all-time in runs scored (2,165) and sixth in total bases (5,752).

Pete Rose broke in as the National League's Rookie of the Year in 1963. He led the NL in batting in 1968 (.335), 1969 (.348), and 1973 (.338). He was the league's Most Valuable Player in 1973. On the all-time list for most consecutive games played, Rose is both number eleven (with 745 games) and number fifteen (with 678). In 1978, when he hit in forty-four consecutive games, Rose tied the National League record previously held exclusively by Willie Keeler. His lifetime average, accomplished over twenty-four seasons, was .303.

Rose's Cincinnati Reds won the NL championship in 1970,

1972, 1975, and 1976, capturing the World Series in the last two years. Traded to the Philadelphia Phillies, Rose was a member of the World Series champion team of 1980 and the NL-winning team of 1983.

Nobody played with more intensity than did Pete Rose. But you can play with too much intensity, and on occasion he did. I saw him in the All-Star Game in which he ran over catcher Ray Fosse and ended Fosse's career. I couldn't believe that one baseball player would risk—and cause—severe injury to another, especially in a game that is in many respects just an exhibition.

I believe that despite his denials, Pete Rose did bet on baseball. It was never proved beyond a reasonable doubt, but saying Rose wasn't guilty is like saying O. J. Simpson isn't guilty of the crimes with which he was charged: everybody—including people who know him well— thinks Rose bet on baseball games. Whether he did any harm to anybody by betting on his own sport is beside the point, because betting on baseball was a violation of his contract. So while Rose was a competent, hustling player, in many people's eyes Rose is not a hero.

Pete Rose's remarkable life in sports began normally enough, in the footsteps of a father who played many sports, including semipro football:

I was just barely walking before I started into sports, not just baseball. I was very fortunate that I had a father who was an athlete. Everywhere he went, he took me with him. He exposed me to all sports. Wintertime he played football, summertime he played softball, autumn time he played basketball. I was always either the water boy or the ball boy for the baseball team.

Whenever it was Sunday morning, me and my daddy had a football game to go to. He didn't have to look for me. I was in the car waiting for him to get in and go to the football game or to the baseball game if there was a baseball game on Friday night, or to the basketball game if there was one on Wednesday night. He didn't have to worry about where Pete was. Pete was in the car waiting to go, because I got to practice with him before the game and I got to be part of it. Just watching was part of it.

I've only idolized one person in my life, and that was my father. I always tried to live up to his expectations and his dedication and his work ethic. I learned those things by watching him. He was a banker in Cincinnati for about thirty-seven years, and he was on time to work every day and he worked until the job was done, and he was very consistent. I think in any sport, in any way of life, if you can develop consistency and if the talent's there, you're going to end up being number one.

Probably the most important thing he made me realize was the difference between winning and losing. At the same time, he made me realize that you weren't a sore loser if you got beat. He made me realize that if you got beat, you concentrated on the things and the reasons why you got beat, so if the situation came up again, you would win the next time around.

Everybody loses in different things, but there again, losing is a very easy habit to get into because obviously every year there's more losers than winners in every sport. And if you accept losing, you're in for a long career. You're in for a long life.

Rose's dad influenced not only his son's values but also the way he hit:

When I was nine years old, my father told the coach that he wanted me to be a switch-hitter. My uncle had been in the minor leagues and hadn't become a switch hitter until he was thirty. And that's when he enjoyed his biggest success in baseball.

So my father made a pact with the coach, and he said, "Hey, I want Pete to be a switch-hitter, no matter whether it's a championship game, an all-star game, or a regular-season game. And I'll never take him away from you during the season as far as going on a vacation. He'll be here at every game."

When I was in high school, football was the number-one sport for me. I was always a lot better football player than baseball player. I wasn't the best player on my Little League team. A guy by the name of Eddie Brinkman, who signed with the Washington Senators, was the best player on our team.

If I really would have liked going to school, which I didn't—and that was my mistake—I would have gone to the University of Tennessee to play football.

But I really loved baseball, too, and I had an inside in baseball. The inside was my uncle, who was a scout with the Reds. To be honest, if my uncle wasn't a scout for the Reds, I probably wouldn't have gotten a chance to play baseball, because when I graduated from high school in 1960 I was about five-foot-ten, five-foot-eleven, but I only weighed one-fifty, one-fifty-five.

My uncle somehow convinced the Reds that everybody in my family physically matured late. My dad was twenty-one years old and weighed a hundred and five pounds. He became a hundred-ninety-five pounder. My uncle convincing the Reds that I would grow eventually enabled the Reds to give me a shot, a chance to play baseball.

All through my Little League career I was a catcher. Then all of a sudden, I become a sophomore in high school, and they put me at second base because of my size. And when I was a senior, I was ineligible to play baseball. So I had only my first sophomore year, my second sophomore year, and my junior year.

In my senior year I played in an AA amateur league up in Dayton, Ohio. There were older men. I hit off a guy thirty-five years old who was a former minor league player. I was a catcher.

And the rest is history.

Pete Rose's history as a professional baseball player started with the Cincinnati Reds:

It was exciting signing my first professional contract, especially because growing up in Cincinnati, three or four miles from Crosley Field and wanting to be a member of the Reds your whole life, all of a sudden you get an opportunity to go to the minor leagues and play with the Reds.

In those days they didn't have a draft or anything like that. It was first come, first serve. Because of my size, a lot of teams turned me down.

Rose was not courted by many teams, yet he became a great success. He explains how that can happen—in particular, how a player not drafted high can nonetheless become a star:

You get a lot of top players who were not drafted high. Let me tell you why. I think because a lot of scouts are caught up in the stopwatch. They're caught up in how hard a guy can throw. They're caught up in how far a guy can hit a ball instead of whether a guy can hit a ball consistently to all fields.

If he runs a four point five from home to first, they just put an X by his name. But if he runs four point zero, they put a big C by his name. They want him. They don't put a guy's heart into the situation. They don't put a guy's attitude into the situation.

I was just an average runner, and I could hit from both sides, but I was too small, so I was overlooked by most everybody. Everybody except the ones who made an in-depth study into the type of attitude my family had and the kind of heart my family had.

They really put a lot of work into how was I growing up, what instructions I was getting, what kind of man was my father, what kind of an athlete he was.

I was the manager of the Reds for four or five years, and a

lot of times there was a lot of guys with a lot of ability, but I'd rather have a player who's got more heart and half as much ability, because he's going to get the job done. Ability doesn't always win. If you've got ability against ability, then ability will win. But if you've got ability against ability and heart and soul, heart and soul's going to win.

Pete Rose started his pro career with the Cincinnati Reds rookie league A team in Geneva, New York:

I graduated from high school on a Friday, I signed with the Reds on the Saturday, and I left on the Monday to go play minor league baseball. It was the first time I'd ever been away from home. I got on an airplane and flew to Syracuse and took a bus from Syracuse to Geneva, New York.

I thought I had a license to steal to go to New York and play baseball: here I was, nineteen years old, and they were going to pay me four hundred bucks a month, and I had played baseball for free every year for nineteen years.

You know, I was happy as a pig in slop being able to go play baseball every day instead of just Mondays, Wednesdays, and Fridays (or Sundays). I was going to be able to play Monday, Tuesday, Wednesday, Thursday, Friday, Saturday, and Sunday, so I was as happy as I could be.

I don't know if I was nervous. I probably was on cloud nine. I did O.K. I hit .277. I played as hard as I possibly could. I only played the last two months of the season. I remember I won two Samsonite suitcases for the most popular player on the team as voted by the fans. So I sort of made my mark with the fans from the first day I reported to Geneva, New York, to play for the Geneva Redlegs.

I had to work on my defense because, like I said, I had been a catcher all the way until my sophomore year in high school. I took as many ground balls as I could.

I know how to approach the game. I know how to play the

game the way it's supposed to be played, and I applied myself the right way. So it wasn't hard for me to practice extra. It wasn't hard for me to take ground balls for forty-five minutes. I worked hard in the cage, too; that's why I was always the last one to leave, because I was really a dedicated type of ballplayer, whether it was defense or offense.

I understood from an early age that if you got a glove on your hand, you got to think about defense and if you got a bat in your hand, you got to think about offense. And if you got a glove on your hand, you don't worry about being 0-for-four. Or if you've got a bat in your hand, you don't worry about making an error your last inning you were out on defense. It's very simple. Keep it as simple as you possibly can, and you have less chance of getting confused.

How did Pete Rose build himself up physically?

Right behind Crosley Field there's a railway express. I remember it like it happened yesterday. I made two dollars and eighty-three cents an hour unloading boxcars, and I worked from twelve o'clock at night until eight in the morning. I just did it to survive. But it built me up. I went from one-sixty-five to one-eighty that winter. And the next year, when I went to Macon, I went from one-eighty to one-ninety. And the next year, when I went to Cincinnati, one-ninety-three or one-ninety-five. And I played one-ninety-five to two hundred the rest of my career.

You know, I always did have big guns. I always was able to hit the ball out of the ballpark, but I wasn't a pull hitter. That's why I got so many hits, because the outfield couldn't play me like a Punch and Judy hitter. They had to respect the fact that I could hit the ball out of the park, but I just didn't pull the ball enough to be a home run hitter.

I think the size of my arms and the size of me as an individual was the reason I got so many hits. My body enabled me to play a lot of games and not get tired. I was rugged and I didn't get hurt. I missed ten games in the course of the ten-year period from 1970 until 1980.

They looked at me as a singles hitter because I didn't hit thirty home runs a year, but I'm sixth on the all-time list in total bases, and there's some pretty impressive names ahead of me. I got more doubles than anybody. And I got over a hundred and fifty triples. I got a hundred sixty home runs, but there are a lot of guys who don't have a hundred home runs. So I'm one of the very few players who have over a hundred home runs, over a hundred doubles, and over a hundred triples.

Some players ignore the fans. Not Pete Rose:

I think I'm one of the guys that understand the importance of fans. Fans make the whole thing revolve. What the hell is the sense of playing baseball if you don't have fans?

I've always appreciated the fans. I've always tried to cooperate with the fans, and sometimes you can't. I'm sure there are fans who will say I snowed them on an autograph. I've had people yell at me for autographs when I've got a base hit and I'm standing on first base. But I think overall I've signed as many autographs as any player that ever played the game.

I played all out, all innings of the game, and as long as I was out on the field I played like it was my last game, because it might have been my last game. Once the fans understood I was legitimate, they accepted me because hey, this guy's an animal. He's out there and he's playing hard, and he's playing every day and he's trying to give us our money's worth.

I used to wonder why I got booed every time I went to another town, but now I know why. I used to get booed louder than anybody when I went to Philadelphia as a Cincinnati Red, but when I played for the Phillies for five years, I never got booed in Philadelphia; then I got booed in

Cincinnati. I convinced myself that if I played for the town that was booing me they wouldn't boo me, and I proved that to myself in two different towns, Montreal and Philadelphia.

Pitchers might try to intimidate Pete Rose, but they wouldn't succeed:

I didn't try to intimidate pitchers. All I tried to do was to make clear when I was in the batter's box, home plate was mine. A guy knocking me down wasn't going to make me scared. I was going to hop back up and get a little closer to the plate.

I didn't do it to try and intimidate guys. I just did it because I was aggressive, and I think players understood I was aggressive. I was never thrown at purposely, because they knew it wasn't going to hurt me. What it was going to do was make me try harder. And that's the last thing in the world you want me to do is try harder against you, because if that was the case you weren't going to have a chance.

Rose had remarkable statistics, but even he depended on others:

The only thing I never worried about was who was ahead of me in the lineup, because I knew it was the pitcher. But other than that, you're only as good as the guy behind you. All those great years we had, I had Morgan behind me or I had Griffey behind me, then I had Bench and Perez coming up and Lee May. Davey Concepcion used to hit eighth and then the pitcher; that's why we had so many opportunities to knock in runs.

You see, baseball is an individual sport because you get paid on what you do individually. But it's also a team game because the end result is a win or loss for the team.

At Cincinnati we had probably one of the best teams in the history of baseball because we all complemented each other and we all did the things that we could do. See, everybody in this life has things they can do and things they can't do. And I didn't try to do the things I couldn't do. I didn't try to hit home runs. Bench didn't try to bunt with a man on third and two outs. He did the things he could do on a consistent basis, and that's why we won more games than anybody else.

Pete Rose became the first "singles hitter" to make $100,000 a year:

I really shopped for that because I got tired of people telling me that I couldn't make money in Cincinnati hitting singles and doubles. I said if you can hit enough singles and doubles you can make money anywhere.

I was the first hundred-thousand-dollar non-home-run hitter. They just called it singles, but I hit forty doubles every year. I led the league in doubles every year.

Rose wasn't just a tough ballplayer. He was a tough negotiator:

I held out every year. You know why I held out every year? Because I was fair. Because I wasn't one of those guys who asked for eighty thousand if I wanted fifty-five. If I wanted a hundred I didn't ask for a hundred and fifty.

That's why I held out, because if I wanted fifty-five thousand, I asked for sixty just to give them a little room. And you know, right away when you ask for sixty they think I wanted forty, and I wanted fifty-five. That's why I always had to hold out.

They wouldn't have a chance with me today if I go to arbitration. They wouldn't have enough money to pay me if I could go to arbitration like these players can.

In 1978, Rose hit in forty-four consecutive games, tying the all-time National League record. He was honored by President Jimmy Carter and the United States Congress:

PETE ROSE • 247

You know, it was fun for me, because I didn't understand
what everybody was making a hullabaloo about, because I
was getting paid to get hits and score runs. I just happened to
do it forty-four straight days. It was fun. It did a lot for me
nationally. It did a lot for me worldwide. It helped baseball. It
helped some teams get some attendance in. The Braves had
the biggest walk-in sale they ever had in their life. They sold
twenty-nine thousand tickets the day that I got number forty-
four off of Phil Niekro.

*Rose did not feel well treated in Cincinnati, and in 1979 he
became a free agent. He signed with the Philadelphia Phillies. It
worked out well for both parties:*

It was great. I wouldn't trade places with anybody for the
five years I spent in Philadelphia. Philadelphia's a great town.
We went to the playoffs three times, went to the World Series
twice, and won a World Series in 1980. I loved the fans in
Philadelphia. They're tremendous sports fans.

Mike Schmidt was the best player I ever played with.
When I went to Philadelphia in 1979, I think Mike Schmidt
was the best player in the league four days a week. And when
I left in 1983, I think Mike Schmidt was the best player seven
days a week. I think I taught him the importance of both
phases of the game of baseball, the defensive part and the
offensive part.

You can't hit home runs every day, and if you don't hit
home runs, you've got to do other things to help your team
win. He can do other things. He can field. He can run. He can
lead. He can do a lot of things, and that's why he's the best
player I ever played with.

Once he watched me, he understood that adversity
didn't bother me. My job was to play baseball. His job
became to play baseball, and he liked to play the game of
baseball.

Then it was ninety-five games in Montreal and then back to Cincinnati:

It was an opportunity for me to go back as a player/manager, and I think being in charge of something like that really rejuvenated me. I really caught fire again. When I went back to Cincinnati on August sixteenth or seventeenth, something like that, in 1984, I hit .365 the rest of the season, playing every day. I was playing great defense. And the next year, '85, was when I beat the [career hits] record, and I did well that year. Dave Parker led the league in RBIs and I was one of the reasons he did, because I only hit .265 or something, but I walked ninety-two times.

When Pete Rose got hit number 4,192, he eclipsed the record set by Ty Cobb:

Ty Cobb is the greatest hitter ever to live. No question about it, but I think I could have hit back in the teens and twenties just like he did. And I think he could hit in the seventies and eighties just like I did. I'd have to argue with people that believe that if Ty Cobb broke in in 1963 when I did that he'd have a .367 lifetime batting average.

I disagree with that. I've faced better pitchers than Ty Cobb did. I honestly believe that, but I don't take anything away from Ty Cobb. I'm just the guy who got the most hits. That means something. I give him credit as being the best hitter ever to hit a baseball. Obviously, he played twenty years and hit .367. You got to be a pretty good hitter.

But there's things I could do that he didn't do, and there's things that he could do I didn't do. We were totally different type ballplayers. I think the only similarity is we both hated to lose, and we were both very aggressive.

I'm a little different. I'm a little tough to compare with most guys because one, I'm a switch-hitter, and two, I played a lot of different positions. But then again, he did all that hitting.

I still played more winning games than anybody in the history of baseball. That means a lot to me, because the only thing I ever tried to do is to hit, score runs, and win games.

In 1989, the commissioner of Major League Baseball, A. Bartlett Giamatti, banned Pete Rose from the game for life on the ground that he had bet on sports, with an unofficial but public conclusion that he had bet on baseball and on his own team at that. How much did this upset Pete Rose?

The only thing that upset me is you could have told people I was a mass murderer and some guys would have wrote it without any verification or without any substantial evidence at all. That's the thing that disappointed me, the liberties the press took in some things. It's a wonder they didn't say I caused the earthquake in San Francisco or I sent the iceberg that got the Titanic. Any of that stuff could have come out, and people would have believed it.

There's a lot of bad writers, incompetent writers that don't know what the hell they're doing. They don't know how to come up with something positive and truthful. It was amazing to me how they carried on with anything they heard. I'm talking about friends of mine, guys that I cooperated with over the years. I just couldn't believe some of the things that they believed and some of the things that they wrote.

But once they write it, I can't do anything. You know, people got on me because I didn't comment on any of the stuff. But at the same time, they didn't realize that Commissioner Giamatti put the gag rule on me, told me not to say anything. And I was criticized for saying "No comment," yet that was what I was told to do by the commissioner's office. So nothing really went right for me in 1989 because my hands were tied.

An Ohio bookmaker, Ron Peters, said Rose had bet on baseball with him. Giamatti signed a letter to the court that tried Ron Peters on drug charges; the letter attested to Peters's "truthful cooperation" in the commissioner's investigation of Rose. Rose filed suit against Giamatti, Major League Baseball, and the Reds, seeking to have the commissioner replaced by "an impartial decision-maker" because of what they called his "displayed bias and outrageous conduct":

That letter is the only reason I wanted to go to court, because it was obvious to me that he had already made up his mind. And if you're the judge, jury, and executioner, you can't do that. You can't make up your mind like that. That's the only reason I didn't want to go in front of him. Not because I was worried about what he was going to do, but because he had already made up his mind.

The only thing that could have disappointed me with the commissioner was the way he handled his press conference. Because here's a man who reads a piece of paper, an agreement signed by him and I, and the agreement says there will be no finding that Pete Rose bet on baseball. And he puts the agreement down, and he turns around and looks at the press and smiles and says, "But I conclude that he did."

That's like a judge saying, "Pete Rose, you're not guilty of murder in the first degree, but I think you killed a person." The commissioner's conclusion should have remained to himself, because how dumb does that make someone look who signs an agreement saying there's no finding that he bet on baseball and then turns around and says I did? If he feels so strongly that way, why didn't he go to court and try to prove it, because he couldn't. It's just like I can't prove I didn't bet on baseball, because you can't prove a negative. But, I might add, no one can prove I did.

Rose finds it odd that athletes who use drugs are treated more leniently than those who gamble:

I know what my problem is, and I got it under control. It just seems like if you have a drug problem, you get four or five chances. If you have a gambling problem, you only get one chance, one chance and out of here.

It's not the same with drugs. They just send you away for thirty days and you come on back. Do it again, go away for sixty days and come on back. You know, I had one gambling problem, and I'm out of here for life. Now you tell me the justification of that. I don't understand it, but I made some mistakes, and I'm taking my punishment like a man. I'm not complaining to anybody. All I can do is not make the same mistakes again, clean that act up, and realize what I was punished for. And if I do that, and if I apply for reinstatement, I have to see the reason why they're not going to reinstate me.

But what if Rose had bet on baseball? So what? Would it be fair to punish a man who bet on his sport but didn't fix a game?

I'm a firm believer in this: if I bet on baseball, I shouldn't be allowed in baseball. I agree with that rule. But I can't believe that I'm banned from baseball for life because I bet on a football game, because I know a lot of guys who bet on football games. I know a lot of guys who bet on basketball games, and that's what I did.

I admitted that to then-Commissioner Ueberroth, then-Commissioner-to-be Giamatti, and then-Commissioner-to-be Fay Vincent. And you know what they told me when I said that? "We're not here to worry about any sport but baseball."

I said, "Well, sir, I did not bet on baseball." So the focus started out that I bet on baseball and the more months that went by, the focus changed because they knew they didn't have any proof. So the end result was they got me for just betting in general.

Though banned from baseball, Pete Rose was never banned from the hearts of his fans:

There's no question about that. I go to car shows, they sell out. I go to banquets, I get standing ovations because I think people could care less if I bet on a football game or a basketball game, because they see the odds in the papers every day, and they can go to Vegas, or they can go to Atlantic City, or they can go to Reno and do it. People understand that people are playing lotteries. People are playing bingo. It seems like everything around the country revolves around gambling. I get the impression that people think, "What did the man do? Let the man go on with his life. Don't hang him up because he bet on the Super Bowl game. What's the big deal?"

All told, how content is Pete Rose?

I've gone out and I've tried to accomplish things in a baseball uniform, which I have. I've dedicated myself. And it's amazing how many people in the media would forget about that because you bet on a football game. You start talking about "I'm not going to vote for him for the Hall of Fame because he bet on football, basketball," that's ridiculous. I think that's totally ridiculous. It's not like everybody in the Hall of Fame is an altar boy.

I had a gambling problem. No one can seem to understand that. If I told them I had a drug problem, they'd understand it. They'd give me all the sympathy in the world. Or if I had an alcohol problem, I'd get all the sympathy in the world. But now you have a gambling problem, you don't get no sympathy. I'm a good person with fans, good person with kids, good person with charitable events. I'm a good citizen.

MONICA SELES

When you write a book like this one, you go back over interviews. You read transcripts of interviews, you listen to tapes of interviews. You select whom to include, what excerpts to include. It was a little hard to listen to the tape of Monica Seles. The interview with her occurred in 1990. That was before.

Monica was sixteen then; so young, so bubbly. It doesn't show up in the excerpts here, but she punctuated most sentences with a little laugh, the modest, enthusiastic laugh of a young player who had not yet collided with all the realities of the world. Her accented speech was fast; more enthusiasm.

By 1993, Monica Seles was only nineteen, but she was the greatest woman tennis player in the world. Seemingly going all out all the time, emitting her trademark grunt as she pounded both forehands and backhands, Monica had already won eight Grand Slam singles titles, tying her for ninth on the all-time list. She had won thirty-two tournaments, also placing her ninth. The Yugoslavia-born star had won the Women's Tennis Association Tour Championship tournament in 1990, 1991, and 1992. She had won the Australian Open in 1991, 1992, and 1993, the French Open in 1990, 1991, and 1992, and the U.S. Open in 1991 and 1992. When she won the French in

1990, she became the youngest player to win a Grand Slam title in the twentieth century: she was sixteen.

Monica had beaten Germany's Steffi Graf in three Grand Slam finals and in 1991 had displaced her as the number one player in the world. That was the "crime" for which she was to pay dearly.

On April 30, 1993, things were to change for Monica Seles. She was still number one, and she was playing in a tournament in Hamburg. During a changeover, an unemployed German lathe operator named Gunter Parche came out of the stands and stabbed Seles in the back. He said he did it to make fellow German Steffi Graf the number-one women's player again.

They say that crime doesn't pay, but Parche got his wish: Graf won six of the following ten Grand Slam tournaments and was number one in 1993 and 1994. Amazingly, Parche received only a two-year suspended sentence.

Things did not go so well for Monica. At the time of the attack, she had won seven of the previous eight Grand Slam events she had played. As much as she wanted to, she was too traumatized to return immediately to tennis.

She was treated by Nevada sports psychologist Jerry Russel May. For more than two years, she avoided competition and the crowds that came with it. The Women's Tennis Association dropped her from its rankings. After all, though it wasn't her fault, she couldn't play.

In 1995, as Monica approached her return to competitive tennis, the WTA held a meeting. The issue: what ranking should Seles hold when she returned? The WTA finally decided that Seles and Graf would be co-ranked number one. The result: hard feelings in the world of women's tennis.

Martina Navratilova took Monica's side: "What's frustrating to me is that the players benefited from Monica's absence. They won more money, they won more Grand Slams, because she wasn't around, and now they're not willing to give back to her a little of what perhaps they gained by her absence."

Seles returned to tennis, but not a tournament, on July 29, 1995, almost exactly two and a quarter years since the stabbing. She played an exhibition match in Atlantic City against Martina. Monica won, 6–3, 6–2.

That must have helped: two weeks later, in her first tournament since the assault, she won the Canadian Open in Toronto. In the semifinals, she beat the great Gabriela Sabatini, 6–1, 6–0; in the final, she routed Amanda Coetzer, 6–0, 6–1.

Monica said, "I wasn't sure I'd ever be back to play tennis again. It's been such a struggle to get to this point, but from that day to this day, what a difference!"

On September 9, 1995, Seles met Graf in the final of the U.S. Open, the first time in thirty-one months that they had faced each other in a Grand Slam final. The hard-fought match took an hour and fifty-two minutes. The ending was not from the storybook: it was Graf who won, 7–6 (8–6), 0–6, 6–3.

Injury and illness kept Seles out of other tournaments in 1995. In January 1996, she won the Peters International Tournament in Sydney. In February, she won the Australian Open for the fourth time. This gave her a career match record of 28–0 in the Australian. A shoulder injury kept Monica out of play from February to May. In May, she won a match at Madrid and then had to default because of the shoulder. Later in May, she lost in the quarterfinals of the French Open. Again she won the Canadian. Again she lost to Graf in the U.S. Open final, this time 7–5, 6–4. At least for the time being, she retained her co-number-one ranking.

Once Monica has fully recovered from the long layoff and then the shorter ones caused by the shoulder injury, and as long as she has the desire to compete, I think her future will be just about unlimited. I think she's probably as physically talented as anybody. She can run, she has matured physically, and she has become a player whom nobody will likely approach as long as she can stay at her top level.

The interview came at the U.S. Open in September 1990, just as Monica was becoming a top player. More innocent times. She answered the interview questions in English that was not perfect but remarkably good for a Yugoslavia-born girl of just sixteen. Monica started tennis very early, but at first it didn't appeal to her:

I started when I was six, and I played for a couple of weeks, and I really got bored with it. And I just told my dad I didn't like the sport. Then we started again when I was seven and a half or eight years old. My brother won the national championship; he was pretty good. At that time we started playing tennis plus watching mainly Borg winning so many Wimbledons. Those small things added for me to start playing tennis again.

I think I was probably around eleven, twelve years old when I thought maybe one day I could make it into professional tennis. I went to a lot of junior tournaments. I played twelve to thirteen tournaments a year, which is a lot for a young age of myself, and we traveled. There was one tournament that was in Disney World, the World Championship for the juniors, and I loved it. Unfortunately they discontinued to use that. And that's mainly how I really started seeing pro tennis, and then a couple years before playing at the U.S. Open, I came here to watch the Open.

Then going to the French Open and just playing there, that's how I slowly started understanding what the tennis is, I mean the ranking system. I still don't understand it a hundred percent, but I'm slowly understanding a lot more things than maybe a year ago, when I was just a first-year on the tour.

If Monica couldn't have played tennis, she might have starred in other sports:

If I wouldn't have been a tennis player, I could always be a basketball player, because I love basketball, and I think I'm a pretty good basketball player, too. Besides basketball, I just recently took up European football, which is a fun sport.

I was in Italy, and it was the World Championships, and everybody was talking about football, so I said, "Let's try this sport," and I just really liked it. As recreational, it's probably swimming.

The year before the interview, 1989, Seles had been named the Tennis *magazine Rookie of the Year and the Rolex Rookie of the Year:*

I didn't think I was one of the rookies; I don't know which magazine decided that, but I just had a great year last year, I mean coming from really zero ranking to number six. I still can't believe how well I'd done for the first year, because everything was new, but last year I really never had a down part. I was always doing so well each tournament, when everything was new. A lot of times I love to look back at a tape, and I was so young, and it was a lot of fun times last year for me.

In only her second tour tournament, Monica defeated the legendary Chris Evert:

I think that's where it all started for me, the Virginia Slims in Houston. I will always remember that tournament, because I was getting ready to play Chris. I watched Chris for so many years on television, but it's different when you see her live and you're supposed to play her. It was a really long match, it was very hot, we were playing like around noon, the hottest time of the day, and I just won it in three sets.

I remember when I won the match point I was like, "Wow, I've done it. I've beaten her at least before she retires, once, I can say that." I think it was my first pro career, first tournament win too, so that moment will always stay special for me.

Although she was already on the brink of becoming the number-one ranked woman in the world, Monica didn't think she was yet even close to her prime:

My idea is probably still very far away, but a hundred percent, nobody knows. I just try to take usually each day at a time and trying to improve some things which I think I need some improvement. But hopefully I'm far away, how good I want to play in my mind, I'm very far away, 'cause my intention is not to miss the ball, which probably I'll never reach that goal. But looking forward to maybe reaching it maybe one day, but as long as I'll take each tournament and everything, just work, probably time will bring it I guess.

Monica didn't much vary her "game plan" from opponent to opponent:

Most of the times, most of the opponents I by now know, because I played almost any of them or I watched them play. A lot of the Grand Slam tournaments, you meet someone who you really don't know, you never played, and then it's a little different. But I may send out somebody from my family, or my coach, to just see how they play, but usually I don't have much of a game plan. I just try to stick to my game and try to pressure her into playing with me, not try to tactically play a lot. What I play, I want to bring that to her, so she plays the same way, too.

Perhaps Monica's greatest victory was her win over Steffi Graf in the 1990 French Open final:

I think it was just my first Grand Slam final. I played Steffi a week before in Germany. I think that's where I got a lot of confidence, beating her there and then going into the French knowing I can do it, and that helped me a lot. It was a great day for me, winning my first Grand Slam, 'cause the whole French Open I had such a tough time getting to the finals. It was always every match I was down in the first, 4–1 or a match point, down everything, just kept coming, coming back, and I realized, "Wow, the whole tournament is finished," and how up and down I had a tournament and I still won it. It was just unbelievable feeling for me.

At sixteen Monica had lofty goals, goals she has very nearly achieved:

I think I would love to win all four Grand Slams. Even just to win once each one, you can say you won all four of them. It's pretty tough. I mean for Lendl, probably he's won everything except Wimbledon. I would rather win everything once, I can say that. But I usually never try to put goals, I just try to play tournament by tournament and see how well I do.

As a tennis star and as a clothing model in several magazines, Seles was to some teenage girls a role model as well. When asked, Monica had some advice for these teenagers:

Oh, yeah, the first for me, always school was like the most important. I still try to do that, I'm just so little at home. I think school tries to keep your feet on the ground a lot of times, because when you come back from a big tournament and everything, it just helps to go back to your friends. Even if you do well or you do badly, they will always be there for you, and sports and everything else comes second.

But I still believe I have a lot of friends who can help me off the court when I'm finished from the match, and just forget about tennis. And that's why I liked to do a lot of other things, not be just very into tennis oriented. 'Cause a lot of times, a lot of players, when their careers are over, they just suddenly don't know what to do, because their whole life was depending on tennis.

And they're much more close because for a tennis player, you travel so much from hotel to hotel that you're very close. You can't do many things during a tournament, and when tennis life is over then a lot of times you can run into small trouble there.

FRANK SHORTER

More than any other person, Frank Shorter gave distance running the popularity it enjoys today. Before Shorter's victory in the Olympic marathon in Munich in 1972, distance running was an obscure sport that drew few spectators and few participants. After Shorter, distance running became nothing less than a craze, as tens of millions of Americans embraced it as a means to fitness and to the uplifting emotional state known as the "runner's high"; many also entered races from five thousand meters through ultramarathons. At the same time, marathons, especially in New York and Boston, began to attract huge crowds.

In 1972 Shorter became the first American to win the Olympic marathon since Johnny Hayes did it in 1908. Shorter's gold medal time was 2:12.19.8, only 8.6 seconds off the Olympic record set by the immortal Abebe Bikila of Ethiopia in 1964. Shorter returned to the Olympic marathon in 1976 in Montreal. He nearly repeated his gold medal performance of four years earlier but came in second to Waldemar Cierpinski of East Germany.

Shorter earned his law degree, became an attorney, and made a part-time career as a TV commentator at track meets and marathons.

Oddly enough, in Shorter's most important race, the Olympic marathon of 1972, he was not the first runner to be seen by the crowd that packed the stadium in Munich. There was an impostor:

There was this fellow who timed it so that he jumped off a cart that his buddy was driving—it was a cart that refurbished the pop stands—and ran down the tunnel into the stadium about 250 yards ahead of me, as a hoax. I heard a big cheer as I was just outside the tunnel. I was just about to go in, just about to make a right-hand turn and go down a grade, because the track was lower than the level of the street.

When I heard this roar, I thought maybe someone had set a record in the high jump. Then I came through the tunnel, out onto the track, and waited for the roar. Silence. There was nothing. I mean, I came out on the track and I heard this mumble-mumble-mumble-mumble through the crowd. What occurred to me was, "Geez, I'm an American, but give me a break!"

I figured maybe there's some anti-American sentiment because an American is winning this race that normally, at least at the time, could be won only by someone from Africa, or maybe a British club runner, a country that had a tradition of distance running.

I didn't quite know what to think, but I said, "Well, I'm winning the race, so that's enough." Then I started around the first turn, and I never saw the impostor, because, given the forty-second lead that he had, he was always just far enough ahead of me that, as I would start to make turns around the track, he was never in my field of vision.

So I got to the first turn, and this great midwestern American voice came out and said, "Don't worry, Frank!" It was Erich Segal [the author of *Love Story*], whom I knew from Yale, where I had gone to school and where he had taught; he was working for ABC. I thought to myself, "Why should I worry? I'm winning the Olympic marathon."

Then it began to dawn on me that something was going on, because I started down the backstretch, and people began to whistle. I thought, "Boy, this is really strange," because in Europe, whistling is booing. So finally, I looked over, and I saw some commotion around the finish line, but I still didn't make much of it. I got through the finish line, and someone immediately walked up to me and said, "Well, what did you think of that guy?" Then it all fell into place, and I knew what had gone on—that someone had jumped in ahead.

In retrospect, what's interesting about it for me is that since I never saw this person, I never had any feelings while I was running the race; I always knew I was winning. Whereas I think the millions of people who watched it felt an empathy for me and thought that I had seen this person and that I must have felt, "Oh my gosh, maybe something's wrong, maybe somebody passed me, maybe I'm not winning." I think they were feeling for me and still continue to feel for me. I think that's why people still remember it. Everybody has a sense of fair play in competition. In a way, I don't remember it as much as other people do.

Shorter did not run the marathon in college. His first exposure to the race was a painful one:

I started to run the marathon because of a friend of mine named Kenny Moore, who had been on the 1968 Olympic team in the marathon, who is now a writer for *Sports Illustrated*. Kenny convinced me to run the marathon as a hedge against making the Pan-American team at ten thousand meters, in 1971.

He and I ran the marathon trial in Eugene. There is a certain humor in the race, in that I'd never gone that far before, either in training or running in a race. We were running side by side at the start, and I wanted to go hard, and he was saying, "No, no, hold back." He was teaching me how to run the race—you have to run easy at the start. We got to ten miles, sixteen miles to go, and I said, "I've gotta go—I'm goin'!"

So I left, he went with me, we pulled away from the pack, started running along, got about a minute-and-a-half, maybe two-minute, lead on the next person. Then at about eighteen, nineteen miles, I began to "discover" the marathon, the way most people do. At twenty miles, we made a right-hand turn into a headwind, and Kenny tucked in behind me, to let me break the wind. I turned around and said, "Ah, come on, don't do that."

So he starts running up next to me. I lasted about another mile. At twenty-one miles, I turned to him, and I swear I said, "Kenny, why couldn't Phidippides have died here?" Phidippides is supposedly the ancient Greek who ran from the Battle of Marathon to Athens, a distance of twenty-five or twenty-six miles, and said, "Victory is ours over the Persians," and dropped dead. So I figured I would have been much better off if the distance thousands of years ago had been twenty-one miles instead of twenty-five.

In the 1972 Olympic marathon, Shorter employed the unusual strategy of trying to break the race open not with a mile to go or ten miles to go but after only one third of the race:

The pleasure of winning the race was that I did everything right. I'd trained properly, I'd focused correctly, I'd used a strategy that worked. I took everyone by surprise, going very early in the race, ran very, very hard in the middle third of the marathon, probably as hard as or harder than it's ever been run by anyone. So even though the overall time of the race was relatively slow, because the first and last thirds were very slow, the middle I ran probably somewhere around 4:45 or 4:46 a mile, for eight or nine miles, which had never really been done before.

That was my strategy, and to do that, you have to train for

it, and I had. No one else in the race had, and they hadn't expected it, so physiologically, they couldn't go with me when I started to run that fast early in the race.

It was the perfect strategy, and even though in the last third of the race I had to slow down significantly, I had such a lead by that point that mentally I'd won the race, even though someone might have been able to catch me had they really tried. I was literally out of sight and out of mind—I was just too far ahead.

If I was innovative in any respect in the marathon, I think I was the person who introduced the idea of not just waiting for the lead pack to simply dwindle in numbers but to actually assertively do something early on in the race, to break the whole pack open. I was the first runner to really do it that way.

Frank Shorter was successful over a broad range of distance events:

I couldn't've been world class at anything under about five thousand meters. I ran four-0-two for the mile, which is a good college time. But then when you went to two miles, which isn't that much longer, I actually held the American record indoors for awhile. At three miles, or five thousand meters, I actually broke the American record once, and I held the American record at ten thousand meters as well. So I had a pretty good range, and I think that's what helped me run the marathon the way I did, because I ran it more like a track race than I did like a long-distance race.

When you have exams done and they take biopsies of your muscle tissue and analyze it, you have two types of fibers: slow-twitch and fast-twitch. The slow-twitch is an endurance fiber, the fast-twitch is a sprinting fiber. Long-distance runners tend to have predominately slow-twitch, sprinters tend to have eighty, ninety, a hundred percent fast-twitch.

So the old adage that a sprinter is "born" is true. But the sprinters, these people with this fast-twitch fiber—they can become marathon runners, too, because over time you can teach these fast-twitch fibers to take on an endurance characteristic. But you can't go the other way: you can't teach one of these long, thin, slow-twitch fibers to get faster, to actually contract faster. So in that respect, distance runners can never become sprinters. But sprinters can become distance runners.

The 1972 Olympics in Munich are remembered not only for inspiring victories like that of Shorter and those of American swimmer Mark Spitz, who won seven gold medals, but also for the tragic killing on September 5 of eleven Israeli athletes by Black September terrorists. Two were killed in the Olympic Village and nine at a military airport. The International Olympic Committee, headed by eighty-four-year-old Avery Brundage, suspended the Games for twenty-four hours and held a memorial service at the main Olympic stadium that was attended by eighty thousand. Then the IOC ordered that the games continue. Shorter was all too close to the action:

The tragedy with the massacre of the Israeli athletes in 1972 was really, when you think about it, the first international terrorist act. It was the first really long-range, premeditated strike of that kind. So the world really wasn't familiar with it, they weren't ready for it, no one believed it could happen.

I was actually sleeping on the balcony of our room because they had so many of us all in these apartments, and I figured it was better to just take my mattress, go outside, and sleep outside on the floor. I heard the gunshots because the balcony of the Israeli apartment was on the same floor level, a hundred yards across the courtyard.

I had a direct line of sight. So I heard the gunshots, but I just figured it must be something, and I fell back asleep. I remember waking up; there was an eerie silence. There was not the noise of activity that you normally had in the Olympic Village. You could just hear people moving around.

So I got up and looked around. There was no one in the courtyard. It was just still. I knew something was up, and then Kenny Moore came out, said what had happened, and told me that there were hostages taken. We could see the terrorists, with the masks over their faces, standing on the balconies a hundred yards away. So it made it very, very real, and we kind of held a vigil that day. We kind of sat around and waited for whatever to happen. And we knew that people had been killed—the word had gotten around.

It was amazing how quickly the news could spread through the Olympic Village, and actually it was fairly accurate, as to how many and what had gone on and everything else. Usually these rumors are just totally distorted.

Then, finally, they brought in some helicopters, and these helicopters came and landed right in the courtyard, behind the building. A few minutes later, they took off again. They were all going to the airport, and some of the people out on the balcony watching sort of breathed a sigh of relief and said, "Well, that's over!"

I distinctly remember turning to Kenny and saying, "I don't think this is over." And then, a short time later we got the word that they had all died. They tried to do something at the airport; one of the terrorists had released a grenade in the helicopter and killed all the rest of the hostages.

The effect, I think, was that all these athletes, who had never come into contact with that aspect of the real world, were very deeply affected. And the initial reaction on the part of these kids—and they're all kids, most of them—was, nothing's worth this human life, we should just go home and stop this.

Now we know—and what I think the athletes realized very

quickly—was you couldn't do that, because that was just giving in to the demands of the terrorists. If you stopped the Olympics, you were doing exactly what they wanted, and so you couldn't do that. But this was the first time this had ever happened. So it took about a day for people to get over that kind of feeling. And they had the memorial ceremony, and then the Games went on. But there was a certain subdued aura about the Games after that. I think the perspective of all those athletes changed dramatically.

O. J. SIMPSON

Orenthal James Simpson, for the most unfortunate of reasons, may now be the biggest celebrity in the United States, in or out of sports. But not long ago, he was a huge celebrity for his football exploits alone. Some consider him the greatest running back of all time.

I saw him play. I saw him do things that no one else did, that no one else could do. There was talk of taking him out of the Pro Football Hall of Fame in Canton, Ohio. In my opinion, you can't. My opinion has nothing to do with the crimes with which Simpson was charged and of which he was acquitted. You can't take him out of the Hall because the reason he is in the Hall is what he accomplished on the football field. I feel strongly about this and have made my views known to the directors of the Hall of Fame.

O. J. Simpson was fast enough to run on USC's world record 440-yard relay team. On the football field, he combined his speed with an elegant running style that featured both grace and a trademark hesitation. After transferring to USC from the City College of San Francisco as a junior, Simpson was the top rusher in the country two years in a row, gaining 1,415 yards in 1967 and 1,709 in 1968. All this made him the Heisman Trophy winner in his senior year. His

USC teams went to the Rose Bowl both years he played, and the 1967 team was number one in the country.

Simpson was the first choice in the 1969 NFL draft. With the Buffalo Bills, he became the finest outside running back in the history of the National Football League.

He was the first runner to amass 2,000 yards in a season, earning 2,003 in 1973. That year he averaged 143 yards a game, still the NFL record. He led the NFL in rushing in 1972, 1973, 1975, and 1976. He is the only player ever to rush for 250 or more yards in two different games, topping out at 273 against Detroit in 1976.

Three times, Simpson was named AFC Player of the Year; in 1973 he also was NFL Player of the Year. In 1975 he led the NFL in points with 138, on twenty-three touchdowns, seven of them on pass receptions. His eleven-year NFL career, which ended with the 49ers in his hometown of San Francisco, accounted for 11,236 yards and sixty-one touchdowns on the ground and 2,140 yards and fourteen TDs through the air.

O. J. Simpson was a tough kid growing up in the tough Potrero Hill section of San Francisco. He ran with a gang before channeling his energy into athletics. Simpson recounts his childhood and his later accomplishments in tones and words that show a certain humility that one might not expect in one of the greatest athletes of the century. He sounds like the affable O. J. of not long ago, one of the most popular players in the history of football and the man Americans liked so well as an actor, Hertz spokesman, and sportscaster. (His interview was completed before the occurrence of the crimes mentioned earlier.)

Though he was to make his name in football, he first concentrated on baseball:

My friends, they thought I would end up a pro baseball player. I was the best baseball player in all the leagues that I had played in. Willie Mays was my absolute hero. As a kid I went to all the Giant games.

I also played football. Football was always easier for me. We played on the playground up in an area called Potrero Hill in San Francisco. And at the top of the hill was a huge facility. I mean baseball diamonds, a football field, a gym. It was great.

That was the focal point of the neighborhood. And your prowess in the neighborhood is directly related to your prowess as an athlete. If you were the best athlete, you were the leader, whatever the game was.

Early in life, when I was eight, my cousin, Dwight Tucker, was the best athlete on the Hill. And they were racing one day, and I beat him. Everyone thought it was a fluke. Then we raced again, and I beat him again. I think that's when I first realized I had some talent, some ability.

I think when I got to high school, football started to take over a little bit. It was a little more challenging, the girls would go to the football games, they didn't really go to baseball games. The cheerleaders were at the football games and not at the baseball games.

At that point, I was a big 49er fan, and I grew up watching them. One of the saddest days in my life was when they traded Y. A. Tittle to the New York Giants.

In his early teens, Simpson was to cross paths with Jim Brown, whose NFL rushing record the younger man would one day break:

I never missed a 49er game for ten years, until I went to SC. When the Browns came to town, they were like one of the two, three best teams in football every year. You'd go to the stadium, and the guy you'd want to see is Big Jim. Jim was awesome. I mean for a kid it was like even in the park you couldn't emulate Jim Brown. You could be Willie Galimore and get the knees really high, you could try to be Hugh McElhenny and the style that he ran, and Joe "the Jet" Perry with his compact style.

But it was hard to emulate Jim Brown, and nobody would try to because he was awesome. You go there and you watch Jim, how he dominated the game. The defense, they were totally concentrated on him. Anything someone else did was like a condiment on the side. It was not the main course. Jim was the guy.

I used to go to all the games, and we used to pick up all the cushions. And we'd get a nickel a cushion, so that's how I would make my money for the week. I'd make a couple of dollars picking up cushions. When the game was over, we'd go and buy hot dogs and ice cream across the street.

It's easily an hour, two hours after the game, and we go into the ice cream place, and Jim Brown was in there, and I think he was with another guy. But you see him—bam, that's Jim. None of my boys are gonna say anything because I was the guy, the man of my group.

Maybe I was thirteen or fourteen, but you know me, I ain't gonna say, "Hey man, you are great." So I say, "Man, you think you're tough."

He'd had a rough game that day. He needed one yard for a first down, and Dave Wilcox made a great stop on him, and they didn't get the first down.

I may have said something about that play to him, and he said something to the group. And I said, "Man, you ain't so tough. Look, you remember my name. I'm gonna break all your records one day." Something a kid just says.

Jim was pretty cool about it. I reminded him about it when I was at USC. He called me up to his house the first time I had met him. Picked me up, took me to his house. I said, "You know, I met you once. I told you I was going to break your record. I was a cocky little kid." I don't think he remembered it. I'm sure it happened to him many times; it has certainly happened to me since then a number of times.

Simpson was always a star in football, but his first team was anything but successful:

We ended up going to a high school called Galileo that's in the North Beach section of San Francisco. Chinatown was right next to North Beach, so my school was about seventy to eighty percent Oriental. So they weren't basically big students. I was the second largest guy on the team, and we didn't do well. We lost all our games in three years, even though I made All-City. My love for football had grown more and more.

I had almost given up. I would end up going to college. I knew you had to go to college to play professional football. I was going to start playing some American Legion baseball or go into the Army. A buddy of mine, Ronnie Patterson, quit school. He was the top athlete on the Hill. Went to the Army, went through Vietnam, lost a leg. When he came home, the hard facts hit us. The Army wasn't The Audie Murphy Story, and it wasn't as glamorous as we thought it would be.

Fortunately I got to the City College of San Francisco. I entered junior college with the intention of playing football or baseball. I played football, and after three games—we had some talented players—I had just about every college in the country after me. I had broken a couple of records in the first few games, and it was interesting, because I wasn't starting at halfback, and the returning running backs were still there, so they were starting. One was in a car accident before a game and then the other one got hurt in the first half. I came in and had a great half—ran for something like two hundred yards, and, like they say, the rest is history. I had all the colleges coming after me.

And then there was O.J. the track star. It was a fight that determined that he would run the third leg when he ran on relay teams:

Back then it was almost impossible to play two sports. The athletes had no rights. These unions have gone a long way for helping the athlete, but back then there was no rights. I broke my hand at the plate, I was a catcher in my senior year at high school. That's when I went over and ran track, because I had a cast on my hand but I could still run.

It was a revelation again. I was wondering where all the students went after school. You know, football is a crowd game; I never thought about track that much. And there they were, all the girls that I kind of liked, I used to flirt with them in class. Guys that you'd seen around, they didn't live in my neighborhood, but they were guys that I had seen around in school, they were at the track meet. Plus, people that I would see around town from the other schools were there. I ran track for the rest of the year, and I did real well.

So when I got to City College, we had a great baseball team, we had won the state championship. I was going to play baseball, but because of some of the guys that were on the football team, they said, "Come on, run track. We can break this record and everything."

I got into a fight right after football season. I was playing basketball. I got into a fight with a friend of mine named Donald McGee, and I broke my thumb—see the scar here? So I had to wear a cast.

Once again, I can't play baseball, I had to wear a cast right to the next football season, and I ran track. And that's really how I wound up running third man on the relay team, because of the left-right handoffs. I couldn't get the baton in my left hand; I had to get the baton in my right hand. I ended up running track and fortunately did real well, ran in the state meet, won the state thing. Our team won the relay.

Once again I played another year of football, and I did real well. I went to USC and all the guys were there, [hurdler] Earl McCulloch, [sprinter] Lennox Miller. They said, "Man, if you run on the relay team, we could break the world record." Boy, the Olympics were coming up. I thought I had a chance. I always dreamed about being a decathlete, but I didn't have the time to train for that.

As Simpson tells it, his decision to go to USC all came down to one day when he was watching football on television:

In '62, I was watching the Rose Bowl on New Year's Day [actually, the game was on January 1, 1963, after the 1962 season]. It was raining outside in San Francisco, and you're watching it on TV, and there's no pro ball on TV. There was always college ball and the only California team was SC, and they were playing against Wisconsin. That turned out to be a great football game. Every time SC scored, this white horse came out. I saw that horse, and I said, "That's where I want to go to school." And then I followed SC after that. I kept my eye on them.

I really had gone to only two college football games before I went to SC, but I noticed that Mike Garrett was featured, and I saw that Mike was a black guy. I said, "Boy, that's really nice. They're really backing this guy." And he won the Heisman Trophy. And I was impressed by that.

Then when I did so well in my first year in junior college, and all the schools recruited me and I went to SC, to be honest I was shocked. I thought this would be like Cal: just this huge school with thirty thousand students, many of them black, with different persuasions. And going to San Francisco, it's such a racially mixed town. Every school you went to, there was a large contingent of blacks, Japanese, Chinese, Mexicans, you name it.

I go to SC, and all of a sudden I'm looking at a handful of our guys. I said, "I've heard of most of these guys," but it turned out that the only blacks at the school were on the team. They were on scholarship, and this was a very expensive, rich, basically white school. I was shocked by that.

There was only nine thousand undergraduate students, and they were winning all these national championships in baseball, track, and football. I think there may have been two guys in the whole school that were black that were not on scholarship, and maybe three girls. I was kind of shocked.

I was also shocked by how they welcomed me with open arms when they were recruiting me. How they wanted me to be a part of the heritage of the school. At that time a lot of things were going on around the country with black identity. Guys wanted to wear naturals, and they were having trouble on the Cal campus and various campuses around the country with black student unions, black identity on the teams, blacks wanting to wear facial hair and dress in a more traditional fashion, ethnic fashion.

All these schools were having problems, and I noticed SC wasn't having any. [Coach John] McKay was allowing the guys to express themselves. As long as you showed up for practice and went to class, if you had to express yourself in a certain way, you could. I like that attitude, and I felt that I needed the polish that I could get from a school like this.

I realized that I wouldn't get wrapped up in a lot of those things and that I needed to focus on football. I was a young man who grew up in a rough neighborhood. My brother and the guys had joined the Black Panthers, and that was very active in the Bay Area at that time—all the things that were going on with the Liberation Army and the Patty Hearst thing. A lot of things had gone on, and I had grown up in the middle of it. I felt I had to get away from it. I needed to go somewhere where I could focus on what I needed to focus on. SC gave me that environment. That's the main reason I went.

Simpson says he was helped by the demands made upon him by USC:

SC kind of made things easy. Things became easy because I liked college better than high school. When I went to junior college, as long as I was around the campus and I was working toward getting my grades, I could go on to the school of my choice. Other schools were going to get me in after my first year on some kind of grant or special government thing. SC told me I had to reach all their requirements. It took me another year of junior college.

One of the reasons I missed my sophomore year playing major college ball was because I had to make up some math stuff. I wasted another half year in my sophomore season making up those grades so I could go to SC. Other schools could have gotten me in, but I realized SC was what I always wanted, and I didn't want to shortchange myself.

Other schools were offering me a lot of things: money, cars, the whole shebang. Back then it was pretty common. A lot of people don't believe it, but SC was the only school that didn't offer me anything. I liked that. They said, "We're going to offer you the opportunity to be a Trojan, and if you come in and play up to your ability, you'll get more than you ever would from those schools."

It turned out that it was the only school that didn't guarantee me that I was going to play. And what I liked, the other schools that were recruiting me were recruiting against SC. They kept telling me that Marvelous Marv Motley was there. That Steve Grady was there. All these great backs who had come out of junior college, and that I may not play. And that zoned in on me.

I said, "What do you mean, I may not play?" That made me want to go to SC more. It was great because I could study things that I wanted to study. You have your electives. As an elective I took a little cinema. My teacher's name was George Lucas, and you could see this man was going to be a talent. He was making movies while at SC. It was easy to cheat on the tests because this guy was not paying attention. And when you go to class at seven o'clock, who walks in and sits on a bed on the stage, you know you've got Mae West in your class. I ended up doing a skit with her.

Simpson resisted an offer to leave USC early to play pro ball:

I had already been offered large sums of money to go to Canada. A good friend of [Chicago Bears owner George]

Halas came to me in San Francisco after my first year in junior college and put about fifteen thousand dollars in cash on the bed and told me Mr. Halas wanted me to go to Canada, then come down. Play up there for a couple of years and then they would bring me down to be on the Bears. And I'm thinking, "Yeah, and then what are they gonna do with Gale Sayers?"

But by then I knew Joe Namath had signed a big contract, so by then I knew football was where I wanted to go. It didn't really bother me not to play baseball.

Simpson looks back on 1967 as a pivotal, wonderful year in his life:

My junior year, the whole year of '67, was just an incredible year for me. You gotta realize in January I'm living at home with my mother and my sister. My brother's away in the Army, and my other sister's married. But we're living in a three-room apartment in an attic above a friend of my mother's home, that they had converted into an apartment. Now I'm at SC. And in that year I ran on the track team that won the national championship; we broke the world record in the four hundred meter and four hundred forty yard relays. I got married a week after we broke that world record, and I brought my wife down to Los Angeles. And here comes football, this is why I'm here.

I didn't know what I was going to play at SC. I thought I would be a wingback. In junior college I caught as many passes as carries. I went a week in spring ball, and McKay had me carry the ball eight times in a row once, and I was exhausted, but I guess he liked what he saw. He told me to finish running track.

In the fall I was the starting tailback, right away. I didn't really have to compete beyond the spring with all of those other guys, those famous junior college guys, guys who were more famous—I don't know if they were more famous than me in junior college; by the time I came out I was pretty famous in California anyway as a junior college player.

Simpson recalls the biggest game of his career in college or the NFL as being USC against UCLA on November 18, 1967. The Bruin quarterback was Gary Beban, who, along with Simpson, was a favorite to win the Heisman Trophy. Going into the game, USC was fourth in the country at 7–1; its only loss was 3–0 the week before at Oregon State in what O.J. calls a "monsoon." UCLA was number one in the country at 7–0–1:

It was two teams playing for the national championship who just happened to be in the same city. Most of the people are going to one school or the other. It happens they have at the time what was considered the top two athletes in the country, at least the two leading candidates for the Heisman. It was like what else could you ask for? Crosstown rivals, winner takes all. Go to the Rose Bowl, win the national championship.

And it was a great football game. I had some big plays in the game, I scored some big TDs, especially the last one, which is still the biggest one in my career: a sixty-four yard touchdown in the fourth quarter to beat them. We won 21–20. Won all the marbles.

And it's still, even more than the two-thousand-yard season, the highlight of my career. Because, in the locker room, it wasn't like I was happy for the quarterback or he was happy for me or you're happy for the guy who breaks the record. We were happy as a team. Everybody was equally happy. It wasn't that "Juice, boy, you had a great season," I got a lot of that: "Boy, you made All-American" or "Boy, you won the Heisman," which is nice. But it was like, "Boy, we did this," so everybody was equally happy, and I never really felt anything like that since.

Simpson looks back on USC football as being fun, fun with mean-ing:

The best football I ever played was junior college football. It was really a kick, it was no pressure. My first year at SC was a revelation: that you can have so much fun and feel like you're accomplishing something at the same time. It's almost like sex, except that it was meaningful, it seemed to be meaningful—not that sex isn't, but not always.

USC won the game against UCLA, but Beban would go on to win the Heisman, edging out Simpson, 1,968 votes to 1,722. USC went to the Rose Bowl, where it beat Indiana, 14–3. The team ended the season as national champion:

It was unbelievable. It was just a total high. My senior year was just the opposite. We didn't have a great football team. We were undefeated, going into the Rose Bowl, but to this day I think we were the worst undefeated team ever. For me, it was just too much pressure. Not that I didn't respond to it—I broke all the rushing records and ended up winning the Heisman.

But there was pressure because we weren't a well-balanced team—we had a lot of talent, but it was such young talent—if I didn't play well, we had no chance of winning. So every game I went into, not only was I a marked man, we had an inexperienced offensive line. I carried the ball I think something like thirty-six times a game. And if I didn't play well, we didn't win. And that's a tremendous amount of pressure. I think after four or five games, I was the only guy on our team who perhaps scored a touchdown. Shows you there was a lot of pressure on.

When that year was over, it was a relief. By the sixth or seventh game, I could not wait for the year to get over.

*In that year, 1968, Simpson led USC to a regular season 9–0–1
record and the number-two ranking. Simpson easily won the
Heisman Trophy, with 2,853 points to 1,103 for second-place Leroy
Keyes of Purdue. On New Year's Day, USC lost to number-one Ohio
State in the Rose Bowl, 27–16. In two years at USC, Simpson rushed
for an average of 164.4 yards a game, making him second in the history of NCAA Division I-A (the leader, Ed Marinaro of Cornell,
played in the Ivy League, facing much weaker teams than those that
confronted Simpson).*

*Simpson was the number-one pick in the 1969 draft. Chosen by
Buffalo, he had the mixed experience of personal stardom but team
mediocrity. Things were particularly frustrating in his first three
years, when the Bills were coached by John Rauch, a man who
restricted O.J.'s role, using him more in third-and-one situations than
in plays that might yield long gains:*

It was just like three years of a total waste of time. I was
the wrong guy and in the wrong place. Obviously, it wasn't a
happy time for me because here I am, as far away from home
as I can possibly be, playing in an area I didn't choose to go
to, playing for a coach who doesn't really want me. Yeah, it
was a tough three years, but I've always felt you have to work
through those things, and good things happen to you, and
fortunately a great thing happened to me. John Rauch quit or
got fired.

I spent one year with Harve Johnson, which was just a
waste of time year; he wasn't really a head coach, and
everybody knew it—he was just kinda holding down the fort,
and the next year they brought in Lou Saban. So I felt I had
wasted four years in the NFL, three years at least, till Lou
Saban showed up.

*Lou Saban knew about running attacks, and he brought to
Buffalo a host of quick, aggressive linemen who could block for
Simpson. O.J. went on to lead the league in rushing four times. The*

*team had a record of 1–13 in 1971 but went 9–5 in both 1973 and
1975 and 8–6 in 1975. Still, they made the AFC playoffs only once,
when another 9–5 record earned them a wild-card slot in 1974. The
1967 USC-UCLA game remained Simpson's biggest thrill. Still,
when O.J. became the first NFL rusher to run for more than two thousand yards in a season (and still the only one to do so in a fourteen-
game season), it meant a lot to him:*

> I think that when I knew that I had made my mark in pro
> ball, that I was part of the legacy of the game, was after the
> two-thousand-yard season, immediately after. As a matter of
> fact, the season wasn't over yet, there was about three
> minutes to go. But after I had gone over two thousand yards,
> they took me off the field, and I was in the locker room. I
> called my wife in L.A. and said, "I did it." Because the game
> wasn't televised there.
>
> As I walked into that locker room, I had a feeling of
> accomplishment, a feeling that I did something. I knew then
> that that record would eventually be broken—all records
> are—but I was the first to do it. And I knew then that no
> matter what I've ever done in football, long after people had
> seen me play, that the memory was gone or they were gone,
> that I will always be the first guy who went over two thousand
> yards.

*Disillusioned by what he saw as Buffalo's lack of commitment to
winning, and following a knee operation, Simpson was traded to his
hometown San Francisco Forty-Niners:*

> After I got to San Francisco, I had the same knee problem
> even after I rehabilitated it. It was in the back of my knee, and
> it was a cyst, and I think now if they would have taken the
> cyst off, I wouldn't have had to do the major surgery, and,
> who knows, my career might have gone on a little longer. But
> it was apparent that I was damaged goods at that point.

San Francisco was a team, like my early years in Buffalo, a team in transition. And I was no longer—with the bum knee, even at just twenty-nine or thirty, all my other skills seemed to be there, and I had a couple of good games for them. But it was a case that I couldn't carry a team anymore. I always thought in my career I could carry a football team, that if they played defense, give me the ball on offense, just have the guys run to the right places and, hey, I'll get the points that we need to win. I knew that was gone.

TED WILLIAMS

T ed Williams may have been the greatest hitter ever to hold a bat. He achieved many amazing statistics, but perhaps the most stunning is that he won the American League batting title in both 1941, when he was twenty-three, and 1958, when he was forty. He won the AL title six times despite spending the 1943, 1944, and 1945 seasons as a World War II fighter pilot. These years came at the peak of his career: he won the AL batting championship both shortly before (1941, 1942) and shortly after (1947, 1948) his military service.

Williams's lifetime batting average is .344, ranking him sixth on the all-time list for both leagues. All of the players ahead of him played decades before he did. Ty Cobb played his last game in 1928, Rogers Hornsby in 1937, Shoeless Joe Jackson in 1920, Ed Delahanty in 1903, and Tris Speaker in 1928; Williams finished up in 1960. It's doubtful the five ahead of Williams could have hit as well as Williams did if they had played under the conditions he faced.

Williams is the last player to hit more than .400, having posted a .406 in 1941. Less well known is that he also hit .400 or higher in two later seasons, 1952 and 1953, but in 1952 he had only ten at-bats, and in 1953 he had only ninety-one, neither enough to qualify him for *the batting championship or to have his mark considered for the title of most recent average of .400 or greater.*

In 1957, when he was thirty-nine, Williams hit .388; with five more hits, he would have hit .400 that season, too. Slowed by the years, he had only nine infield hits. (Mickey Mantle, who until late in the season contended with Williams for the batting title, hit .365 but had forty-eight infield hits; Mantle was not quite twenty-six.)

Williams had a beautiful, natural-looking swing that thousands have tried to emulate. He hit not just for average but with great power: he won the AL home run title in 1941, 1942, 1947, and 1949, hitting forty-three in the last year. He is tied for tenth on the all-time list for home runs, with 521 in nineteen seasons.

Ted Williams had the most RBIs in the American League in 1939, 1942, 1947, and 1949. He is tenth on the list of RBIs in a career with 1,839, giving him an astronomical .80 RBI per game. He won the AL Triple Crown—by leading the league in batting average, home runs, and runs batted in—in both 1942 and 1947, making him the only AL player ever to win the Triple Crown twice (the only other player to win a league Triple Crown twice was Hornsby).

Williams has the second highest slugging average in baseball history. His .634 is exceeded only by the .690 earned by a man named Babe Ruth. Williams is second on one more list, and again Ruth is first; this is the list that speaks loudly about the respect pitchers give to hitters. The list is for most career walks; Williams got 2,019, Ruth 2,056.

In fact, Ruth is Williams's greatest competitor for the title of Greatest Hitter Ever. Whom you pick is a matter of taste; if you like power more than you like batting average, you choose Ruth. If your preference is for average over power, Williams is your man.

I didn't have the good fortune to watch Ted Williams play at his peak, but I did see him at the end of his career. Even then I was impressed with what a great hitter he was, what a student of hitting he was. You have to respect the man's courage and his desire after the adversity he's had, such as the recent stroke. You have to respect how he has come back.

The longer I'm around, the more I hear what a gentle person Ted is, what a concerned human being he is, and how loyal a friend he has been to some friends of mine. I've learned that down beneath that hard-core shell that he has presented, or has seemed to present, there's a very gentle man.

Looking back on his life, Ted Williams feels fortunate to have grown up in Southern California:

I've always said I was so fortunate as a young kid to have been in San Diego, California. Greatest weather in the states. A lot of baseball played there, and I had a chance to play baseball every day of my life. And about the age of thirteen, fourteen, even though I was playing softball around the playground, I really started taking a real big interest in baseball. As a result, I started to play baseball, and all my time was spent at a playground a block away. I had a wonderful opportunity to meet fellows who had been pretty good ballplayers who could throw a little bit of advice toward me once in awhile.

Through extensive practice, Ted Williams perfected his model swing:

That all goes back to practice, practice, practice. I practiced and played all the time. So my error in judgment should have been a little bit smaller than most. I think it was. I think the key is concentrated practice. Not just swinging the bat and letting it fly. Concentrated practice. Trying to do it perfect every time. I think by doing that, you develop a little more finesse than if you're just wailing away. I developed some pretty good practice habits. Nobody told me about them, it was just something I happened to fall into.

Growing up in California long before the Giants and Dodgers journeyed West, Ted Williams didn't dream of the major leagues:

I didn't even look at the big leagues. The big leagues were three thousand miles away. Sixty years ago, that was the end of the world, pretty near. I'd keep the scores of the games, didn't have any national radio and certainly no television. So, as a result, we weren't as close to it then as a young kid in San Diego today would be.

Now they've got a major league team, they see it on television, they see all the highlights, they see all the players. That should give some of them an advantage because they get a chance to look at all the styles and pick out what they think is good and what they like.

But I started to see some hitters that I liked to look at. I thought they looked good. Everybody wants to look good. I could see these hitters hit a ball, and they were in good balance and quick, and that impressed me. So I was lucky. I look back and say, "Boy, I was lucky that I could decipher a good swing, one that looked good, and one that was productive." As a result, I tried to copy a lot of things I saw.

Later called the Splendid Splinter, Williams at eighteen was six-foot-three but weighed only about 150 pounds:

I thought I was a little late in developing, and I think at age seventeen, eighteen I was really just a little boy. Eighteen, nineteen, I started to really come. My year at Minneapolis, I was nineteen years old, and I was really getting some strength, and I really was coming into my own, real, real fast.

Williams started out in the majors competing with players who had played near the start of this century and ended up playing with a few who would make it into the 1980s. For instance, there was Hornsby, who began his career in St. Louis in 1915. Williams met up with him in Minneapolis:

He was a rough, tough old guy. He had a reputation that
he was hard to get along with, and he wasn't too diplomatic.
I've got to say that as a young kid, he couldn't have treated
me nicer, and I felt like he was interested in me. He used to
stay after practice at spring training, and we'd be the only two
there: the great Rogers Hornsby and a young kid. He was
really great to me, and I always had a real deep, warm feeling
in my heart regarding Rogers Hornsby. He knew a lot about
hitting, probably as much as anybody.

*Williams, of course, spent his entire major-league career with the
Boston Red Sox. But at first it looked like he might become a New
York Yankee:*

Bill Essex was a great Yankee scout. As a matter of fact,
he offered us the nicest contract of any of the people that
were interested in me, including the Detroit Tigers. Of
course there wasn't that big a rush for me, because I was just
a real tall, skinny kid. But they did offer me the best contract.
I look back now and I say, "I wonder why."

Well, the reason was because they wanted me to go to
Binghamton, New York. Of course, that was thirty-five
hundred miles away. It was a long way, and I'm seventeen and
we just felt like I'd be better off in San Diego. We were
getting a lot of pressure to sign with San Diego, because they
were in the Pacific Coast League, and it was my home town.
That's eventually where I went. I don't think it was a mistake,
because the Red Sox had an affiliation with San Diego, and,
during one of their trips, they put an option on me. The first
year they got it, they sent me to Minneapolis. From there I
went to the Red Sox.

*The Red Sox held spring training in Florida. There Williams
encountered more legends:*

They were great to me. Jimmy Foxx and Joe Cronin and Lefty Grove and the other veterans on the club couldn't have been nicer to me. I certainly didn't mean to be a pop-off-type of kid but, apparently, I threw that feeling out, and I was really scared to death like all young kids would be. But I was so lucky. It turned out great for me, and I've always been appreciative of the fact that I did get with the Red Sox. I had my career there and that was the end of it.

Williams was thrilled to be playing professional baseball:

I was playing the sport I loved and getting paid for it. Traveling on trains, getting the best food I'd ever eaten in my life, having some success, and certainly I was having a great time. A good enough time that I made up my mind, more than ever, that I was going to make a success out of this.

The year 1941 was a remarkable one for Williams—that was the year he hit .406—but he was more impressed by the accomplishment of another American League player:

Joe DiMaggio had such a great year in 1941, hitting in fifty-six straight games. I hit .400, which is super for me, but nobody had ever hit in fifty-six games. Only ten years before, somebody else had hit .400 [more precisely, eleven years before, 1930, when Bill Terry of the New York Giants had hit .401].

But that .400 looms a little larger all the time. I still think there's going to be other .400 hitters, but that's probably my greatest accomplishment in baseball, and I'm glad, more than ever, that I did, because I never had the chance to do it again.

He nearly didn't do it the first time. Going into the last game of the season, Williams was hitting .399 and a fraction, high enough to be rounded to .400. He took a sure thing and turned it into a risk:

The last game of the season, [Red Sox manager] Joe Cronin said, "You know, you don't have to play today. You're officially .400, and if you don't want to play, I can understand that."

I didn't even give it a thought. I'd never thought about it all season and certainly not that day. So I went up, but a funny thing happened. Just before the first pitch, [Hall-of-Fame umpire] Bill McGowan turned around and he wiped home plate and he said, very softly, "In order to hit four hundred, you gotta be loose."

He just broke the spell a little bit, and the first ball I hit, I hit a bullet to right field, a base hit. Then, I hit another ball to right field, and then, I hit the horns for a home run and then I was on my way.

Ted Williams was named American League Most Valuable Player in 1946 and 1949. He might have won the award the next year too, but for an accident:

In 1950, I was doing everything better than I was in forty-nine and—bam!—I ran into the wall and I broke my elbow, and I was out the rest of the season, and that was the turning point in my career because, in my heart, I don't feel I was quite the hitter after that that I was before.

It seems odd that Williams didn't win more MVP awards than he did:

I never won a Most Valuable Player award when I won a batting championship. I never won a Most Valuable Player when I won a Triple Crown. Two Triple Crowns and six batting titles, and I never won a Most Valuable Player. It was always those other years. So you don't really know the answer, but I think '47 [Williams' second Triple Crown season] is my most bitter feeling about a writer, when he didn't acknowledge me with even a tenth-place vote in 1947.

There was so much competition in the sporting pages in Boston—I'm talking about fifteen, twenty writers right in the Boston area, trying to get a lead, trying to get a story. Then there were some controversies that developed, and I wasn't very smart about it, and as a result, everything got on the wrong foot. I think a lot of that was due to my hardheadedness and immaturity.

On the other hand, Williams looks back at the seasons directly after World War II as the Golden Age of baseball:

That period of baseball was a great era, and I think it's going to go down that those five years will produce more Hall-of-Fame players than any other five-year era in baseball. There were a lot of good teams, there was a lot of competition, a lot of great players.

People had been starved for three years for baseball as they knew it. The old names were coming back. It was just like a homecoming for a lot of the great players, and I think, as a result the fans got into it a little bit more, and everything was getting bigger and better, and good times were starting and all the rest of it, and it was a great era.

In his nineteen years in the majors, Ted Williams faced some of the most fearsome pitchers of all time:

They all had a particular pitch. Lemon's ball was as alive as it could be. Ford always got it in the good spots. Feller had the most stuff. Wilhelm had the unhittable knuckleball. I didn't hit it. They were all tough for me.

In a career of wondrous individual achievements, Ted Williams' chief disappointment was the failure of the Sox to make it to more than a single World Series. During his career their one trip was in 1946, when they lost to the St. Louis Cardinals in seven games:

Those were the most heartbreaking years of my career. They were the most exciting and, certainly, the most productive for me, but the most heartbreaking because we didn't win the World Series. We never got back into it; we won the pennant by eleven or twelve games [12] in '46 and, with the same club, we lost our three starting pitchers. And when you lose three starting pitchers, you have to start all over again building your staff. It took us a couple of years to do that.

Despite that, we played the Yankees even from '46 to '50. But they beat us a little bit on the road. But the big thing was, for two years, we played the last day of the season for the pennant, and we lost both times. [In 1948, Cleveland and Boston ended the season with identical records of 96–58; the Indians beat the Sox 2-1 in a one-game playoff to win the AL pennant. In 1949, the Yankees won the league with a record of 97–57; Boston went 96–58.]

The hitter of hitters advises batters to let the first pitch go by 95 percent of the time:

Only the first pitch. I see his fast ball, probably, and it's a ball or a strike. At least I see his speed. It's just better to at least look at one pitch. Then you get a chance to see two or three or four more pitches, which tells you a little bit about his overall stuff. Gives you a little bit of an idea how he wants to pitch you. Then, you compound that a little bit more and say, "Well, if the first nine hitters did that, he's pitched a third of a ball game in three innings and, if he gets into problems, then he's really going to start throwing a lot of balls."

Williams may have been the best hitter, but the man with the best lifetime average was Ty Cobb, at .367. Cobb ended his career in 1928; Williams's first year in the majors was 1939. So it would seem they would have had no contact. In fact, however, Williams began to receive letters from Cobb, and sometimes Cobb would deliver his opinion in person:

Cobb used to plead with me to hit to left field. I had a hard time hitting to left field. [Williams hit left-handed.] He was a natural, through-the-middle, left field. He'd look like he was drooling when he'd tell me, "Boy! If they ever did that to me!"

I guess he'd have hit .600, I don't know, but it was hard for me to go to left field at that particular time in my career. I was right on the plate and I was pulling the ball and I was still hitting, leading the league sometimes. So it was hard for me to think about doing other things, but that shift hurt me, and I'd hit real bullet-type balls to right field and there was somebody standing there. No way they could get through. There were just too many people over there. The only guy that wasn't over there was the third baseman and the left fielder.

Finally I learned to get away from the plate and push the ball to left field. Then everything was away from me. I'd go to left field enough to break it up, but it still took a long time.

They finally decided, "Gee whiz, this guy can't pull the ball anymore." This was in the spring, and I had a heavier bat. So I could see them loosening up. All of a sudden, it's getting warm again in July and boy, I was a good hitter in hot weather. I could see them loosening up and then I got my regular, little, lighter bat and boy, I was pulling balls.

That was the year Mantle and I had the batting championship down to the last two weeks, and I had more holes that year than I had had in fifteen. So it proved to me that, certainly, take advantage of the whole field if you can. It's a little bit harder to do it for a hitter like I was, but you've got to take advantage of that whole field. If you hit a ball good, you've got a better chance of getting it through.

JOHN WOODEN

John Wooden is the most successful college basketball coach of all time.

He is a great leader of men. I think he succeeded especially because he spent as much time on detail as anyone I've ever met or read about. His detail work was focused not on the opposition but on his own team, on practice habits and requirements.

His UCLA Bruins, featuring a fast-break offense and often a full-court-press defense, set records never seen before or since. Wooden won more NCAA championships than any other coach: his teams of 1964 through 1975 won ten NCAA championships; the runners-up, Adolph Rupp and Kentucky, won four. His UCLA teams were undefeated four different times, maintaining identical 30–0 records in 1964, 1967, 1972, and 1973. Wooden's teams established the longest winning streak in NCAA history, winning eighty-eight straight games in 1971–74.

UPI named Wooden Coach of the Year in 1964, 1967, 1969, 1970, 1972, and 1973. He recruited, trained, and coached players like Kareem Abdul-Jabbar (known at UCLA as Lew Alcindor), Gail Goodrich, Mahdi Abdul-Rahmad (Walt Hazzard during college), Marques Johnson, Bill Walton, Sidney Wicks, and Jamaal Wilkes (previously Keith Wilkes).

Wearing glasses, known for his meek smile, and preaching honored American values of industriousness and loyalty, Wooden has been called "Saint John." Nevertheless, when the coach was in his forties, opposing players would complain of the vicious insults he screamed at them through a rolled-up game program. One USC player was so upset by Wooden's remarks that he stopped a game. National championships seemed to make the coach a calmer man.

Little known is the fact that not only is Wooden in the College Basketball Hall of Fame as a coach; he's the only coach named to the hall as a player as well. He was a three-year All-American guard at Purdue and in 1932 was named College Player of the Year.

Wooden has observed basketball for more than sixty years and has seen it change:

There is far more showmanship in the game today. The dunk has made players more individualistic, and that's got to have taken something away from team play. As the players have become better individually, coaches have permitted the great individual ability to take over at the expense of team play.

They are permitting the game to be more physical today. Post play in the pros today is more like wrestling.

Wooden was influenced by the legendary University of Chicago football coach Amos Alonzo Staag:

One of the coaches whose philosophy I admire probably as much as any was Amos Alonzo Staag. After he had a great football team at the University of Chicago, a reporter asked him, "Is this your greatest team?"

And Staag said, "I won't know for fifteen or twenty years." What was going to happen to his players after they got out–he had to know that to know whether he had been successful with them.

Wooden was looking for quickness, but more:

I'm interested in quickness. Quickness under control. I've had players that were very quick, but they weren't under control. I recall at one time a reporter said about a certain player, "Boy, he is quick." And I said, "Yes, he is. Never gets anything done, but he is sure quick. He makes his mistakes quickly."

Now obviously you want your post man big, and they aren't going to be as quick as forwards and guards. Well, I want my post men to be quicker than other post men. I want my forwards to be quicker than other forwards. I want my guards to be quicker than other guards. So I'm looking at that quickness in comparison with the position in which I figure they're going to play.

Despite Wooden's singular success, he did not spend much time scouting opposing teams:

I scouted opposing teams probably less than any coach in the country. I wanted to build my own team. My constant is, "Don't worry about the other fellow, let's make the best of what we have." My definition for success, which I coined in 1934, is that success is peace of mind, which can be attained only through self-satisfaction in knowing you made the effort, and did the best of which you are capable. Not to be better than someone else, but to be the best you can be. You don't have any control over how good somebody else is going to be, but you should have control of how good you are.

Many fans will be surprised at how Wooden contrasts his two greatest centers, Kareem Abdul-Jabbar (Lew Alcindor at UCLA) and Bill Walton:

Lewis/Kareem is the more valuable of the two, in my opinion. I didn't say he is the better player. Walton might be the better player. If you took every individual fundamental of the game, say rebounding, passing, shooting, free throws, every fundamental, and based it on one to ten, I believe that Bill Walton would probably rate higher than Lewis/Kareem would. But I still believe Lewis is the more valuable because he forced the other team to adjust more both offensively and defensively than did Bill.

One of Wooden's greatest moments as a coach had nothing to do with winning or losing a basketball game:

I think one of my greatest thrills was after one particular game, a national championship game. There was one reporter looking for angles, and he spoke to one of my black players, Curtis Rowe. I happened to be standing near enough talking to another reporter that I overheard, and the reporter asked Curtis Rowe, "Tell me about the racial problems."

And Curtis Rowe just seemed to straighten up, and he said, "You don't know Coach Wooden, do you?" And the fellow said, "What do you mean?" And Curtis Rowe said, "He doesn't see race. He sees basketball players." I haven't had anything give me a better thrill than that.

I've had an opportunity to talk with many of the players who played for Wooden. They have the highest regard for him as a teacher and as a human being. He wasn't much of a recruiter, but he was a great coach. You can tell by the way his former players talk about him that he was not only a great teacher, but also a very moral man. I think those qualities made him the leader that he was. It means a lot to me that to this day his players still contact him when they have a question about their lives. They phone or they go back to Los Angeles, and they talk with Coach Wooden.